AN INTRODUCTION TO DOMESDAY BOOK

AN INTRODUCTION TO
DOMESDAY BOOK

R. WELLDON FINN, M.A.
Sometime Scholar of Peterhouse, Cambridge

Othertime Gad about town

LONGMANS

LONGMANS, GREEN AND CO LTD
48 GROSVENOR STREET, LONDON W I
RAILWAY CRESCENT, CROYDON, VICTORIA, AUSTRALIA
AUCKLAND, KINGSTON (JAMAICA), LAHORE, NAIROBI

LONGMANS SOUTHERN AFRICA (PTY) LTD
THIBAULT HOUSE, THIBAULT SQUARE, CAPE TOWN
JOHANNESBURG, SALISBURY

LONGMANS OF NIGERIA LTD
W. R. INDUSTRIAL ESTATE, IKEJA

LONGMANS OF GHANA LTD
INDUSTRIAL ESTATE, RING ROAD SOUTH, ACCRA

LONGMANS GREEN (FAR EAST) LTD
443 LOCKHART ROAD, HONG KONG

LONGMANS OF MALAYA LTD
44 JALAN AMPANG, KUALA LUMPUR

ORIENT LONGMANS LTD
CALCUTTA, BOMBAY, MADRAS
DELHI, HYDERABAD, DACCA

LONGMANS CANADA LTD
I 37 BOND STREET, TORONTO 2

PRINTED IN GREAT BRITAIN AT THE VILLAFIELD PRESS, BISHOPBRIGGS

GJ 9081/2

TO
P.F. & S.V.F.

CONTENTS

Contents

Part Three: The Magnates and their Revenues

The farming-out and renting of manors
Leases
Comparison of pre- and post-Conquest valuations
Valuations of complex manors
Artificial values
Renders in kind
Renders for parts of manors
Miscellaneous information

Preface

There has not been published any book dealing solely and comprehensively with the Domesday Inquest and all its products since Augustus Ballard's appeared nearly sixty years ago. Since then, not only has much excellent work on Domesday Book and the allied documents appeared, but some of the conceptions concerning their character and origins have been modified. It is time, therefore, that a new introduction to the contents and to the study of Domesday Book should appear.

The sheer volume of Domesday Book, and the deceptive monotony of its thousands of entries, are discouraging to the inexperienced. These are reasons for attempting to reduce its essentials to more manageable proportions, and, as far as is possible, to segregate each of its definable aspects. But, before these can be considered by the student or the amateur, it is as well to examine just what Domesday Book is, why the Inquest which produced it was held, how this Inquest obtained its information, and in what manner the results were committed to writing. It is also judicious to consider in what manner and along what lines the earliest and most celebrated commentators approached the problems which Domesday Book presents. While this book, for lack of space, does not pretend to make anything but occasional glances backwards or forwards from the time of the Inquest, it is as well to remember that it is impossible altogether to isolate Domesday Book. Much of what appears within it has its roots deep within an England less mature than the kingdom over which the Confessor had reigned: the student must know something of the slow evolution of administrative and agrarian arrangements, of socio-economic divisions, of the beginnings of legal codes and a legal system, before he can hope to understand both its contents and what made its compilation possible. Much which is to be found therein is, without some acquaintance with the history of the Anglo-Norman state, only partly intelligible. But this is an

introduction to Domesday Book, and not a history of some
three hundred years of economic and political evolution.

It is important that those unfamiliar with Domesday Book
should appreciate that it is an incomplete and imperfect series
of documents, and that interpretation of its condensed and
telegraphic style is often a difficult matter. Its omissions—some
obvious, some disclosed only by collation of an entry with other
passages—are numerous; moreover, we can never be sure that
a clerk did not leave out one or more words and so alter the
sense of a passage. We can be sure that the accounts of some
manors were omitted altogether, and often we cannot help
suspecting that information then available went unrecorded in
the surviving documents.

Moreover, when we collate Domesday Book with associated
documents—even though the latter may be copies made some
time after their originals were inscribed—and find statistical or
other differences, we cannot help wondering whether the
Domesday version is always the correct one. Certainly these
texts demonstrate that condensation of the original material has
deprived us of much which we would be glad to possess.

Today the writer of a book such as this has a much easier
task than that of Ballard. Comparatively few volumes of the
Victoria County Histories were available to him, and though the
need for revision of the texts and translations of many of these
is acute, the value of the introductory essays is obvious. Work
on the documents associated with Domesday Book had hardly
begun when he was writing, and the less defensible theories of
Eyton, of Round (and, in some degree, of Maitland), had as
yet hardly been challenged. The *Domesday Geography of England*
volumes are a most valuable quarry and have furnished the
first 'Domesday atlas' for which so many commentators pleaded
in vain.

On the other hand, establishment of the truth that many
earlier theories were over-simplifications of the information
available has made it difficult to be satisfyingly definite about
many aspects of the text. For still we need those analyses and
syntheses which Stubbs and Maitland and others envisaged. To
produce satisfactory tables which are also capable of ready
interpretation is a difficult matter—as Baring found. But the

right tables would prove both illuminating and stimulating. The work of future commentators would be materially lightened and of increased value if we could produce tables—preferably by Hundreds and manors—which showed the special characteristics for both the territorial division and the individual fief or sub-fief, and simultaneously the variations in formulae and vocabulary, and (for example) such things as deficiencies of plough-teams, absence of standard information, and textual lapses.

Moreover, the author of a book such as this has certain difficulties to overcome which are additional to those engendered by the volume and character of his material. Not the least of these is order of presentation, for no grouping of the topics is altogether satisfactory, and the inter-relation of the details makes logical sequence exceptionally hard to achieve. Passages from the text must be cited in considerable quantity, but often without opportunity of adding whether the phrase quoted or the implication it contains is of common occurrence or not. Folio and column references have to be provided, but it must at every point be made clear to which of the numerous documents considered these refer. Thirdly, to give the Domesday or other version of a place-name is often unsatisfactory, since several variants may well occur in a comparatively small space, and to expect equation of the eleventh-century form with a modern name, which it often in no way resembles, is unfair. A reader cannot be expected to know that *Stuterehele* is the modern Libury. The variants of proper names produced by the clerks, too, are discouraging, and often bear small resemblance to their originals. The manner in which an attempt has been made to minimise the two last of these difficulties is indicated on p. xv.

The typescript of this book was in the printer's hands when Professor Galbraith's *The Making of Domesday Book* was published. His conclusions have caused me to delete many untenable suppositions, and to attempt to direct readers to an exposition far more detailed and precise than is possible in a book of this character, but I cannot pretend always to have dealt adequately with what his book has to teach us.

I have to thank Professor H. C. Darby for letting me see

proofs of vols. III and IV of the *Domesday Geography of England* when these were still unpublished, and the authorities and staff of the Library of Trinity College, Cambridge, and of the Colchester Public Library, for many courtesies and help. I am deeply grateful to the Curator of the Wisbech Museum Library, Mr. W. L. Hanchant, for the assistance with texts which he has so readily afforded. I should like also gratefully to acknowledge the help I have received from those who in the past have discussed problems of interpretation of the text with me, especially Professor V. H. Galbraith, Dr. H. P. R. Finberg, Professor R. R. Darlington, and Professor R. S. Hoyt.

Wisbech – Frinton-on-Sea   R.W.F.

Feast of St. Edward, Confessor, 1961

DB   Domesday Book
LE   *Liber Exoniensis* (containing the Exeter Domesday)
TO   *Terrae Occupatae* (a section of LE)
ICC   *Inquisitio Comitatus Cantabrigiensis*
IE   *Inquisitio Eliensis*
VCH   *Victoria County History*

DBB   Maitland: *Domesday Book and Beyond*
Dom. Geog.   Darby (Ed.): *The Domesday Geography of England*
Dom. Inq.   Ballard: *The Domesday Inquest*
DRB   (HMSO): *Domesday Re-bound*
Eng. Hist. Docts. Douglas and Greenaway (Edd.): *English Historical Documents*, 1042-1189
EHR   *English Historical Review*
FE   Round: *Feudal England*
MoDB   Galbraith: *The Making of Domesday Book*
Stud. Pub. Rec.   Galbraith: *Studies in the Public Records*

Folio references

Those of the *Liber Exoniensis* have been italicised to avoid confusion with those of vol. II of Domesday Book, since both are in single column; the column (i or 2) has been included for Exchequer Domesday references, but it must be remembered that some folios in this are not two-column. References to vol. II of DB ('Little Domesday') have been prefaced 'II', except where it is made clear in a long section of Chapter VI that this deals solely with vol. II.

As Hamilton's printed text of ICC and IE is not entirely trustworthy, folio references (to ms. A, as the text most easily available) rather than the customary pages of his edition have been included.

A reference is normally to the folio on which an entry begins.

Place-names

Where possible, the modern equivalent of the Domesday name has been given, though distinction has not always been made between, e.g., North and South Tawton, where the text gives no indication as to which is meant. Since many Domesday forms are altogether unlike their modern equivalents, it has at times been necessary to give both examples, e.g., *Bisobestona* and Montacute, or to use the DB form only. Where a name is still unidentified, or the identification is in serious doubt, the DB form has been used, in italic type.

Proper names

If these are always rendered in conventional form, it is frequently difficult to identify the person concerned by means of the Domesday orthography, and accordingly in some instances the Domesday clerks' versions have been given.

Part One

PRINCIPLES
OF THE DOMESDAY INQUEST
AND DOMESDAY BOOK

CHAPTER I

Domesday Book and the Domesday Inquest

DOMESDAY Book is the name by which an elaborate description of the England of 1086 has been known ever since the twelfth century. Yet how or why it got that name no one knows. It is unlikely that it was because of association with the *Domus Dei*, or House of God, at Winchester, its earliest home, though there is an early reference to it as the *Liber de Wintonia*, or 'Book of Winchester'. There might be an association with the *dooms* or judgments given by the local public courts whose members had much to do with its production, but the most probable reason for its name is that given in a document of about 1179, the *Dialogus de Scaccario*, a description of the work and functions of the Exchequer. For England's Treasurer, writing less than a century after its compilation, says that 'the book is called by the natives "Domesday", that is, metaphorically speaking, the day of judgment'. To those who had experienced the thoroughness of the Inquest which produced it, it may well have seemed comparable to 'the book by which the dead were to be judged according to the things written in it'.[1]

Domesday Book, however, never calls itself by that name. It styles itself in a few passages *descriptio* (e.g. on fols. 3ai, 252ai, 269a2), and the word can mean a 'writing-down' as well as a description. It does so in the colophon at the close of the Suffolk section (II.450), and the statement here that,

> In the 1086th year from the Incarnation of Our Lord, in the twentieth of the reign of William, this description was made, not only for these three counties but for others also.

is one of the principal reasons for thinking that not only was the Domesday Inquest held in 1086 but that Domesday Book was written in that year also. It refers to 'the year in which this

[1] Rev. xx. 12.

descriptio was made', and speaks of none of the inhabitants of a certain manor coming to this *descriptio*. The earliest mention of it, where again it is referred to as 'the description of the whole of England', is in a writ of the reign of the Conqueror himself.

Reasons for holding the Domesday Inquest

We are never expressly told *why* it was made. The explanation given in the *Dialogus* is that

> when William the Conqueror had subdued the whole island, he decided, to prevent further trouble, to place the government of the conquered on a written basis and subject them to the rule of law . . . to round off the work he sent men of proved discretion on circuit throughout the kingdom. A careful description was made of the whole country by these men, of its woods, pastures, and meadows, employing the usual agricultural terminology; this was gathered into a book.

The *Anglo-Saxon Chronicle*, under the year 1085, says that

> at midwinter the King was at Gloucester with his counsellors . . . and afterwards held a great council and very deep speech with his wise men about this land, how it was held, and with what men.

Probably this is the most satisfactory brief explanation of why the undertaking was begun. A recent threat of a Danish invasion had obliged King William to billet an army of mercenaries upon his barons, and had shown how little the authorities really knew about the social and economic resources of the country, and how desirable it was to acquire adequate information.[1]

But while this may have been the prime reason, other motives were probably contributory factors. The fact that there were three divisions of English law – the Mercian, the Danish, and the West Saxon – made codification of the systems highly desirable, though there is no evidence that a revised conflation of them was then undertaken. So much, in the England of Edward the Confessor, was still a matter of custom and oral tradition rather than of written law, and in many

---

[1] See Sir F. M. Stenton: *Anglo-Saxon England*, p. 609.

aspects unfamiliar to the newcomers and alien to their conceptions, that to record Anglo-Danish arrangements in a national record was desirable, though Domesday Book is no legal treatise or code.

Thirdly, the past twenty years had shown how much doubt there was regarding the rightful possession of estates. The King and his Council, on becoming masters of England, had laid down definite principles for the transfer of estates from natives to newcomers. In the great majority of instances, the lands of an Englishman who was to lose them were granted to a royal adherent who was to be regarded as the Englishman's heir and who was to succeed to all the privileges and responsibilities which had been his. His title to these was the King's writ, the formal putting of him in possession of them, of 'seizing' him of them, by the King's representative, and notification to the local authorities of the grant. But many men had obtained estates since the Conquest, forcibly or through the actions of the royal agents, to which they had no legal right, and the complexities of English land-tenure had frequently resulted in more than one claimant to a holding. In these twenty years there had been numerous enquiries into disputed possession. We have record, for example, of the attempt by Lanfranc, Archbishop of Canterbury, to establish his rights against Bishop Odo of Bayeux, the King's half-brother, and of an enquiry into the claims of the Bishop of Worcester against those of the Abbot of Evesham. Somewhere between 1071 and 1075 a royal commission was directed to enquire into the losses experienced by the Abbey of Ely; the enquiry had to be reopened in 1080, and it was then reported that still further evidence and investigation was needed to settle outstanding problems. Domesday Book is full of passages referring to *placita* or pleas held during the reign, and to claims and disputes in the local courts.[1]

But well into the present century the opinion of commentators was that there was no doubt that DB was a financial document; that it was constructed to show for how much land-tax, for how much geld, men were responsible, and that this formidable body of statistics was acquired so that a King

[1] For further details, see pp. 33–6.

whose love of the red gold was notorious could obtain all he possibly might collect, seek out those who were avoiding their liabilities, and wherever possible increase assessments and so his income. It was rightly pointed out in 1948 by Professor V. H. Galbraith that while the Domesday Inquest was conducted by men obviously interested in the individual's liability for geld, Domesday Book as drawn up was virtually useless as a means either of collecting or of re-assessing geld.[1] The amount due from each shire, as J. H. Round had shown, had been distributed among its vills in round figures or combinations thereof, and the issue was confused by the fact that the majority of vills were composed of several holdings, each with its own quota. DB is drawn up by fiefs or fees, and to discover from it the total liability of a vill is not only sometimes impossible, but moreover might entail searching the record of an entire county to extract the information required. The government knew perfectly well how much geld each sheriff had to collect if no land was exempted from payment, and the sheriffs' records must have indicated who was liable for geld, and for how much. Though entries in DB demonstrate that such records must have been far from perfect, the Domesday Inquest was far more elaborate than a mere revision of these warranted.

The holding of the Inquest

Nor are we told *how* DB was made. The *Anglo-Saxon Chronicle* merely says that the King 'sent his men over all England, into every shire, and caused to be made out how many hundred hides were in the shire, or what land the King himself had . . . or what dues he ought to have in twelve months from the shire'. We do indeed possess, in the form of a twelfth-century copy in the *Inquisitio Eliensis* of an earlier document, what may have been the 'terms of reference' of those who conducted the Inquest, a reflection of which is found in the account of the *Anglo-Saxon Chronicle* which says that 'the King caused them to write down . . . what or how much each man that was settled on the land in England held in land and cattle, and how much it was worth'.

[1] V. H. Galbraith: *Studies in the Public Records*, pp. 91–103.

Here follows the inquisition regarding lands made by the King's barons, viz. by the oath of the sheriff and of all the barons and of all their Frenchmen and of the whole Hundred, of the priest, the reeve, six villeins of each village. That is to say, what is the name of the manor, who held it in the time of King Edward, who holds it now, how many hides are there, how many ploughs in demesne and how many are held by the tenants, how many villeins, how many cottars, how many slaves, how many freemen, how many sokemen, how much wood, how much meadow, how much pasture, how many mills, how many fisheries, how much has been added or taken away, how much the whole was worth then and how much now, how much each freeman or sokeman had there or has. All this three times, namely, in the time of King Edward, and when King William gave it, and as it is to-day, and if it is possible that more can be obtained how it is to be obtained.

The undertaking was obviously an unpopular one; the chronicler complains that 'he caused the survey to be made so narrowly that there was not a single hide or yardland, nor – shameful to relate . . . – was there an ox or a cow or a swine left out, that was not set down in his writing'.

There is, too, apart from references to the Inquest in other chronicles, an account of it written in the year in which it was held by Bishop Robert of Hereford, who must have been thoroughly familiar with the circumstances. It includes aspects which the above does not, notably ploughlands, services, and payments, and differentiates between 'those who dwelt in cottages and those who had their homes and share in the fields'. This, too, tells us that the first set of investigations was followed by a second, and that the King sent men into parts of the country unknown to them, and where they themselves were unknown, so that they could check the first reports and if necessary denounce their authors and their guilt to the King. It adds that 'the land was much troubled by many calamities' arising from the collection of money – possibly a reference to the imposition of a concurrent geld.

The extreme north of England, not then shired, and under local administrators rather than the central government, is unrepresented in Domesday Book, though parts of Cumberland, Westmorland, and what is now north Lancashire were included

with the territory of the West Riding of Yorkshire, while south
Lancashire is described as the land 'between Ribble and
Mersey' and follows the Cheshire section.

We shall see (p. 39) that each existing shire formed an
independent unit for Inquest purposes, but that the shires
were at some stage combined in groups, each of which seems
to have been dealt with by a different body of royal Commissioners and their clerks, headed by one or more Bishops
from distant sees and by lay royal nominees of substantial
position. How the statistical information was furnished we
do not know – perhaps by the stewards of fiefs and by the
bailiffs and leading men of each manor and vill. We do not
know whether the Commissioners held a meeting in each local
administrative division known as the Hundred or the wapentake, or whether there was merely a shire-moot attended by the
representatives of each of these. But we do know from many
passages in Domesday Book that the members of the shire-
courts and Hundred-courts gave evidence on doubtful points
where this was required, and that interested parties, in person
or through their local representatives, also gave evidence,
written and oral. There survive for Cambridgeshire and for
three of the Hertfordshire Hundreds the names of those who
composed the Hundred-juries, eight men for each Hundred,
half natives, half newcomers; they are men of neither negligible
nor lofty status. But we are told also that evidence on oath
was given by the sheriff and by local landowners and their
men and by all the best – that is, reliable or influential –
men in the shire. It is extremely probable that at different
stages, as the information was furnished and the record
compiled, the priest and reeve and the six inhabitants of each
vill had to swear that it was a true one, and that at a later
date landowners and shire- and Hundred-juries did so also.

The vast mass of statistics which make up the bulk of DB
could never have been elicited and written down in open court,
nor could the officials of the Hundred have provided them,
save perhaps as regards geld-liability. The only persons who
could have done so would be the owners of the manors themselves, whose nominees must have furnished them in between
the sittings of the court (perhaps indeed in part before the

formal opening of the proceedings) through local representatives. The function of the shire- and Hundred-juries must have been to give their sworn testimony on points of disagreement or difficulty on which the Commissioners required additional evidence.

The making of Domesday Book

In what form the results were first inscribed is another of the things about the Inquest which we do not know. We have about four-fifths of a twelfth-century copy of what may have been substantially an early draft for the county of Cambridge, known as the *Inquisitio Comitatus Cantabrigiensis* (ICC). This is arranged by Hundreds, and, within each, by the vills composing it, but there is no proof (and indeed a large amount of contradictory evidence) that this was a method adopted elsewhere. The Commissioners had been obliged to use shire and Hundred as the basis of their Inquest, for these ancient administrative units alone would serve their initial purpose, but Norman feudal-mindedness demanded that the ultimate presentation of the material should be in terms of the individual landowner's fief, his 'honour'; indeed, it is not impossible that returns were demanded also from the major fiefs, irrespective of local divisions within the shire, and their material compared with that of the hundredal returns.

The survival of the ICC caused Round to consider that 'hundredal returns' were the basis of the information to be found in DB, and were in fact the 'original returns', sent to Winchester and there transformed into DB. But it is quite incredible that the 'original returns' were laboriously written out in the form of the ICC, by Hundreds and vills and the holdings within them, and then equally laboriously converted into an account for each fief within the individual shire. Nor is it at all likely that both hundredal and independent feudal full returns were required, compared, and then jointly transformed into the material of DB. The Hundred, however, may well have supplied a list of the manors within it, checked against the other information provided. If we speak of 'hundredal returns', we must not think of these as elaborate written documents.

The probability is that the authorities for each fief provided accounts of the manors within it, and that for convenience, especially as the Commissioners must have summoned Hundred-juries, one by one, or in groups, to give the evidence required of them, the manors were grouped according to the Hundred in which each lay. The 'first draft', furnished to Inquest clerks independently of sittings of the court – whether orally or in part at least in writing we do not know – must have consisted of a somewhat chaotic collection of manorial accounts, possibly (but by no means certainly) grouped by Hundreds. From these a 'second draft' – the first really useful material – was constructed, the basis of which was the individual fief. What this was like we can see by studying the ill-arranged, voluminous, and somewhat muddled text known as the *Liber Exoniensis*.

For the second drafts were roughly in the form that was taken by Domesday Book as we possess it. The material for the whole shire was arranged in a collection of *breves* or 'chapters', one for the fief of each tenant-in-chief holding land within it, or for groups of minor landholders, irrespective of geographical administrative units; but from the way in which the name of the Hundred in which a holding lay was included in Domesday Book, and from the fact that all a man's holdings in the individual Hundred normally come together, hundredal returns would seem to have been in part their ultimate source.

The record for Essex, Suffolk, and Norfolk has always remained separate from the remainder, and is very much more detailed than the latter; e.g. it contains the number of livestock, as does the ICC, which was later omitted for the rest of England. Round thought that this was the portion of the record first to be compiled, and that when the royal officials saw how vast was its bulk, they ordained that the material for the remainder of the counties should be substantially reduced in volume by the omission of certain features – e.g. demesne livestock, sobriquets of under-tenants and former landholders – and by the use of formulae more contracted than those of the 'provincial Domesdays'.[1] But this, as Professor Galbraith demonstrated, was 'a rash theory

[1] J. H. Round: *Feudal England*, pp. 140–2.

which . . . will not really bear examination', and which ignores the survival of that other record which in form and character so strongly resembles the eastern counties' text, the Exeter Domesday.

For there exists, in a collection of documents known as the *Liber Exoniensis* (LE), a record of the Inquest for the greater part of the five south-western shires. It strongly resembles the eastern counties' Domesday: like it, it is drawn up in single column, the handwritings are unprofessional, the technical terms used are often alien to those of what we normally call the Exchequer version of DB, and it includes the livestock, sobriquets, and formulae less contracted than those of later texts. This 'Exeter Domesday' was later condensed on the lines of the surviving record of other shires, and the counties it covers appear with them in what is usually thought of as Domesday Book. Professor Galbraith's compelling conclusion was that the Exeter Domesday was a 'second draft', a rearrangement of the manorial accounts and hundredal information by fiefs; it is demonstrable that it was copied and slightly revised and an improved version used for the making of the Exchequer text.[1] The eastern counties' material is a 'third draft', comparable to the revised version of the Exeter Domesday: it is a good deal neater, better arranged, and less full of errors and corrections and postscriptal additions than is the Exeter Domesday. For some reason, probably lack of time, it was never converted into 'Exchequer' form.

The *Anglo-Saxon Chronicle* tells us that 'all these writings were afterwards brought to the King'. The initial interpretation of this statement was that it was a vast mass of 'original returns', a *descriptio* by Hundreds and vills, which was sent to the royal Treasury at Winchester, though there is no evidence of this, and that there the returns were made into Domesday Book. There is indeed no proof that any part of DB was constructed there. Indeed, it looks as if not only the second and third drafts but the Exchequer text also were produced in the

---

[1] Galbraith: *op. cit.*, pp. 92 *et seq*. The true relationship between the Exeter and Exchequer Domesdays was first demonstrated by F. H. Baring in 'The Exeter Domesday' (*EHR*, vol. xxvii) and developed by R. Welldon Finn in 'The Immediate Sources of the Exchequer Domesday' (*Bulletin of the John Rylands Library*, vol. xl., no. 1.)

provinces, and for the most part while the Inquest was still in progress (p. 89). The 'writings' brought to King William were most likely DB as we have it, and it is just possible that when in August he exacted at Salisbury an oath of fealty from all the principal men of the country, they swore also to the justice of the record it contained. The 'writings' must have been brought to him before 1086 ended, for he left England, never to return, towards its close.

Seven months, three of them winter months, as Eyton pointed out, may seem an impossibly short time for the holding of the Inquest and the writing down of its voluminous products.[1] But Domesday Book at every point shows how hurriedly, and at times carelessly, it was compiled. The accounts of a good many towns, including London and Winchester, are missing from it – not, in all probability, because they were never constructed, but because they never got beyond the now lost drafts. For space was left for them; three whole columns were reserved for the accounts of each of the premier cities. Occasionally matter was at first omitted, and later inscribed on loose sheets, partially filled, and slipped in as near the appropriate place as possible. The accounts of some manors known to have been in existence in 1086 are omitted altogether; much of the indexing is highly imperfect; and there are numerous blanks, e.g. where figures were apparently not available at the time of inscription, though sometimes the clerk made a marginal note to point out that enquiry must be made about the missing quantity with a view to filling in the gaps. The whole gives the impression of having been produced with a time limit ever in mind, and handed over before it was completed.

Many of the deficiencies of DB will be exposed in later chapters. It must be appreciated that it does not include material which we know should be in it, and that it contains duplicate passages which contradict each other; it convicts itself of errors in figures, and consequently we are often uncertain whether the figures we have are correct. We can never be sure that the clerks did not inadvertently omit a phrase or a figure, and we do know that often the name of

[1] R. W. Eyton: *Domesday Studies: Somerset*, p. 13.

the wrong Hundred was inscribed at the start of a batch of entries. We have no account in it of certain vills, e.g. Abingdon and Ramsey, which are known to have been in existence in 1086; in the Claims section of Yorkshire, and in the Yorkshire Summary, vills are recorded which are not mentioned in DB, and the reverse is true also. We have itemised figures which will not produce the totals stated, and quite often no details at all for certain settlements which were constituents of large complex manors; frequently these constituents are unnamed. In some counties the number of ploughlands is not given, and in others they are frequently omitted. On fol. 19b2 the clerk wrote *unum Ferlang*, as though a furlong, or a ferding or 'fourth part', were meant, but he should have written *Ferleg*, the village of Fairlight. To list all the manifest errors and omissions would occupy many pages, and there must be many of which we can have no knowledge.

It looks too as if work on DB suddenly stopped short, and as if it then stayed untouched.[1] Perhaps the occasion of the cessation of work was the Conqueror's departure from England; in less than a year he was dead, and the troubles of his son's reign were no time in which to reopen the many disputes about ownership of land the Inquest disclosed. Yet, despite its imperfections, the Exchequer text of Domesday Book displays evidence of considerable and thoughtful planning and execution. The Exchequer volume consists of large sheets of parchment, doubled for sewing together (though there are occasional single sheets plus sewing margins), brought together in forty-seven gatherings or quires, frequently of eight leaves, though we find examples of four, six, and ten also.[2] Only three times does the account of a shire open elsewhere than at the beginning of a gathering, which strongly suggests that the account of each shire was individually produced, and within its borders. The sheets are approximately 22 × 15 in. in size, making a page of about 15 × 11 in. when doubled. They are, save for

[1] There is one addition to the body of the text, but inscribed appreciably later, the fief of Robert de Bruis 'which was given to him after the book of Winchester was inscribed' (fols. 332bi–333ai).

[2] e.g., the account of Berkshire is contained in sixteen pages (folios 56–63); that of Wiltshire in twenty, with an additional leaf, making twenty-two, at the end (fols. 64–74).

some of the insertions, written on both sides in double column; there are in all 383 folios, with many of the headings and initial letters rubricated, and with place-names and proper names underlined in red. How many clerks contributed to the work it is impossible to say; the handwritings are neat and uniform, but there are appreciable differences in the appearance of individual counties, and occasional suggestions of alien hands appear in some. It does not look, e.g., as if one man wrote the accounts of both the south-western and the northern shires, and it is highly doubtful if some folios, or indeed the accounts of some manors, were all written by a single clerk. Fol. 239a does not look as if it was all written at one and the same time, nor does the account of the Church of Worcester's land on 172b; other instances can perhaps be seen on 87bi,2, 123ai,b2, 124ai,2. Postscriptal material might well not be added by the clerk who had originally written the column.

The style is telegraphic, and the word-forms are highly contracted: *tempore regis Edwardi* is almost always shortened to T.R.E. and *manerium* to M̄, *cotarii* to *cot.*, *valebat* to *valb.*; an initial often stands for a proper name already mentioned. The condensation of the matter often makes translation difficult. Each separate fief has or was intended to have a rubricated and numbered cross-heading; and an index, often imperfectly constructed, prefaces the feudal sections in each county.[1]

The fiefs appear in a logical and workmanlike order; first come the royal estates, *Terrae Regis*, sometimes grouped according to the previous holder, then the lands of the Church and churchmen – archbishops preceding bishops – and then the religious houses, which usually appear in an order governed by national or local importance. There follow the lands of the earls, and after them come those of the other lay tenants-in-chief, roughly in order of the extent of their local possessions, and sometimes on an unsystematic alphabetical principle. Usually at the very end come tenures in sergeancy (headed *servientes regis*), followed by the lands of the English thegns. Men precede women; the lands of the *comitissae* or countesses often close the list.

[1] The indexes were perhaps made from the 'second drafts', whose contents and order were often altered when the Exchequer text was made.

There seems to be method, too, about the order of appearance of the shires, but this depended on the first binding of the loose gatherings.[1] We begin with the five south-eastern counties; then come the five south-western; each group runs roughly from east to west. In turn we find south midland, west midland, east midland, north-western, and northern shires. The order is not completely logical, for Warwickshire comes between the east midland and north-western groups, and it is doubtful if the order altogether represents the Inquest groups of shires – Huntingdonshire, for example, would seem to have been associated with the northern counties rather than with Cambridgeshire and Bedfordshire.

This, however, is not necessarily the order in which the circuits and shires were inscribed by the Exchequer clerks. If – of which I am by no means convinced – one man wrote the whole, or nearly all, of the Exchequer text, he may have begun with Middlesex and the circuit in which it lay, passed thence to the northern shires, and then to the south-east.[2]

The smaller volume, containing the three eastern counties, is almost all on vellum sheets, approximately 11 × 8 in., written on both sides in a number of rough hands in single column, in fifty-seven gatherings, almost all of eight leaves, containing in all 450 folios. Rubrication is less generous than in vol. I. The order of appearance – Essex, Norfolk, Suffolk – is somewhat illogical, and while the fiefs appear in much the same sort of order as they do in volume I, there are occasional lapses; e.g. lay sometimes precede ecclesiastical tenants-in-chief. This is probably only because it was not a final text, but it occurs in Nottinghamshire also. It is distinctly unfortunate, in view of its volume, that this eastern counties section, always bound separately from the rest, has become known as 'Little Domesday'.

Other Inquest products

There still exist a number of records which, though not incorporated in the Exchequer Domesday Book, are products of

---

[1] Though there have been five bindings at various times, there is no reason to suppose that the order of counties has been changed from the original make-up (see *Domesday Re-Bound*, p. 20: H.M.S.O., 1954).

[2] See Galbraith: *MoDB*, pp. 202–4.

the Inquest. The *Liber Exoniensis* includes, besides the 'Exeter Domesday', over thirty folios headed *Terrae Occupatae* (TO), which seem to represent lists of points in dispute or of tenures judged to be illegal in Devonshire, Cornwall, and Somerset. It contains also copies of abstracts of the geld account for each south-western Hundred for a year in which the rate was six shillings upon each hide; according to internal evidence, this was 1083–4.[1] Bound up with these, at the end, are Summaries of the material for a few of the fiefs.

Three twelfth-century copies of the *Inquisitio Eliensis* (IE) exist. They give accounts, differing slightly from each other, of the estates held or claimed in 1086 by the Abbey of Ely in the six counties in which she held land; at times they supplement the information of Domesday Book and of the ICC. They include Summaries in the style of those of the *Liber Exoniensis*, and, among other information duplicated elsewhere, a schedule of the Abbey's claims against usurping barons, and (in one ms. only) notes of claims made at the enquiry of 1071/5 into infringements of Ely's rights to lands and services.

The original of the *Inquisitio Eliensis* was certainly constructed, not, as Round thought, in part from 'Little Domesday', but from draft returns to the Inquest which, as regards the eastern counties, became, when amended, vol. II of DB. The bulk of the information it contains must have come from inhabitants and servants of the monastery at Ely, and the Ely authorities saw the wisdom of retaining the original or copying it for their own use. Professor Galbraith thinks that in the form in which we possess it, it is 'a return demanded by Rannulf Flambard in 1093, when Abbot Symeon died and the possessions of the abbey were taken into the king's hands'.[2] The basis of any such return would certainly be the information provided seven years earlier.

There are also contemporary surveys for the lands of the individual religious house, surely originally connected with

---

[1] The Chronicle, *sub anno* 1083, tells us that the King in this year levied a 'mickle geld' of six shillings upon every hide. These geld accounts certainly relate to a year when this was the rate of imposition. But in 1950 Professor Galbraith suggested ('The Date of the Geld Rolls in Exon Domesday'; *EHR*, vol. lxv) that they belong to 1085–6, and are a product of the Domesday Inquest – see p. 249.

[2] Galbraith: *MoDB*, p. 141.

the holding of the Inquest, and perhaps in part constructed from the returns to it, incorporated in documents belonging to Christ Church, Canterbury (the *Domesday Monachorum*), and Bath Abbey. The surviving records of other monasteries suggest that they include material inspired by the Domesday Inquest. It is unfortunate that some of these have been styled 'satellite surveys', for they are in origin Inquest products.

The Commentators

Domesday Book has remained of official interest and use throughout its history (see Chapter V). Local historians, from the seventeenth century onwards, adopted the practice of including a transcript of it in their compendiums, and the ideas of a facsimile edition, and also of an official and complete text, were mooted before the end of the eighteenth century. The printing of an exact transcript, reproducing the abbreviations, was agreed to by Parliament in 1774 and completed in 1783. In 1811 a volume of Indexes was issued, reprinted five years later with a general introduction to the study of Domesday Book by Sir Henry Ellis (revised in 1833). In 1816 a fourth companion volume, including *inter alia* the *Liber Exoniensis* and part of the *Inquisitio Eliensis*, was issued. Between 1861 and 1863 a facsimile edition for each county was produced by means of photozincography.

Until such texts were available, study of Domesday Book could but remain unscientific and unsatisfactory, and little more than extensions of the contracted text and unscholarly translations had been attempted. The *Victoria History of the Counties of England* began publication in 1900, and for each shire an adequate annotated translation, with a substantial critical introductory essay, was included.[1]

The commentators' labours were greatly facilitated by the published work of J. H. Round and Professor F. W. Maitland. It was Round who, in *Feudal England* (1895), taught us how to interpret Domesday Book and who, in a host of scholarly papers, set the standard for all subsequent research on matters of detail. Maitland, in *Domesday Book and Beyond* (1897),

---

[1]Dorset is a county the Domesday of which has not yet been included in the *VCH*.

enquired into its legal and social implications, and produced a study which, if some of its conclusions are now obsolete, remains the best detailed study of the text as a whole. Sir Paul Vinogradoff, in *English Society in the 11th Century* (1908), though not primarily concerned with the record itself, furnished the student with a vivid picture of conditions before and after the Conquest. A 'Domesday Commemoration', which produced papers of unequal merit (but some of Round's most vital studies), had been held in 1886.

Ellis's *General Introduction* had been anticipated, imperfectly, by R. Kelham's *Domesday Book Illustrated* (1788) and was followed by W. de G. Birch's *Domesday Book* (1887). The only other short book for the general reader has been A. Ballard's *The Domesday Inquest* (1906); Ballard had already produced a work on *The Domesday Boroughs* (1904).

No other major work concerned principally with Domesday Book was to appear for a considerable time. Study of it was confined largely to the Victoria County History (*VCH*) Introductions, many of which were contributed by Round, and others by Professor Sir Frank Stenton, Charles Johnson, William Farrer, Professor J. Tait and L. F. Salzmann, and to analyses of the material of the individual county. Pioneer work in this field had been produced by R. W. Eyton (Dorset, Somerset, and Staffordshire), and was continued by O. J. Reichel (Devon), T. W. Whale (Somerset and Devon), C. S. Taylor (Gloucestershire), F. H. Baring (certain south-eastern and south midland counties), G. H. Fowler (Bedfordshire), and others. In 1955 Professor R. R. Darlington's article in the Wiltshire *VCH* set new standards for treatment of the individual county record.

Work, too, on the 'satellite surveys' had lapsed with the issue in 1876 of N.E.S.A. Hamilton's edition of the *Inquisitio Comitatus Cantabrigiensis* and *Inquisitio Eliensis*. Professor D. C. Douglas published in 1932 a scholarly work on the Feudal Documents from the Abbey of Bury St. Edmunds, and followed this with a critical edition of the *Domesday Monachorum* (1943). Critical editions of the ICC and IE are still badly needed.

A feeling had grown up that Round was infallible (an atmosphere thickened by the character of his writings and his outspoken criticism of the work of most of his contemporaries), but a long article by Professor V. H. Galbraith on *The Making of Domesday Book* (1942), followed by his *Studies in the Public Records* (1948), showed that some at least of Round's deductions were demonstrably incorrect, and that there was still much to be discovered about the manner in which the Inquest was held and Domesday Book made. It is in these directions, and in scientific analysis and synthesis of the material for the individual shire and group of shires, that future knowledge lies.

Professor Galbraith has now developed and materially enlarged the suggestions made in his earlier papers, and in *The Making of Domesday Book* (1961) he produced a new and compelling hypothesis, admirably documented, regarding the Inquest procedure and the construction and inscription of Domesday Book. Earlier in the same year my book *The Domesday Inquest* had attempted to correct some of the deficiencies of earlier works less concerned with why and how the Inquest was conducted, and the results inscribed.

The statistical elements of Domesday Book are now being considered, and pictured in maps, in the *Domesday Geography of England*, publication of which, under the editorship of Professor H. C. Darby, began in 1952.

So far the palaeographer has unfortunately played only a small part in the study of our oldest public record, and very little work has been done towards discovering how and when and where the Inquest documents were constructed.

CHAPTER II

The Norman Conquest and its Consequences

THE Normans and their allies were not, when they invaded England in 1066, seeking to master a country entirely strange to them. Duke William had possibly visited his cousin King Edward; his intimate friend William Malet was of semi-Saxon parentage; he had received a constant stream of English visitors to Normandy and there had long been English hostages at the Norman court; traders and clerics had brought him information regarding internal conditions in England. The half-Norman Edward had during his reign appointed foreigners to high office. The Norman William was Bishop of London; Giso, a Lorrainer, Bishop of Wells; the brother of the Norman baron William fitzOsbern was one of his chaplains, in the next reign to become Bishop of Exeter; the Breton or Norman Robert fitzWymarc was his Essex sheriff; his nephew Ralf had been Earl of Hereford. Many leading Normans must have been well acquainted with the principal figures of Edward's England, and have possessed some knowledge of its social and economic system.

The Norman theory of the Conquest

It was a convenient assumption that the invasion was not a conquest at all, but that Duke William had merely come to claim the kingdom promised to him by his cousin, and that Harold Godwineson had never been more than a usurper. It followed that those who had opposed William's coming were rebels, and the accepted penalty for rebellion was loss of lands and office.

This is the attitude adopted by those who compiled DB. Only twice did they slip and speak of King William 'conquering' England, or of Harold 'reigning'.[1] Ever at pains to stress

---

[1] Whitlingham (II.124b); Soberton (38a2). On the latter folio they speak of Harold 'invading the kingdom' (Hayling).

the continuity between the current reign and that of the Confessor, they make reference not to the period of Harold's supremacy, but to 'the time of King Edward', *tempore regis Edwardi*, shortened in DB to T.R.E., or speak of 'the day on which King Edward was alive and dead'. The Norman régime is referred to in such phrases as 'after he (Duke William) came into the country' or 'into England'. Harold is never styled king, but always *comes*, earl.[1]

Domesday Book, indeed, tells us nearly as much of conditions under the Confessor as of those under the Conqueror, and thus its value to us is greatly increased. For tolerance, or at best resigned acceptance of the Norman and his allies, could best be secured by continuance where possible of the state of affairs as they had been in Edward's day. Continually we are told of the composition of manors, of the conditions of tenancy, of privileges and responsibilities and penalties, as these had been in 1066: often nothing is said, but merely implied, about their continuance under Norman rule. But, in the absence of evidence to the contrary, it is safe to assume that where it is said that certain customary obligations of a shire or borough or of the individual were current in King Edward's day, they had been continued after 1066, though the text may not say so.

It is questionable whether it was also assumed that because William's coming had been actively opposed, the whole of England was forfeit to him on the grounds that this resistance was rebellion, or whether in accordance with Norman feudal theory the whole of the land was considered to be ultimately the king's. Neither DB nor the early documents of the reign gives us much information about this. The abbot of Bury St. Edmunds was indeed ordered to surrender the holdings of those of his tenants 'who stood against me (King William) in battle and were slain there'. The *Anglo-Saxon Chronicle* records that in 1066–7 'men paid taxes to him and afterwards bought their lands', and this might imply that estates adjudged

---

[1] e.g. on fols. II.13, 87, 102b. Ballard (*The Domesday Inquest*, p. 3) was of the opinion that the use of *comes* was a deliberate slight on Harold. But if the theory was that Harold had never legitimately been king, then 'earl' was the correct title. The word may have been interlined, as it was also for his father and brothers and other earls, to distinguish these from lesser namesakes.

to be forfeit could be redeemed only by purchase. DB once mentions recovery of Edmundsbury holdings on an occasion 'when the English redeemed their lands', and speaks of its abbot 'redeeming land'.[1]

The Church lands

It is highly improbable that the Church lands were held to be forfeit, although one abbot at least, and Winchester monks also, had taken part in the battle of Hastings. William had received the Papal blessing on his enterprise, and besides being a faithful son of Holy Church, needed the support and counsel of the leading ecclesiastics. He did, however, replace those who were English by foreigners as opportunity offered. DB does not show us bishoprics and abbacies losing land at William's instance, though we see them suffering severely at his barons' and sheriffs' hands. We might think, however, that confirmation of title to their lands was required, for DB constantly gives the value of a bishop's or abbot's lands 'when he received it', *quando recepit*. But since there were so many new ecclesiastical appointments early in the reign, the implication may be that instead of giving the values in 1066 and when the King gave the land, as the orders for the Inquest demand, the figure for the moment of the change of office was provided.

King William did not, however, materially increase the Church's possessions during his reign. He did indeed endow the foundations at Caen, St. Stephen's and Holy Trinity, built to expiate his uncanonical marriage with Matilda, with English lands, and also the Abbey of the Battle instituted to commemorate his victory at Hastings, but most of the gifts to foreign churches recorded in DB are those of his lay magnates. We do sometimes find ecclesiastics holding land which had not been their predecessors' in 1066, but these might be personal gifts unconnected with official position. Bishop Osbern of Exeter, for example, was holding *Tetinges* (31a2), though

---

[1] Stonham (II.360b), Ixworth Thorpe (II.367b). Other passages possibly implying redemption are to be found under *Sudberie* (50ai), an unnamed estate on 50bi, Southill (215b2), Saxlingham (II.217). The Saxon owner of a Sharnbrook estate (213a2) had it given *back* to him by King William.

he had not held it T.R.E., and Buckland (58bi), tho
did not belong to his bishopric'. Certainly there are in
where after the Conquest the Church acquired what was not
rightfully hers. St. Paul's, London's cathedral, had illegally
obtained Navestock (II.13a), and had got possession of Fanton
'by means of a forged writ' (II.14). Seaborough (*154*) had
been part of the royal manor of Cricket St. Thomas; in 1086
it was in the hands of Bishop Osmund of Salisbury, but it is
noted that 'it is not of the bishopric of Salisbury'. King William's
writs, and the numerous enquiries instituted to ensure that
the Church should not be robbed of its estates, make it clear
that he had no intention that she should suffer from his
advent.

Redistribution of lay estates

But the redistribution of the remainder of English land entailed
difficulties. Of the way in which it was done, we know little.
The only record is the note in the *Chronicle* that when the
King returned in December 1067 from a visit to Normandy he
'gave away every man's land'. Until then, many Englishmen
were left in possession of their lands and offices.[1] It may be
that the revolts of 1068–9 against Norman rule were in part
inspired by a large-scale transference of estates. The revolt in
1075 of the earls, Ralf II of East Anglia, Roger of Hereford,
and Waltheof of the east midlands, must have necessitated a
further distribution of the lands of those implicated in this
rising.

The King's first care was obviously to secure his new position.
His lines of communication with the Continent were ensured
by bestowing the earldom of Kent on his half-brother Odo,
and each of the rapes or local divisions of Sussex on one of his
most trusted companions. His other half-brother, Robert of
Mortain, later succeeded a Breton noble, Brian, in a dominant
position in Cornwall. William fitzOsbern, in addition to

---

[1] An early writ of the Conqueror's is addressed to two Englishmen who held
extensive estates in the west, Edric and Brictric; other Englishmen attest his
earliest charters. English sheriffs remained in office for some time after the Conquest,
and William's councillors included Edwin and Morcar, the former earls of Mercia
and Northumbria, Earl Waltheof, and Archbishop Stigand. Copsi, the friend of
Earl Tostig, was despatched as earl to Northumbria.

controlling the Isle of Wight, was made Earl of Hereford, and also commissioned to defend the eastern counties against a threat of invasion from Denmark, though quite early in the reign an East Anglian earldom was given to the Breton Ralf the Staller.

We cannot be sure whether the greatest fiefs we find in DB were bestowed on their holders in 1067–8 or not until after the series of revolts which broke out almost everywhere in England in 1068–9. Certainly in DB we find a number of men who have been given broad lands which would give them virtual control of a district and minimise the risk of future revolts. The counties of Cheshire and Shropshire, except for the Church lands, were given to Hugh of Avranches and Roger of Montgomery as earldoms in 1071 and before 1075 respectively to contain the unpacified Welsh. Castles were quickly built, especially from 1068 onwards, to overawe the natives, and the aggregation of lands granted for the maintenance of a castellan and as a sphere of local influence appear frequently in DB. In a Summary of the lands of Earl Alan of Richmond, the manors are divided into those which are within his *castellaria* and those which lie outside it (381a2). Sometimes DB uses a different term; Hugh de Montfort, sheriff of Kent, had a group of estates known as his *divisio*, and Richard fitzGilbert had his 'lowy' based on Tonbridge.[1]

In almost every county where there is no earl we find that two or three of the barons with land in it have far greater possessions than have fallen to their fellows, and it may be that they too had virtual castleries, though they are not so called. Juhel has vast lands in south Devon, and in DB is styled 'Juhel of Totnes', the castled seat of his barony; Alfred is always 'of Marlborough', though his lands extended into several shires.[2]

But these major gifts still left a huge number of estates of

---

[1] The Sussex rapes referred to above are in DB styled *castellariae*. Others mentioned are those of Roger of Poitou (332ai), William fitzAnsculf (177a2), Ilbert de Laci (373bi), and those of Caerleon, Monmouth, and Ewyas in the Welsh borderland. 'Odo of Bayeux had a Kentish *divisio* (1062); the Sussex rape of Robert of Eu is also *divisio*.'

[2] DB does not record a castle of Marlborough. But there is good reason to think that one existed before 1086.

which to dispose. The principle very frequently adopted seems to have been that a newcomer should receive the whole of the estates of one or more natives, what is occasionally styled his 'honour', wherever they may have lain. Thus, though Merleswegen had been a leading Lincolnshire thegn, he had manors in Somerset and Devonshire also, and these as well as his Lincolnshire lands were bestowed on Ralph Paynel. Alfred of Marlborough received the lands of a certain Carle in a number of counties in the south and west. But the principle was not rigorously pursued. While as a rule King William took to himself the estates of all the members of the House of Godwine, there are numerous instances in which we find other holders of them in 1086. Some of the Buckinghamshire lands of the House of Godwine, for example, went to the leading bishops. In Herefordshire Alfred of Marlborough got Earl Harold's lands. King Edward's widow, Edith, seems to have been allowed to retain her estates, and to bestow them before her death in 1075 on whom she pleased; e.g. Puriton (91a2), Chesham (153ai).

It seems to have been thought that the estates of some men were too extensive to pass to the individual; we find in 1086 at least five different holders, including the King, of those of Edric of Laxfield. Sometimes there was perhaps no single landowner with estates in a shire commensurate with the size of the gift the King wished to make. Seventeen different men had held the twenty-one Lincolnshire manors Robert of Stafford was holding in 1086 (368bi,2). In the north and east, where an immense number of free men had held manors which were often minute ones, it would be impossible to allot lands according to their owners in 1066.[1] The individual holding was here often of small value, and so we find estates insignificant in themselves being absorbed into a neighbouring one 'to make up a manor', *ad perficiendum manerium*, irrespective of former ownership, or a number of free men (which presumably implies their holdings) being 'delivered' to 'make up a manor'.[2]

---

[1] The implications of the term 'manor' as used in DB are considered on pp. 45–51.

[2] e.g. Dersingham (II.245b), Egmere (II.170). (*De*)*liberatio* is the technical term for formally putting someone in legal possession of his land, which was 'delivered' to him by a royal officer.

There is, however, one serious difficulty which makes consideration of principles of inheritance and the bestowal of land a matter for partial speculation. This is the fact that in 1086 many landholders were in possession of estates not by reason of royal grant or policy, but because they were renting them from the owner. This is a point considered in Chapter XIII, but which must throughout be borne in mind.

It was formerly thought that the results of distribution disclosed by DB were by reason of deliberate policy, a policy which would prevent the individual potentially rebellious baron from acquiring too much local power. But it is plain that most of the leading English families had accumulated lands in several shires, and that even within the single shire their estates rarely formed uninterrupted blocks of territory.[1] We cannot perfectly trace the principles involved, for often DB does not tell us who held a manor in 1066; often enough, indeed, it gives as the pre-Conquest holder an Englishman, e.g. Earl Godwine or Earl Ælfgar, known to have been dead well before 1066. It does not always indicate post-Conquest grants; e.g. the Dorset geld accounts show that the Abbey of Préaux had the manor of Stour Provost, but in DB this is listed in the fief of Roger of Beaumont, who gave it to the Abbey, which is not mentioned at all in the Dorset Domesday, (*22*, 80a2).

Domesday Book does not include information which charters and other documents of the period give us. For example, certain grants to the Abbey of St. Evroul are certainly pre-Inquest in date, but DB does not record the Abbey's ownership of the estates in question.[2] It is possible that no return of these comparatively recent acquisitions was made by their owners, and the clerks placed them in the fiefs of those whose lands they had been. DB also gives as landholders men and women who certainly were dead before the Inquest finished; e.g. Adeliza, the wife of Hugh de Grentmesnil, who died 11 July 1086, and Hervey of Helléans. This may make us think either that formal seizin of their lands had not yet been granted to

---

[1] Ælfstan of Boscombe was holding 230 hides, distributed over eight shires.

[2] References to these will be found in *VCH: Leicestershire*, vol. I, p. 291, and in Tait: *Domesday Survey for Cheshire*, p. 46.

an heir, or that the return of their property had been made at an early stage of the Inquest, which then would be in process in the spring or summer of 1086.

We do not know if some Englishmen were permitted to hold their lands for some appreciable time after the Conquest, perhaps with a foreign feudal superior between themselves and the king, or what estates passed *after* 1067–8 on the death or disgrace of their English holders. For the rebellions of 1068–9, 1070–1, and 1075 must have resulted in the transfer of a whole host of manors, and it is clear from DB that not all Earl Waltheof's manors, for example, were retained by his widow the Countess Judith. There is much about land-ownership of which DB does not tell us. Haimo de St. Clair is never mentioned in the Suffolk Domesday. But the IE (70a2, 273, 207a2) shows him to have been a well-endowed tenant of Bishop Odo of Bayeux.

We find comparatively few natives with holdings in chief of any magnitude in 1086; only Thorkill of Warwick, its former sheriff, is conspicuous. Not all those who held in 1086 as well as in 1066 may have been native-born, e.g. Grimbald and Theodoric the goldsmiths, though Odo the treasurer and his brother Ældred probably were. The most likely people to remain in undisturbed possession of minor estates were tech-nicians, and we find in 1086 a number of huntsmen bearing Old English names holding land, for the newcomers would hardly have had time to acquire the local knowledge these possessed.

Principles of inheritance

But despite its deficiencies, DB makes one principle entirely clear to us. King William had come to England as the legiti-mate heir of Edward the Confessor, and in full realisation that, save where military necessity dictated policy, his best hope of minimising native opposition was to retain the laws and customs of Anglo-Saxon and Anglo-Danish England. Accord-ingly, every newcomer was to be regarded as the heir of the relevant displaced or defunct Englishman, who was to be considered to be, as DB calls him, the *antecessor* of the new lord of the manor, and the Norman or other foreigner was to enjoy all the privileges, and discharge all the responsibilities, which had been his predecessor's.[1] Thus at the Domesday Inquest we constantly find someone claiming a manor because it had belonged to the man who had been named by the King as his *antecessor*, or being adjudged to be in illegal possession because his *antecessor* had not possessed the land. Hugh de Port's tenant argued that a holding (44b2) should belong to his manor of Chardford 'because he was his predecessor's heir', *per heridatem sui antecessoris.*

While this system of organiséd descent of land had obvious advantages, equally it produced complexities and difficulties where land was merely being held on lease or where conflicting connections existed. For example, William of Warenne had been granted the lands of a thegn named Thorkill ('Tochi'). Now Thorkill had been tenant of some of the thegnlands of the Abbey of Ely, and William, and before him his dead brother-in-law Frederic, had`taken possession of these thegnlands, which the Abbey sought both at the Inquest and earlier to have restored to them.

'Thegnland' was land leased to a subordinate and which reverted to the owner as demesne land on the death of the lessee or the termination of the lease. Presumably grants of thegnland were made in consideration of the provision by the tenant of military or other service's. At Durnford (67b2) three Englishmen had been holding land of the nunnery of Wilton, two at a money-rent, the third by rendering 'such services as are due from a thegn'. Often it is noted that such tenants 'could not separate from the Church'; that is, the holding could not be alienated, and the lessee had no power to dispose of it.

The thegn of pre-Conquest England we meet with continually in the folios of DB. The term covers many gradations of society. There had been King's Thegns who owned no lord but the monarch, and who must often have held their land from him in respect of public office or performance of definite ministerial duties. There were land-owning thegns who, in

---

[1] Indeed, in two passages, the newcomer is styled the 'heir' of his Saxon predecessor (Worthy, 46b2; Bartley, 175a2). Often DB refers, without naming him, to the *antecessor* of the holder or former holder – obviously the officials knew who had held each estate in 1066.

return for the protection of a man more powerful than they, had 'commended' themselves to him, had 'become his man', rendering services (often, perhaps, military service) in consideration of his patronage.[1] DB is full also of minor landholders who had been commended to an earl or to a great ecclesiastical institution, who had been the 'men' of Earl Harold or of the Abbot of Ely. But the system entailed no permanent bond: it seems that men could transfer their commendation as it pleased them; they could, as DB tells us, 'go with their land to what lord they would', so long as the land they held was not inalienable thegnland. Indeed, more than one lord might simultaneously have the partial commendation of the minor thegn.

To possess a man's commendation, however, was not necessarily to have the right to receive the profits of the execution of justice done upon him, to have soke-right over him. By royal grant, or by ancient custom, the leading landholders, lay and ecclesiastical, had obtained the right of jurisdiction, or of receiving the fines for trespasses committed, over lesser men; they had 'sake and soke' over them. This, however, did not necessarily imply that a man must commend himself to the lord who possessed soke-right over him; moreover, transference of commendation did not imply transference of soke. Over and over again we are told that a man could 'go with his land', but that if he did so, the soke-right remained with its original owner. In such circumstances two men might well claim the same piece of land, the one in right of the commendation possessed by his *antecessor*, the other by virtue of the soke his *antecessor* had possessed.[2] The sokemen of three Northamptonshire manors which had been given to William Pevrel had been 'Burred's men', and on this account Bishop Geoffrey

---

[1] T.R.E. a certain man held an estate in Surrey (36ai); the Hundredmen had never seen the King's seal or messenger to put Walter of Douai in seizin of it, but the man had voluntarily 'submitted himself into the hand of Walter for his defence' – had, we may think, 'commended' himself to him. After the Conquest a thegn who T.R.E. 'could go to what lord he pleased, of his own accord turned to' Arnulf of Hesdin (Chedglow, 70a2).

[2] DB never specifically says which was regarded as taking precedence; though it frequently says that someone had 'only the soke' over free men (e.g. II.250b), it is not implied that the possession of commendation gave the better title.

claimed their *hominatio* – as he had inherited Burred's estates, he seems to have claimed their commendation.

DB shows us, too, that men had been acquiring, on a large scale, land to which they had no shadow of just claim, and had been taking it out of one manor and placing it in another as their own economic or administrative advantage suggested. The disclosures of the Domesday Inquest regarding illegal occupation of land, and the methods used to acquire it without sanction, are more conveniently considered at a later stage (p. 61), but it must here be stressed that ambitious men had largely negatived the royal policy. The sheriffs, too, either to their own advantage, or because they were unwilling to restrain a local magnate with whom it paid them to be on good terms, had perpetrated or countenanced a formidable collection of illegalities.

King William's sheriffs appear to have been uniformly unscrupulous, and DB bears frequent witness to their illegal actions. Eustace of Huntingdon robbed St. Benedict of Ramsey of a church and a house in Huntingdon, and gave them to Bishop Geoffrey of Coutances (203ai); Ralph Taillebois took possession unjustly of a woman's land at Houghton Conquest 'when he was sheriff' (217b2). Froger of Berkshire added Pangbourne to the royal feormland *absque placito et lege* – without judicial enquiry and against the law (58ai). Their offences were so extensive and notorious that in 1076–7 King William appointed a commission to enquire into their thefts of Church lands and other illegal transactions.

But there may well be instances of what the bald text of DB would seem to indicate were usurpations by a sheriff or a pro-sheriff which were in fact perfectly orthodox transactions. Picot the sheriff of Cambridgeshire and Hardwin d'Eschalers had obtained numerous estates which are noted as being rightfully Ely Abbey's. But certain of the surviving royal writs, and passages in the IE, show that, though credited in DB with the land, they had had to admit the Abbey's superiority over it. They are said to hold some of them 'under the Abbot', or 'serving the Abbot and holding of him by the King's command'; indeed, in the Summaries in the IE they hold 'by the grant and order of King William', and 'have made agreement with the Abbot by the King's permission'. They seem, too, to be holding these Abbey thegnlands and sokelands with all the responsibilities pre-Norman tenants had incurred. Also, when it looks as if illegal occupation has taken place, but the land is said to be 'in the King's hand', this is probably unexceptionable, for where no grant, or re-grant, of the land had been made, the land was 'in the King's hand', and who other than the sheriff or a royal reeve should administer it on his behalf?

The machinery of redistribution

The King had wished that all land transference should be done in order and give no cause for legitimate complaint. It is to be presumed that lists of properties, which must have been at the disposal of every sheriff for the collection of geld and determining other responsibilities, were used for regulating the distribution of estates. It is clear from DB that land-transference was intended to be confirmed by charter or the King's writ, and that the procedure was that a royal official should formally put the recipient in lawful possession, 'in seizin', of it, and that the appropriate Hundred should be notified of the King's gift by having the writ read to it at its moot or meeting and being shown the King's seal which established its validity.

In DB we naturally hear most often of occasions when the holder of a manor could *not* produce the necessary evidence of title to it. But a certain Edward could show the King's writ entitling him to Hinwick, and the Hundred-jury confirmed his claim (218a2). The Canons of Beverley could produce charters from both King Edward and King William (374ai). Azor the steward, a pre-Conquest landowner, was holding an estate in Wantage Hundred of Robert d'Oyly, but the Hundred-jury said he ought to be holding it directly of the King, because when at Windsor the King had restored the land to Azor, and had given him his writ (62a2).

The number of writs concerned with land transfer issued may have been very large, though unfortunately few of King William's have survived. One writ, no doubt, would serve for all the lands granted to a baron in the individual shire.[1]

---

[1] Professor Galbraith, however, is of the opinion that these grants were made orally, and *sine carta* (*MoDB*, p. 46).

How the recipient treated these once the gift in bulk was made probably interested the King not at all: the creation of sub-tenancies, furnishing the means of subsistence to his household and fighting men, was the baron's own affair. But it seems as if he expected his sanction to be sought when for their own convenience his magnates made exchanges of lands, or wished to grant them away from the fief. Some of these exchanges, which appear continually in DB, may have been made to try to conceal imperfect title: e.g. Stambridge and Paglesham were said to be in exchange for Coggeshall, but also the owner is said to have 'invaded' them (II.99b).[1] The King did not wish land to be granted in such a way that a baron might in consequence have one less trained soldier to furnish to the feudal host; thus we find Frome in Mordiford being given by Walter de Laci to St. Peter's, Hereford, 'with the consent of King William' (182b2), and Earl Ralf and his wife giving Hoveton to St. Benet's Abbey 'by the King's leave' (II.158b).

Whether, during his frequent absences in Normandy, the King despatched instructions for grants, or whether his regents sometimes acted on their own responsibility, we do not know. It seems as if Bishop Odo himself issued writs, from the phrase in DB *per praeceptum episcopi Baiocensis*, by his writ (Porringland, II.278), and South Carlton (342ai) is said to have been transferred 'under the seal of Odo'. The King's men (*barones regis*), Ingelric, Bishop William of London, and Ralf the Staller, dealt with certain Edmundsbury lands (Ixworth Thorpe, II.367b). The King's writs, as well as DB, show him instructing his leading men to convey land; he instructs Robert d'Oyly that Hugh de Bernières is to hold Berners Roding from Geoffrey de Mandeville if Geoffrey can prove it belonged to his fief, which Geoffrey had done earlier than 1086 (II.60b).

Many of those who dealt with transfers of land seem to have been the men of Bishop Odo, intermittently regent for his half-brother, for we frequently find them as his sub-tenants. Chadwell (II.98) was held 'by the leave of Hubert de Port';

---

[1] These exchanges are frequently recorded in *Terrae Occupatae*, which is primarily a record of illegalities; *invasio* or *occupatio*, or the use of *capere*, 'to take', always imply an unsanctioned action.

the same man seized the Bishop of land at Ashfield (II.377). Hugh de Port, probably a connection, adjudged land at Aspall 'free' (i.e. ungranted), though William Malet claimed to be seized of it, and put the Bishop in possession 'because the free men used to hold it'. DB frequently tells us *who* formally put the holder in possession of his land; he is described as the *saisitor*, or *liberator*, of it – the man who put him in seizin of it – and who was often appealed to at the Inquest to vouch that he had done so, to act as the claimant's *advocator, guarantor, tutor* – to warrant his legal right to it.

But the natural recipient of a royal order regarding the bestowal of estates was the sheriff. Durand, sheriff of Gloucestershire, put St. Mary of Pershore in seizin of part of Dyrham (167a2) by the King's orders. Ivo Taillebois (in 1086 sheriff of Lincolnshire) delivered a Norfolk holding to Earl Alan (Islington, II.149). Hugh the sheriff delivered property at York to Bishop Walcher of Durham 'by the King's writ' (298ai). When Ralph Taillebois was sheriff of Bedfordshire, he placed six estates (218bi) *in ministerio regis* which were not so held in 1066, and in 1086 were held by King's reeves, who then claimed to have them by grant of the King.

Power tends to corrupt, and DB convicts lesser men also of dishonest dealings in land. A reeve, especially a King's reeve, had both opportunity and power to traffic in land: we hear of a reeve at Ewell providing his friends with an estate (30bi), of another at Broughton who acquired a mill (38bi), of the King's reeves acquiring part of the manor of Mottisfont without the sheriff's knowledge (42a), of a Canterbury reeve taking dues unjustly from foreign merchants (2ai).

The testimony of DB that during the twenty years of the reign there had been extensive unlawful transactions is clear and voluminous, and a great many of these had given rise to a variety of official enquiries and trials about which we unfortunately know very little. Some are incidentally mentioned in DB; about others it is silent.

Pre-Inquest territorial disputes

How soon after the initial redistribution of lands legal proceedings regarding ownership may have begun we can have no

4   I.D.B.

idea. But that during the score of years preceding the Inquest they were of frequent occurrence, DB and other documents of the reign bear vivid witness. Some seem to have been confined to the authorities of shire- and Hundred-courts, but equally some appear to have been regarded as of major, almost national, importance. The rapacity of Bishop Odo of Bayeux within his earldom of Kent caused the Archbishop of Canterbury to institute proceedings for recovery of episcopal and monastic lands; the case was heard at the shire-court which met on Penenden Heath.[1] The Bishop of Worcester's claims to lands and services were challenged by his neighbour the Abbot of Evesham, and in connection either with this dispute or one less localised there was an enquiry 'at the four-shire stone' during which the Bishop established his claim to certain estates.[2] Odo, presumably when acting as regent during an absence of his royal half-brother from England, mistrusted a verdict by the Cambridge shire-court and summoned a fresh jury to London to give evidence about disputed inheritance of the manor of Islesham.[3]

The number of pre-Inquest proceedings was far greater than cursory study of DB would suggest. Yet there we read that King William had 'ordered a trial to be made' regarding an estate lost by St. Petrock, and 'the Church in justice to be re-seized of it' (121ai). Edward of Salisbury and Robert d'Oyly, in 1086 sheriffs of Wiltshire and Oxfordshire respectively, 'proved their right' to Malden against Richard of Tonbridge (35a2), and as neither was a local magnate, we may suspect that they were acting as royal commissioners. Ældred, brother of a pre-Conquest treasurer, proved *his* right to Compton 'before the Queen, after the King crossed the sea' (48b2); Archbishop Ældred his to Cutdean 'in the time of King William' (173ai). Picot, sheriff of Cambridgeshire,

---

[1] Our information about this is not derived from DB, though it is referred to therein, e.g., on 5b2. See M. M. Bigelow: *Placita Anglo-Normannica*, pp. 5–9.

[2] Accounts are available in *Monasticon Anglicanum*, i. 602, and Heming's *Chartularium Ecclesiae Wigorniensis* (ed. T. Hearne), i. 77–83. DB references are *Ildeberga* (Evenlode, 175b2) and 238bi: Bishop Wulfstan is noted in DB as establishing his claim to Alveston 'before the Queen and four shires', and as having 'King William's writ and the testimony of the county of Warwick' to this effect.

[3] *Registrum Roffense*, pp. 149–52.

adjudged two 'invasions' of Aubrey de Ver to be illegal, and the wording of DB does not suggest that this was in 1086 (190ai, 199b2). At some unknown date there had been a 'plea' at *Hodiham*, and on the same folio we are told of legal proceedings between Bishop Odo and the mother of Robert Malet.[1] A writ which its editor dates as 1066/76 orders Swegen, sheriff of Essex, to ensure that Maurice 'receives his rights according to the award made when his charters and writs were produced before the justices at Writtle'.[2]

Complaints to the King regarding usurpation of ecclesiastical lands, judging by numerous entries in DB and surviving royal writs, must have been frequent (DB shows they had not been infrequent in King Edward's day). It would be only too easy, where bishopric or abbey had let some of its land to laymen, for a newcomer to ignore the fact that it was merely leased in consideration of payment of rents and services, and claim that he held in chief because the former occupant was his *antecessor*. Loss of ecclesiastical thegnlands constantly appears in the collection of documents which form the IE, and we know that between 1071 and 1086 enquiries into Ely losses had been ordered by the King.[3] There survive a number of royal writs ordering laymen to make restitution of Church property illegally acquired. Hugh de Montfort was ordered to surrender Barham to Ely; the King ordained that the Abbot of Ely should have his forfeited house in Norwich.[4] Lisois de Moustières, who was dead before 1086, had acknowledged that Lakenheath and Brandon, which he had illegally occupied, were part of the Ely demesne.[5] DB several times tells us that Ely had proved her right to certain manors in the presence of the Bishop of Coutances, and had recovered them, or had forced usurpers to admit that they held land as tenants only;

---

[1] II.450b. *Hodiham* is not necessarily Odiham in Hampshire.

[2] C. Hart: *Some Early Charters of Essex* (Leicester University Press, 1957). Maurice was the King's clerk who in 1085 became Bishop of London.

[3] The documents are printed in Hamilton, *op. cit.* See also E. Miller: 'The Ely Land-Pleas in the Reign of William I' (*EHR*, vol. xlii, 1947).

[4] H. W. C. Davis: *Regesta Regum Anglo-Normannorum*, 1066–1154, nos. 43 and 153 (O.U.P., 1913): other examples are given there also. See also DB II.417, 423b.

[5] DB II.403.

not in chief, but 'of' or 'under' the Abbot.[1] Losses similar to Ely's constantly appear in the list of *Terrae Occupatae* included in the LE, and in the Exeter Domesday: Glastonbury seems to have suffered severely.[2]

It is unfortunate that the condensed telegraphic language of DB frequently does not enable us to determine whether reference is being made to a dispute first considered, and about which evidence was furnished, at the Domesday Inquest, or whether the allusion is to some earlier public enquiry. Some entries may well relate to ventilation of claims at a date earlier than 1086 and to what witnesses and shire- or Hundred-court said then about their legality.[3] The number of disputes recorded in most shires is so large that to hear all the arguments and evidence would take the Commissioners of 1086 more time than we can allow them.

The establishment of claims to which DB bears witness may not always have been the subject of special enquiry. When we read of the Bishop of London 'recovering' or 'proving his right to' certain of the manors of his episcopate by the King's orders, this may not necessarily imply that someone had attempted to occupy them in defiance of him. It may imply no more than that 'when King William came into England' he expected all landowners to show in the shire-courts – perhaps on such occasions attended by royal nominees – that they possessed good title to the lands they were occupying or claiming.

From the above, one good reason for instituting the enormous, and surely costly, effort of the Domesday Inquest can be clearly seen. We shall see that deep dissatisfaction with the revenue from levies of geld, and with the discharge of customary

---

[1] DB II.383, 383b. It is equally clear from DB and IE that Ely failed to recover many estates to which she had good title. The King's writs were not invariably obeyed, for DB and IE often show the lands still to be held by laymen with no suggestion that Ely's right to them had been acknowledged.

[2] Frequently as the result of 'occupation' by Geoffrey of Coutances, very often appointed elsewhere by the King to preside over hearings of claims for restoration of lands lost. Was he a mere custodian of them while awaiting the royal award?

[3] When DB merely says that rightful ownership is adjudged to someone, 'the Hundred so witnessing', this might well refer to a verdict earlier than that of 1086, but then confirmed.

royal dues and services, was another, and further reasons have earlier been suggested also (p. 4). But since the whole conception of Norman administration depended on knowing, and being able to establish by the written word, who was legally liable for what, and since so much dispute regarding lawful ownership was current, we may well think that one topic of the 'deep speech' at Gloucester was the means of what Professor Galbraith calls 'getting at the facts', to demand evidence from those best qualified to furnish it about tenancies and inheritances. Obviously piecemeal methods had proved unsatisfactory, and with such a wholesale undertaking in view, a statistical record of every manor and borough seemed the natural concomitant – especially as this should prove the means of materially increasing the royal revenue.

CHAPTER III

The Machinery of the Inquest

The 'circuits'

FROM the earliest days of critical study of DB there has been general agreement that for the purposes of the Inquest the country was divided into 'circuits', but not about how these were composed. The grouping of the shires by those who have studied the matter is based largely on similarities of formulae in the text and the absence of particular categories of information in certain groups of shires. We can, for example, be reasonably certain that Sussex, Surrey, Hampshire, and Berkshire were in some sense considered together, for only these use a formula stating that a holding gelded or 'defended itself' for so many hides 'then' (*tunc*), but 'now' (*modo*) for what is often a different quantity.[1] Kent, which opens DB, precedes these four, and was probably within the same 'circuit'. Since for the five south-western counties, and the three eastern, we have self-contained drafts earlier than the Exchequer text, and since the south-western shires appear consecutively in Exchequer form in DB, these surely formed two other 'circuits'. The quantity of ploughlands in a manor is almost altogether absent from the record for the counties of Gloucester, Hereford, and Worcester, which therefore were presumably handled by a single panel of Commissioners and clerks.

Certain characteristics of groups of shires are easily recognisable. In some the name of the pre-Conquest holder comes early in the entry, in others late or at the very end. In one group he is said to have been able to sell his land, or use is made of a similar phrase; in another he is said to have held it freely, or to have been a free man (*libere tenuit; et liber fuit*). But not all similarities of formulae, or presentation of in-

---

[1] The formulae stating the assessments of holdings, which differ for various groups of shires, are given in Maitland: *DBB*, pp. 404–6.

formation, are as uniform as they are in the above instances. Eyton grouped the remaining shires thus:

(a) Middlesex, Herts, Bucks

(b) Cambs, Beds

(c) Oxon, Northants, Leics, Warwicks

(d) Staffs, Salop, Cheshire, 'between Ribble and Mersey'

(e) Derbyshire, Notts, Rutland, Yorks, Lincs, Hunts.[1]

Ballard reduced Eyton's nine circuits to seven by making a single circuit of (a) and (b) above, and combining the whole of (d), except Staffordshire, which he placed in (c), with that west midland group in which ploughlands are not regularly mentioned. Stephenson followed Ballard except for certain minor adjustments.[2] Cambridgeshire and Hertfordshire, where alone we have the jurors' names, were probably taken together.[3]

The above must not be taken to imply that any such grouping of shires was an initial or essential part of the organisation of the Inquest, though it seems highly probable that at an intermediate stage, and for one definite purpose at least, they were treated in territorial blocks. While we hear much in DB of shire- and Hundred-juries, we never receive the smallest direct indication of 'provincial groupings' of shires. In contrast to similarities of formulae, there are both marked and subtle differences in the treatment and material of almost all the shires. Some of these would be inevitable; the existence of the Sussex rapes, and the fact that many manors lay in more than one of these, meant the employment of special formulae which we naturally do not find elsewhere. Fisheries, common in the other south-western counties, are unmentioned in Wiltshire and Cornwall, and among the midland shires are absent from the Leicestershire text. Meadow is almost everywhere estimated in terms of the acre or by means of linear dimensions, but in

---

[1] Eyton: *Notes on Domesday*, pp. 9–10.

[2] Ballard: *Dom. Inq.*, p. 12; C. Stephenson: 'Notes on the Composition and Interpretation of Domesday Book' (*Speculum*, vol. xxii). Their grouping of the shires, and Eyton's, are given in *DRB*, Appendix II.

[3] Their names were not preserved in DB, but were included in IE and ICC.

a few shires in terms of plough-teams. Pasture is commonly recorded in the Essex folios, but only about a dozen times for the whole of its sister-shires of Norfolk and Suffolk. The treatment of the boroughs differs from shire to shire; e.g. in Wiltshire and Dorset. It is plain that the primary unit was the single shire.

It is plain, too, irrespective of differences of formulae and content, that shires treated their material in different ways. Usually the late Queen Matilda's estates form a sub-section of the *Terra Regis*, but in Buckinghamshire (152bi,2) they follow the fiefs of the leading barons and precede that of the Countess Judith. No matter who was holding them in 1086, the Oxfordshire estates of William fitzOsbern, who had long been dead, come at the very end of the county's record, treated as a fief (161ai). The feudal basis is often most apparent: though the lands of Earl Aubrey, who had resigned his Northumbrian earldom, were *in manu regis*, and had not been re-granted, in most counties they form a separate sub-section, and are not grouped with the *Terra Regis*. DB makes practically no reference to the disgrace of Odo of Bayeux; normally his lands are recorded as being his and unconfiscated. But in one county the opening entry reads *tenuit*, not *tenet* (176ai).

The Hundreds and wapentakes

It is equally clear that in most shires the secondary unit was the Hundred or the wapentake.[1] The structure of DB makes it plain that each Hundred separately rendered its account to the inquisitors, or that returns were re-grouped by Hundreds, and so the holdings in a Hundred normally come together in the account of each fief, and often in a consistent order throughout a shire. The organisers, perhaps conscious that a Hundred's statements might have to be checked, included headings showing in which Hundred a holding was reckoned to be. Unfortunately, they made frequent errors, and omitted a number of headings which should have been included, especi-

---

[1] The possible function of the Sussex rapes or Kentish lathes in connection with the Inquest has not received much attention. The testimony of 'the lathe of Eastry' is however mentioned (13ai).The Ridings or 'thirdings' of Yorkshire and Lincolnshire seem to have held a place intermediate between shire and wapentake.

ally in Oxfordshire. They omitted them altogether from the Exeter Domesday, so that they do not appear for the south-western shires in the Exchequer Domesday.[1]

About a dozen times in Berkshire, and quite frequently elsewhere, they omitted indication of the relevant Hundred (sometimes, indeed, they entered the name of the Hundred instead of that of the manor; e.g. *Nachededorne*), or included a Hundred-name, overlooked the fact that there were in that fief no manors within the Hundred, and continued entries without correcting the ascription to a Hundred. In consequence, there are numerous instances where we cannot be sure in which Hundred a holding lay in 1086.

The use of the Hundred as the secondary territorial unit has left its mark upon DB in other ways also. The clerks frequently treated those classes of the peasantry variously styled *coceti* or *cotarii* and *bordarii* as the same thing; e.g. in the Summaries of the LE and in parts of the IE, what are *cotarii* in the Domesday text are there added to the totals of the *bordarii*. In a number of southern counties we find that some Hundreds contain *bordarii* only, some only *cotarii*, apart from *villani* and *servi*. In Surrey, bordars and cottars never appear in the same entry, and the latter are found here and in Berkshire in certain Hundreds only.[2] No woodland was recorded in eight Berkshire Hundreds, all in the north-west; it may be that no account of it was, through some accident, demanded or recorded. Two New Forest Hundreds have the formula *geldavit*, the rest *se defendit*. The inclusion of a particular piece of information, or of a phrase, is frequently limited within the account of a shire to the individual Hundred, or group of Hundreds, as with the phrase *pro manerio* in Buckinghamshire. Formulae are used for the Huntingdonshire Hundreds of Hurstingstone and Norman-cross which do not appear for the other two Hundreds.

---

[1] In Cambridgeshire the name of the Hundred was seven times omitted; Babraham (199a2) is ascribed to Flendish when the ICC shows it was in Chilford; 'Weslai' Hundred (199a2) is otherwise unknown, and seems to be due to inserting the name of a vill by mistake.

[2] This sort of illustration of the peculiarities of the individual Hundred-account is clearly shown in F. H. Baring: *Domesday Tables*.

The functions of Shire and Hundred

Of the composition of the shire-court and Hundred-court we receive little more indication than is afforded by that passage in the IE which mentions that the enquiry was made 'by the oath of the sheriff and of all the barons and of all their Frenchmen and of the whole Hundred'. It suggests that the royal Commissioners put all these on oath and caused them to swear that what was to be set down as the result of the Domesday Inquest was true, and to give evidence on oath. They, presumably, were regarded as what are described in DB as 'the best men of the whole shire' (177ai), and as 'the men of the country' (*patria*). For the ICC and IE show that the Hundred-juries were composed (in Cambridgeshire and Hertfordshire at least) of eight men, four of whom were 'French' and four English, and many of whom seem to have been possessed of sub-tenancies. But we find also Richard the reeve of the Hundred of Staine, 'a man of the Abbot of Ely', a baron's steward, 'Walter the monk', a priest. These are not the ordinary villager.

The Hundred represents, as a rule, a fairly extensive area, and the Inquest officials could not have performed their task without making use of units of enquiry smaller than this. The components of a Hundred were its villages and manors, and instantly the difficulty arises that the village might represent a single manor, that it might be divided among several manors with different owners, and that the manor might consist of a number of individual villages, not necessarily forming a geographical whole.

The villa of Domesday Book

The first of the questions to be asked, according to the list which prefaces the IE, is 'what is the name of the manor?' This in itself is enough to engender a suspicion that the unit of the Inquest was not, as the form of the ICC might suggest, the vill. DB makes fairly frequent use of the term *villa*, but it is improbable that it had any precise meaning. To those who compiled DB, the prosperous town of Bury St. Edmunds

(II.372) is a vill; so is the borough of Totnes (*334*). But so is the small Dorset settlement of Hurpston (84ai), which has but five recorded inhabitants, with none above the status of a coscet. We can hardly think of a 'vill' of Tidworth, for North Tidworth and South Tidworth were (and are) in Wiltshire and Hampshire respectively. Certainly we cannot think of a 'vill' where a river had given its name to a number of settlements on or near its banks. There are, for example, fourteen entries in the Dorset Domesday under the name 'Tarrant' (not all in the same Hundred); today there are eight parishes so called, with as many miles between the most northerly and southerly settlements. The vill of DB is, it seems, indefinable: no doubt there were places, isolated hamlets or steadings, which men would not have spoken of as 'vills', but any settlement with some community of interests, irrespective of size or character, might in 1086 have been thought of as a vill. In Cambridgeshire a common phrase is 'pasture for the beasts of the vill'; we hear too of the mill, the church, of the vill (Bradfield, II.362).

But the vill, it seems, had been and still was some form of unit. It is plain that when fiscal liability was being cast on the Hundred, the Hundred had apportioned its quota by dividing it amongst what it thought of as its constituent villages; five hides or six carucates to one of average size and prosperity, ten or twelve to a larger village, and so on.[1] The ICC shows this most clearly, and however disrupted the original assessment might have become, as holdings in a vill developed into independent economic and administrative units, it shows us this basis most markedly in Cambridgeshire. It says that a place with a certain name 'defended itself' as a whole for so many hides, irrespective of the fact that many men might own different portions of the vill, each with its own liability. DB itself reminds us of this: 'this vill' it notes of Watton (II.174), 'was in two manors'. The ICC is drawn up according to Hundreds and vills, and with very few exceptions, the vills of a Hundred appear in each fief in DB in the order in which they appear in the ICC. It may be that because its authors thought in terms of vills they recorded only Toft (111ai)

[1] In the north, imposition had been in terms of a unit of six carucates (p. 245).

though both DB (191bi) and IE (43bi) show us that with Toft went the settlement at Hardwick.

Those who furnished the relevant information, perhaps the elders of the Hundred, did not altogether think in terms of the vill. For there seem to have been numerous places, sharing it is true a common name, which were not to be classed as characteristic nucleated villages. For the village is not a static thing: some villages decay; others prosper, and the surplus inhabitants have to break new ground, and, in order to avoid waste of time and energy, construct a new settlement at some little distance from the parent community. We read in DB of *Snareshella* and of *Alia Snareshella* (II.178), of *altera Pichenham* (II.144b), of *Rodeclif, alia Rodeclif,* and *tercia Rodeclif* (301b2), of *Parva Meltuna* (II.204b), of *Litla Livermera* (II.366b), of *Rollandri majore* and *parva Rollandri* (160bi, 155a2), of *Sut* (South) *Cadeberia* (383b) and of *Chenvel Regis* (*1*). As early as 968 we are told of 'the two Holfords', and in the ICC of 'the two Wilbrahams' (79b2). The river Cerne gave its name to a number of settlements, and one offshoot of them is in DB *Obcerne,* Upcerne (75b2), a newer village further upstream. But such names are not, in DB, of extreme frequency; it is rather later that we find neighbouring settlements distinguished by such names as King's Langley and Abbot's Langley, Fonthill Episcopi and Fonthill Giffard, Clyst St. Mary and Clyst St. George, Tarrant Monkton and Tarrant Crawford.

Thus we can see why the vill or village was not an unit convenient to the inquisitors. That it was not used as their unit seems plain. Had the returns had a villar basis, we should expect to find two things common in DB. First, if a landholder possessed several distinct estates in a vill, we should expect them to appear consecutively in his fief. Secondly, we should expect all the woods, meadows, and pastures of the holdings in a vill to be reported in terms of the same unit; all, e.g., in acres, or by linear dimensions. But that is just what, over and over again, we do not find. Two portions of Wootton Fitzpaine were held by a certain Bretel of Robert of Mortain. But five entries for other places separate the two holdings called *Wodetone* (80ai). Nor is there consistency about units of quantity. At Pitcott, for example, wood and pasture for one holding is given in linear dimensions, for the other by acres (89b2, 98b2). Instances of both features are so numerous as to ensure that there was no single report for the individual vill.

There is yet another reason why the vill could not be the Inquest unit. Not infrequently neighbouring villages, all in the same ownership, had for convenience been combined to form an economic and administrative unit. The whole Wiltshire Hundred of Ramsbury, owned by the Bishop of Salisbury, is dealt with in DB in a single entry (66ai), but there were more villages within it than that of Ramsbury; their statistics would be added to those of Ramsbury itself.[1] Moreover not all the holdings in a village, sharing a common name, were within the same Hundred; in course of time landholders had found it convenient to attach an estate to a particular neighbouring Hundred.[2] With the Hundred as an Inquest unit, the vill, unless it was all within a single Hundred, could not also be the inquisitors' unit.

The manor

The unit of the Inquest was what the clerks styled *manerium* or *mansio*, the manor, frequently contracted to M̄. It is hardly, like so many of DB's technical terms, an approximate translation of an Anglo-Saxon word; on the other hand, the conception of the manor was hardly a Norman innovation. The Old English *heafod botl*, 'principal dwelling', had for some time been vaguely equated with not only a lord's house, but also with the lands surrounding it from which he derived provisions and services and money.

It is improbable that either Normans or their predecessors could have defined what they meant by a manor, and, indeed, it is virtually incapable of definition. For the manor took many different forms, and varied widely in character. We find in DB vast aggregations of territory such as made up the manor of Sherborne (77ai), which charters show to have included a large number of villages in north Dorset, none of which is

---

[1] The Hundred of Ramsbury includes, besides the parish of that name, those of Baydon, Bishopstone, and Little Hinton, all of which may have been settlements in 1086.

[2] Some of the holdings at the two Orchestons (69a2, 72b2) are in Dole Hundred others in that of Heytesbury.

mentioned in DB, and which did not lie in a solid block of
territory. We find enormous scattered manors such as Rothley
(230a2,bi), with twenty-two named *membra* or 'members'. DB
tells us that the land of the Northamptonshire manor of
Finedon (*Tingdene*, 220ai) lay in six named Hundreds. The
land of some of the New Forest manors lay in the Isle of
Wight (38b2, 39ai).

There were manors which consisted of the whole land of a
single village, and villages whose lands were shared among a
number of manors; even hamlets and outliers in the hills or
woodlands or marches, each the home of a solitary family,
such as Fernhill on Dartmoor (110ai), were manors. Some of
the East Anglian manors, too, were very small, amounting to
only a few geld-acres.

DB comparatively rarely tells us the names of the settlements
which made up the complex manors, but for the most part
deals with these in a single entry bearing the name of what it
calls the *caput manerii*, *capitale manerium* (377ai), or head of the
manor. Sometimes, indeed, we are told what the constituents
were (e.g. of several manors of Glastonbury Abbey in Somerset), and that certain places were berewicks or outlying portions
of a manor; Hatfield Broad Oak in Essex (II.2) had three
berewicks – Amwell, Hertford, and Hoddesdon – in Hertfordshire. In the northern counties, and in less degree in those of
the east, we often find recorded not only the manors, but also,
immediately following the accounts of them, a list of their
berewicks and also their sokelands; that is, places whose
inhabitants, though not strictly speaking part of the manor,
were within its owner's soke or jurisdiction (e.g. Darley, 272a2).

The Inquest clerks were at great pains to note which holdings
were manors, though at times their imperfections leave us in
doubt as to whether the subject of an entry was a manor, or, if
not, of what manor it was part. In some shires, chiefly those of
the north and of the east midlands, they inscribed against the
appropriate entries a marginal $\overline{\text{M}}$ to show that it was or had
been a manor, and often, if it was not, a B or $\overline{\text{S}}$ to indicate that
it was a berewick or sokeland. Repeatedly they recorded that
a man held or had held a certain estate 'as a manor' (*pro*

manerio); occasionally they are still more explicit and say that someone held an estate 'and it was a manor'.[1]

Indeed, they went a good deal further than this, often writing a figure over the $\overline{M}$ to indicate for how many manors it had been held, or saying that some place was held for more than one manor. For the composition of a manor was something which was essentially fluid. Many of the minute manors which we find recorded must have owed their origins to the division of a landowner's estate among his sons, and what might once have been a single manor would become a number of manors. For the sake of administrative or economic efficiency, a man might amalgamate a number of holdings into a single manor, and this obviously happened in a large number of instances after the Conquest: a landowner, finding himself with a quantity of small and reasonably adjacent holdings, would for his own convenience treat them as a unit.

DB continually records the changes which had taken place in the composition of manors. Before the Conquest, Earl Harold had joined the vills of Latton and Eisy into a single manor (68bi). Three Shropshire manors had been held by three thegns, but when Earl William fitzOsbern gave them to Thurstan of Wigmore, the latter joined them to his manor of Claybury (260ai). Roger of Ivry put *Elinge* (62bi) in his manor of Harwell. The figure over the symbol $\overline{M}$ indicates that what is now a single manor had formerly been as many manors as the figure indicates, and usually we read that it had been held before the Conquest by as many thegns as there had been manors. At Weston (286b2), six pre-Conquest holders are named; 'each had his hall' (to the significance of this phrase we shall come in a moment), and there had been six manors where in 1086 there was one. The Devon and Somerset records contain copious entries stating that a man has added a pre-Conquest manor to another of his manors (and equally we read of portions of manors taken away and incorporated in a manor of the man who has filched them from another). Sometimes small holdings were lumped together to form a new manor: the entry for Sidestrand (II.170b) tells us how such estates were

---

[1] e.g. Ashley (163bi). For M and B we sometimes find MAN, MNR; BER, BR. It is possible that some of these symbols were inscribed after the Inquest was over.

delivered to Waleran 'to make up a manor'. Chilfrome (*48b*) had been held 'for three manors', but at the Inquest William of Mohun claimed to hold it for two. He would not have done so unless to do this was in some way important to him.

Quite obviously it was important to those responsible for conducting the Inquest to know which holdings were or had been manors, and for how many manors a holding counted. In the Exeter Domesday, almost every entry begins with the statement that Y holds Z for one manor; in the Summaries of certain fiefs which we find here and in the IE the number of manors in question is always given, and collation with DB and other documents shows that the number given is that of the holders (which implies the number of manors) in King Edward's time.[1] But why should they want to know this? Manors varied so greatly in content that the number of manors a man held was no guide to his resources or prosperity.

Maitland decided that it was because the manor was the unit of taxation. 'A manor', he wrote, 'is a house against which geld is charged.'[2] Though the vill might have been the unit on which an assessment had once been laid, the vills had been combined to form complex manors, or divided up into a number of manors; parts of a vill, owned by different lords, might be parts of several different manors. The payment of geld was the lord's responsibility (though his tenants were responsible to him for their appointed shares), and while he may have had to bring it to Hundred- or shire-moot, possibly the tax collector journeyed from manor to manor, to the lord's hall which DB so frequently records.

Round vigorously disputed this contention.[3] He pointed out that *manerium* alternated with the colourless *terra*; that indeed, though some entries were prefaced $\overline{M}$, the holding was in fact described as *terra*. He quoted also instances of what seemed to be 'manors within manors', and of holdings gelding independently of the manors to which DB says they belonged.

---

[1] Not every pre-Conquest holding recorded or implied in DB was, of course, a manor. But it happens that this does not seriously affect collation with Summary totals.

[2] *DBB*, pp. 127–8.

[3] J. H. Round: 'The Domesday Manor' (*EHR*, vol. xv, p. 293). See also Tait's review of *DBB* in *EHR*, vol. xii.

But the impression DB as a whole gives is that Maitland's theory is substantially correct. First, DB's imprecision is obvious, and its telegraphic style, on so involved a matter, can easily be misinterpreted. Secondly, in instances such as that in which it is said that Ralf holds of the manor of Whitchurch a manor which is called Freefolk (41ai), this may not mean that Freefolk was a manor in 1086, but that the pre-Conquest manor of that name had subsequently been absorbed in the manor of Whitchurch.[1] Thirdly, where the land of a complex manor was widely dispersed, it may have been an obvious convenience for the geld of the individual member, or of a berewick, to be collected locally instead of centrally, so that what is a component of a manor is said to geld and has its liability stated. *Terra*, land, obviously can have no precise meaning (though sometimes it seems to be used to indicate that the estate in question is *not* a manor), and frequently would be used because the clerk's sense of Latinity forbade the repetition of *manerium*.[2] Often enough, when owing to absorption in a different manor a holding had ceased to be a manor, the clerks, perhaps purposely, styled it *terra* (e.g. *Lamarsh*, II.74a,b; Cray, 6b2).[3]

Just as the clerks noted manorial status, so they recorded when a holding was not or had not been a manor. One estate at *Driteham* (35bi) had been held as a manor, but at the time of the Inquest it did not lie in any manor, nor was it held as a manor.[4] Of two holdings at Stratford (309bi), one was a manor,

[1] The text reads 'of this manor and of these hides' (the fifty hides at which Whitchurch is assessed) 'Ralf fitzSeifride holds a manor which is called Freefolk'. We are also told that Ednod had held it of the Bishop of Winchester, 'and could not go where he wished': this implies he could not take Freefolk out of the Bishop's manor, or leave the Bishop's authority. Thus equally it might be that Freefolk, not a manor in 1066, now was one, but was not now part of Whitchurch.

[2] On two occasions $\overset{7}{T}$ (for *terra*) is noted marginally, just as $\overline{M}$ and $\overset{7}{\overline{S}}$ and B are (206ai,2).

[3] Collation of the LE entries strongly suggests that frequently the clerks used *terra* when a holding was not or had ceased to be a manor.

[4] Maitland's interpretation of this was that it was shirking the geld (*DBB*, p. 123); in the south-west the clerk would probably have said that it was 'concealed'. Were places said 'to be in no Hundred' (157ai, 183a2, 377bi) in a similar position? Dean (48a2) did not 'lie in any manor' of Waleran's: this may mean that he had illegally appropriated it. But it is said both to geld and to have gelded.

the other not. Now one of the essences of the pre-Conquest 'manor' seems to be that it had included the house which its possessor occupied, his 'hall' or 'court', *halla, haula, aula, curia;* we do indeed hear of the 'lord's building', *dominicum aedificium* (Pytchley, 222ai), the 'demesne of the hall' (Langham, 283ai). But we hear also of manors 'without a hall', *sine halla* (e.g. Selling, 12a2); they were frequent in the north (e.g. on 286bi, and 306a2 onwards). At Westmeston (27a2) there had been no hall, but neither had it gelded, as the witnesses report.

It is certainly suggestive that when a holding has been leased to villeins, as at Millbrook (41a2), we are told 'there is no hall there'; at Westmeston (27a2) it is added that they do not geld, which probably means that they do not geld direct, rather than that they have no liability. It seems to imply that neither of these instances is considered to be a manor, but is part of some un-named manor. How difficult it was for the clerks to be precise is well demonstrated by instances of manors which had never been hidated because they paid the *feorm* of one night, and yet portions of these placed 'in the Forest', or taken out of the manor, are expressed in terms of hides and virgates (e.g. Rockbourne, 39ai; Neatham, 38ai). It is difficult to believe they would have inscribed so much about manorial status, and pre-Conquest manorial status, if there had not been some economic or administrative reason for it.

The information about manors and manorial status which the witnesses provided and the clerks recorded is voluminous and catholic. The holding of manors by previous Welsh kings is noted (Bistre, 269a2); so are the holding of 42 houses in Oxford 'as one manor' and the hall Queen Edith had held in Grantham (158a2, 337b2 – how town houses could form a manor is considered on p. 263). The material ranges from noting that Hail Weston (207ai) was a manor by itself and did not belong to that of Kimbolton; that holdings could not be taken out of the manor of which they were part (Wycombe, 144bi); that the pleas of a manor were held in the hall of its lord, not in the Hundred-court (Acton, 265bi). We are told how at Shalford (35bi) two brothers each had his house, yet they dwelt in one court, but that at Barsham (II.168) the two holders dwelt in two halls. In the two Aldrington estates

(26b2) – *in his duabus terris* – there was only one hall, one manor. Three holdings had been manors, but in 1086 were in the soke of Clifton, and thus no longer manors (313a2); the soke of Burton belonged to the manor of Scampton (368b2), 'but nevertheless there was a hall there' – it had been a manor previously. Detailed study of DB can only make us think that present and past manorial status, or the fact that to its authors a holding was not a manor, was of immense import.

The sources of the statistics

We have no direct evidence as to how the material of DB was furnished, and all suggestions can be but conjectures inspired by the information the documents supply. The owners of those small estates which were virtually under peasant proprietorship most likely made their own return of them. Probably the reeve of every manor, or group of manors administered together, provided the details of plough-teams, inhabitants, and manorial appurtenances, and quite possibly did so, not direct to Inquest officials, but to the steward of a local fief.[1]

We must not, I think, interpret the passage from the IE quoted on p. 7 as necessarily implying that the priest, reeve, and six villeins of every village appeared before the Commissioners to render a tale of oxen and meadows and swine. This would take a very long time, and involve problems of travel and accommodation which would seem to be insuperable. It is unlikely that these would have reached perfect agreement about quantities, and royal Commissioners would have had small patience with personal differences. Many a vill, on the evidence of DB, could not muster as many as half-a-dozen villeins, or six men who were not slaves. In many instances, where a village was divided between two or more manors, such witnesses could hardly speak for the village as a whole. Had they done so, we should expect meadow, pasture, and wood to be estimated in the same manner for the whole village. But this is just what we do not find; where a village is divided, we frequently find the woodland of one of its manors

---

[1] The section in the IE known as the *breviate* groups the demesne manors and gives totals for each group. This suggests that the manors in each group may have been administered together.

recorded in acres, of another by linear dimensions.[1] Indeed, the passage does not definitely state that these men furnished statistical details; they are rather coupled with their superiors who are enjoined to 'make oath'. Their function was more likely to have been attending a meeting of the Hundred-court at which the material supplied for the Inquest was read over to them, swearing that what was set down was true, and giving evidence on oath about tenancy where required to do so. For that the ordinary villagers at least upon occasion gave sworn evidence, voluntarily or not, is demonstrated by DB, though it may be, where there was a dispute about rightful possession, that they were sent on to the shire-court from the Hundred-court to do so.[2] But there is no direct evidence that the Hundred-court had any other part in the Inquest proceedings, but that of providing evidence about tenancies.

Some places, however, failed to produce the information required. None of the inhabitants of one of the Woodchester manors (164a2) came to the *descriptio*; no account (*ratio*) was given of 33 of the Bishop of Hereford's 300 hides within Herefordshire; of Hankham (22a2) it had to be written, *inde nullum responsum*.

Ever since the time of Eyton and of Round, however, it had been more or less assumed that the ICC indicates how the Inquest was conducted and the 'original returns' inscribed. The contention that the ICC provided the vital clue arose mainly from the conviction that DB was a geld book, and that since geld-liability had been imposed *en bloc* on the Hundred, and then partitioned by the Hundred among its vills, the original returns were of this order; all the holdings in a village or combination of villages would come together, later to be re-arranged by fees and condensed. Round's theory stayed unchallenged until Professor Galbraith pointed out that such 're-arrangement' made it virtually impossible to use DB as a geld-book, for it 'tore to shreds', in Maitland's words, the divided villages, necessitating a search through the entire county record to establish their individual assessments. He rightly added that the feudally-minded Normans cared nothing for the pre-

---

[1] See also p. 171.

[2] Passages indicating evidence given by *villani*, etc., appear on p. 64.

Conquest organisation by shires and by Hundreds, but only
for one based on the 'honour', the barony; and used the
Hundred – and perhaps the village – for Inquest purposes
merely as a matter of administrative convenience. There had
been no time to evolve an organisation which ignored Hundred
and village.

We do not, indeed, know what form the 'original returns'
took, and it is most improbable that the ICC represents it.
The ICC survives only in an incomplete twelfth-century copy
bound up with ms. A of the IE, and ignores a number of the
royal manors. Its numerous references to the witness of shire or
Hundred rather suggests that, if it is a copy of the original
returns, it is one into which material from the later stages of
the Inquest – examination of claims to disputed estates and of
the truth of the returns – has been interpolated. Its original
may indeed have been a sheriff's copy of the proceedings,
using a hundredal and villar structure because that was the
form which best suited his responsibilities regarding the collection of geld and the discharge of duties to his master the King.[1]

But the DB account of Cambridgeshire could not have been
taken from the ICC, for it includes matter not to be found
therein, and the probability is that a record of the royal
demesne and the fiefs of the tenants-in-chief had already been
made when the ICC was drawn up. Professor Galbraith thinks
that it was 'actually written down in court', or constructed
from the accounts of the holdings already existing and grouped
by fees, 'helped out by notes of additions and amendments
made by the hundredal jurors, the sheriff, and other oral
testimony to the commissioners'.[2] It looks as if Ely Abbey, the
bulk of whose possessions was in Cambridgeshire, saw the value
of this document to itself and obtained a copy of it, which
later was re-copied in the form in which we possess it. The
IE does not treat all the six counties with which it was concerned in the same way, probably because the three circuits

---

[1] The absence of so many royal manors might be because the sheriff, the royal
representative, may have preserved a separate account of the King's estates.

[2] Galbraith: *MoDB*, p. 135. The surviving ICC refers to the *breve regis*, here
implying the DB account of *Terra Regis*, the construction of which it could not
altogether have preceded.

involved had arranged their material rather differently, and because other shires produced (so far as we know) no document comparable to the ICC.

Non-statistical information

While reeves and village headmen *may* have furnished the rest – i.e., the largely non-statistical – of the information demanded, it seems far more likely that this was ultimately provided to the Inquest clerks by a representative of the local fief, a monastic steward or a baron's treasurer. The first suggestion that there may have been returns for the fief was made by Mr. C. Johnson. He pointed out that against some of the fiefs in the Norfolk section appeared the letters *f, n, fr,* etc., which might be indications that the owner had or had not made (*fecit*) a return, and that one holder seems to speak of producing a list of his manors, referring to 'the day on which it was drawn up'.[1]

Another slight suggestion of returns by fiefs is furnished by the MS. known as 'Evesham A'.[2] Its source seems to have been 'an early stage of the enquiry', and 'information collected from tenants in chief and arranged in hundreds in preparation for the hundredal enquiry but before that enquiry took place'. The grouping of the estates is largely by tenants-in-chief, and in one section all the demesnes of Westminster Abbey precede the sub-tenancies, while in DB demesne and sub-tenancy are described in a single entry. The ms. suggests initial returns by fees, with the entries for divided vills or sub-infeudated manors brought together in preparation for examination in terms of the Hundred and vill.

It is indeed to be argued that the largely hundredal structure of DB is deceptive, and that the 'original returns' were in terms of the fief (though probably here too the manors would be grouped by Hundreds), but that at the Inquest villages,

[1] II.276; the word used is *inbreviatus,* but this suggests rather inscription in DB. Similar letters appear against fiefs in the Essex and Suffolk texts, e.g. nos. XV, XXVI, XXXIII, and XL (Essex), and on fols. 378b, 381, 389, 420b (Suffolk), and in the Gloucestershire folios from 166bi–9b2. Professor Galbraith thinks they may be late additions to the text (*MoDB*, p. 82).

[2] See P. H. Sawyer: 'Evesham A, a Domesday Text', in the Worcestershire Historical Society's *Miscellany I* (Worcester and London, 1960).

whether divided or not, were used as units, without harmonising any differences in the manner of presentation of the information. It is highly probable that every landholder did produce a list of his manors and tenancies – it would be prudent, if not essential, to do so – and added information as to how he had come by each, or for what reason he claimed a holding not actually in his possession. The instructions, be it noted, demand that the name of the estate, and who held it in the time of King Edward, be furnished to the inquisitors.

This would at least explain why, in instances of disputed holdings, a note of them frequently appears in DB in the account of the fief of each of the claimants, and this would account for occasional differences in the figures in these duplicate entries.[1] The original explanation of these very frequent duplications was that the clerks were careful, where there was uncertainty about rightful tenure, to include an account in the fiefs of both claimants. In numerous instances, however, they failed to do so, and it is doubtful if this deduction is a valid one. But if they used feudal returns as their guide, the holding would automatically appear in the fief of both claimants, unless rightful possession of it had been determined.

Certain aspects of a large number of entries in DB strengthen a belief that there were returns by fees. Hundredmen or village elders would hardly report, unless asked to do so, the terms of a pre-Conquest tenancy, or in what manner and when the present holder obtained a manor. But the steward of a fief would surely produce a list of all the properties to which it was intended to lay claim at the Inquest, stating which were Church demesne or thegnlands or other leaseholds, noting properties over whose inhabitants the right of soke existed, pointing out that a right to them had been established earlier in the reign, or in what manner they had been obtained since King William's coming. While the sheriff must have possessed a list of all the properties within his territory, with their

[1] E.g. the two entries for the manor of Aston Ingham (179bi, 186a2), one under the royal manor of Linton, one under Ansfrid's lands. Eight Rutland entries appear both on fol. 293bi (Rutland) and also scattered about the Lincolnshire text. In six instances the details differ. Galbraith (*MoDB*, p. 117) has pointed out that dual entries are rarely exact 'duplicates', and sometimes suggest an alternative account given by a Hundred-jury recalled to give further information.

assessments and other liabilities or privileges, it might be the representative of the fief rather than of the village, especially the divided village, who would submit the information about the amount of geld for which each property was liable, and what exemption could be claimed. About a return of plough-lands no suggestion will be made at this point, (the 'terms of reference', incidentally, do not require their number to be given), but as regards the other information demanded, it seems more likely that the representative of the fief rather than villagers furnished details of alterations in the composition of the manor, the holdings of free men and sokemen, and the values at three different dates. Much, too, appears in DB which is not included in those IE terms of reference, and when we come to deal with the miscellaneous information (Chapter X), we shall see that its provision was probably not the affair of the village.

The problem of the borough entries

The instructions do not require that any information be given about the boroughs and their inhabitants. For this any or all of a number of reasons may have been responsible. In the first place, the towns – or the greater part of them – did not belong to any one lord in the sense that a manor did; nor, as a rule, were they included in any Hundred, and therefore it was perhaps no one's strict responsibility to make returns about them. Secondly, it would have been extremely difficult to frame a comprehensive set of questions about urban inhabitants and pursuits and customs comparable to those which dealt with the manor and its characteristics. Thirdly, there was, generally speaking, no one man, or representative of a body of men, who could speak for a borough as a whole. Fourthly, the towns were of such widely different sizes and character and origins that to deal with all on a single principle would probably have proved impossible. Finally, there may indeed have been instructions about describing the boroughs, but since our sole evidence about such instructions is in the IE, and Ely Abbey had only slender interests in any of the local towns, these may have been omitted from a document for which she was responsible.

Yet, since most of the boroughs are recorded in DB, someone

must have been responsible for their inclusion. The most likely official is the sheriff, for among his duties was that of ensuring that the King his master received all that was his due, and it is plain that from most boroughs the King received revenue and services. Moreover, in many boroughs the local sheriff himself had considerable financial and practical interest. Each sheriff may have had quite different ideas about what should and what should not be brought before the King's Commissioners regarding the towns, and this may in some measure account for the unsystematic and varied accounts of them.[1]

The accounts of the boroughs are indeed so diverse, in content and scope, that they have always furnished, and continue to furnish, one of the most intriguing and irritating sets of problems that DB presents. No account of the two chief cities of the realm, London and Winchester, reached the final draft. Towns known to have been of considerable importance, such as Bristol (163a2, 164b2, 88a2) and Tamworth (238a2, 246a2,b2), are unmentioned or appear only incidentally. The account of a town may occupy more than an entire folio, or be limited to some half-dozen lines or less.[2] The material and the manner of its presentation usually varies from shire to shire, and, within the shire, for the individual borough also. Not all of what we can only think of as towns are styled 'boroughs', and there are places with burgesses which we can hardly think of as towns. Almost there seem to be different categories of boroughs, and yet no really satisfactory classification of the various kinds of town, or any system by which we can sharply differentiate one group of towns from another, can be evolved. But that those responsible for DB saw gradations of urban units seems certain.

This is strongly suggested by the structure of DB itself. In the accounts of a considerable number of shires, the description of the major town within it is placed at the very inception of the record, before the Index of landholders within the county,

---

[1] Folio references for the principal boroughs, since the places in which these occur are easy to determine, are here normally given only at the first mention of a town.

[2] Cp., e.g., Chester (262bi) and Bedford (209ai). This again suggests that there were no set formulae and pattern for burghal returns.

and before the royal estates, *Terrae Regis*. This is true, for example, of York (298ai) and Shrewsbury (252ai) and Gloucester (161ai), and of the midland shires, some of which had been the headquarters of a Danish 'army', and round which the north and east midland shires seem to have been formed, e.g. Cambridge (189ai), Lincoln (336ai) Leicester (230ai).[1] Sometimes it seems as though the organisers intended to do this, but that their work ended before the matter was inscribed. Most of fols. 126a,b are blank, as though an account of London should have preceded that of Middlesex. Three and a half columns (37a,b) are void before the Index of Hampshire tenants-in-chief is inscribed; we can only think they should have been filled by a description of Winchester. A blank space occurs at the opening of the Somerset Domesday. A variation of the system is noticeable in vol. II of Domesday; the account of Colchester (II.104a) concludes the Essex material, and Norwich (II.116) and Ipswich (II. 342b) each forms a special section of the King's lands. Had we an Exchequer account of the eastern shires, we should probably find these three towns heading the material for each.

There were counties, however, which contained no place of the character which later would usually be thought of as the 'county town'. Dorset contained four boroughs, which are all described in identical fashion at the inception of its record (*11–12b*, 75ai).[2] Some secondary boroughs are placed, not with the 'county' borough, but in positions of special emphasis. Southampton (52ai), for example, comes between the account of the Hampshire mainland and that of the bulk of the Isle of Wight.[3] But many of the smaller towns, especially those which had not become 'boroughs' until after the Conquest, or those with which the King had no immediate concern, are within the body of the county records, included in the fief of

[1] Huntingdon (203ai) is within the same category, but is the only borough in the shire. The accounts of Derby and of Nottingham (280ai,2) come between those of the two counties, which seem to have been treated as one.

[2] Shaftesbury, Dorchester, Wareham, Bridport (75ai). Wimborne, which from the mention of houses within it, seems to be a quasi-borough, is not so singled out (26a, 80bi).

[3] The King's lands in the eastern Hundred of the Island are tacked on to the account of his mainland manors.

whoever had the principal interest in them. Okehampton, the seat of the new Norman sheriff of Devonshire, which was only just beginning to exhibit urban characteristics with the building of a castle and establishment of a market – it has only four burgesses – is described within Baldwin's fief (*288*, 105b2). Bury St. Edmunds comes within the Abbot's fief (II.372); Taunton (*173b*, 87bi) in that of the Bishop of Winchester. A number of places are described in just the same way as the ordinary country manors are, and the only indication of urban characteristics is that they are said to include some burgesses. But never are these called boroughs (*burgi*) or towns (*urbes*). Four in Wiltshire – Calne, Great Bedwyn, Warminster and Tilshead (64b2, 65ai) – are royal manors, described in detail, save for the number of burgesses in each, just as other rural manors are. Another in the same county is Bradford-on-Avon (67bi), belonging to the nunnery of Shaftesbury. About the accounts of the boroughs, indeed, there is no consistency whatever.

The receipt of the information

It must ever be remembered that, so far as we can tell, the whole work of the Inquest was executed between the closing days of 1085 and some date, possibly Lammas in 1086, when the 'writings' were brought to the King. Moreover, every sheriff had first to be notified, and at his instance every landholder and Hundred and village also, of what was to be required of them. Some reasonable interval had to be allowed before the first returns could be expected; the King's Commissioners had to be appointed, given their instructions and equipment, and despatched on their journeys. We know the names of those for one shire only, that of Worcester (though probably the same men dealt with the rest of the 'circuit' of which Worcestershire was part). They were headed by Remigius, Bishop of Lincoln, who had with him a clerk and two monks, and his co-adjutors were Henry de Ferrars, Walter Gifford, and Adam fitzHubert, the brother of Eudes the Steward. It looks as if Bishop William of Durham headed the south-western panel, and a certain 'Walter' may have been one of his colleagues, for they are recorded as recovering unpaid geld (*1b, 2, 2b; 7b, 8*). If so, these Commissioners were certainly engaged in areas in which they were not major landholders, as Bishop Robert's account of the Inquest suggests was the arrangement.

But we do not know that Commissioners of this importance were actively concerned from the outset of the proceedings. It is perhaps unreasonable to suppose that bishops and barons had small private, or other public, life for a good many months on end, owing to their Inquest duties. It may seem a great deal more likely that the initial stages were conducted, if not in the Hundred-courts, in the shire-court under the presidency of the King's local representative, the sheriff. The interpretation of the Bishop of Hereford's statement may be that the early stages disclosed such numerous disputes, such conflicts of evidence, that it proved necessary to despatch, to districts in which they had no major territorial connections and interests, royal legates of the standing of those of whom we hear in Worcestershire. We can hardly think that they concerned themselves with such aspects of the terms of reference as were not concerned with succession, legality of tenure, customary rights, and the like, but rather that they summoned, to attend a shire-court before them, those indicated in the IE to furnish statements on the strength of which they could make their decisions.

In Round's opinion, the Commissioners made a progress through the shire, visiting each Hundred in turn, but Maitland did not agree with him. The main argument for such progresses is that the appearance of the Hundreds in the ICC, and often in DB, in each fief, follows a regular, orderly, and geographical sequence. But it is highly unlikely that the Commissioners had time – or were willing – to undertake such journeys, and reasonable to suppose that in whatever order the Hundreds were taken, their reports were in most shires considered in an order which had a geographical basis.[1]

---

[1] A consistent order of appearance of hundreds is very marked in Devonshire, and to a somewhat lesser degree in Somerset. See R. Welldon Finn: 'The Making of the Devonshire Domesdays' (*Trans. Dev. Assn.*, vol. lxxix), and P. H. Sawyer: 'The "Original Returns" and "Domesday Book" ' (*EHR*, vol. lxx). The order in which holdings appear has been used to deduce their modern identities by I. S. Maxwell: 'The Geographical Identification of Domesday Vills' (*Trans. Inst. Brit. Geog.*, vol. xvi).

The work of the Commissioners

That the *legati regis* had the authority of royal justices seems to be clear from DB, for a few of their decisions are reported. Probably they gave many more judgments than are noted in the text. The most notable instance recorded is that regarding the manor of Werrington, of which the *barones regis* disseized the Abbot of Tavistock because the English testified that it did not belong to the abbey 'on the day on which King Edward was alive and dead' (*178b, 98*). It had been given to it by Gytha, Earl Godwine's widow, *after* the Conquest, and so the abbey had no right to it according to the principles of King William's settlement. When we read of land illegally 'occupied' that 'we have taken this into the King's hand', we must surely be reading of a decision of the Commissioners (Peldon, II.94b). It was the *legati* who decided that what had been thegnland in King Edward's day, but was later converted into reeveland, was accordingly 'taken away from the King by stealth' (Gayton, 181ai).

When someone other than the *de facto* holder claimed land, or a customary due or service, against another at the Inquest, it seems to have been common practice to ask the opinion of the Hundred-jury, or of the shire-court, about the legality thereof. The number of instances of this record in Domesday Book is considerable. 'The whole shire' testifies that Hadham (135ai) lay and lies in the demesne of the Church of Ely, and lay in it 'on the day on which King Edward was alive and dead'; the Hundred that the owner of an estate at Wycombe (146ai) could not give or sell it in such fashion that it thereby ceased to be part of the manor of Wycombe. The 'thegns of the shire' stated that Earl Harold had unjustly taken four hides at Allington (69ai) from the nunnery of Amesbury; 'the best men of the whole shire' witness that Wulfwine bought Bartley (177ai) from the Bishop of Chester for the duration of his own and two successors' lives. 'The men of the Hundred' said that they had never seen the seal of the King, or his legate, who put the claimant to Tytherley (50ai) in seizin of the manor.

In the accounts of some shires we are told nothing of appeals to the witness of the shire- or Hundred-court; but this hardly implies that they were not made. Though Dorset and Wiltshire, on the evidence of the LE, formed a 'sub-circuit', we hear nothing of either in the former, and in the latter only half-a-dozen times of the testimony of 'the shire', 'the thegns', 'the thegns of the shire' (64b2, 74b2, 71a2). There seems to be no reference to either in the accounts of Leicestershire or Cornwall, and while we hear something of the evidence of the Worcester-shire shire-court (*comitatus, scyra*), that of the Hundred is never mentioned, nor is it in Warwickshire. But it appears frequently in the east and east midlands and north, while, whereas there are a score of instances in Surrey, Middlesex shows only two examples.[1] Their judgment seems to have been accepted, if the term *diratiocinavit* (Mathon, 175bi) is anything to go by.

But some problems the Commissioners were unable to settle. They reserved for the King's judgment 'the claims which Drui de la Beuvrière made upon Morcar's land' (377bi). Bishop Osbern of Exeter claimed to be holding Buckland 'as of his bishopric' (58bi). But the authorities were not satisfied about this, and decided that the case must go before the King for his judgment (Eddington, 6ai).[2] Over and over again we read in DB that someone is holding land, but that someone else claims it, and often we are told the basis of the claim. But hardly ever is it said what the verdict was, though perhaps the fact that often it is said that the shire- or Hundred-jury testifies to the justice of one of the disputants' claims indicates for whom judgment was given.[3] There may, as we shall see later (p. 90), be a reason for this lack of clarity about the outcome.

The mass of evidence about legitimate descent of holdings and of tenancy proffered at some stage of the Inquest amply demonstrates how many questions the Commissioners were called upon to determine. On many occasions it looks as if the witnesses have been asked not only whether a certain state of affairs existed before the coming of King William, or both

---

[1] See Galbraith: *MoDB*, pp. 71–2.

[2] A case at Broughton (38bi) is said to be 'not yet determined'. Hardwin was holding a hide of Ely land at Thriplow (191ai, 199a2) 'until he can discuss the matter with the King'.

[3] The disagreements are often over what may seem to be small matters – e.g. at Chawston (215ai) there was a dispute over 1½ acres of meadow.

before and after, but also 'when did this happen?', 'how long
is it since this happened?' But equally a claimant, to give
additional point to his allegations, may have indicated the
length of time over which an immunity had been enjoyed, or
an injustice suffered. Thrice the origins are said to date from
the reign of Cnut.[1] The representative of the nunnery of
Chatteris complained that Harold Godwineson had deprived
it of Wymondley, making it part of his manor of Hitchin,
three years before King Edward's death (132a2). The Ely
monks alleged that Eustace, sheriff of Huntingdon, did not
take Easton from them until King William's reign was five
years old (208ai). The 'whole shire' can testify that Stigand
had been in possession of Cerney as early as 1055/6 (169ai).
The successor of Abbot Ælfwine is said to have held Witton in
Droitwich for more than seven years; i.e. till 1073 at least
(177b2).

The jurors are often inclined to date events by means of the
period of holding of an office, or of some familiar incident, in
each case establishing that a situation under consideration is
not a novel one. They relate their statements to the periods
during which Baynard or Swegen were sheriffs of Essex
(II.6, 6b, 7); to the time when Geoffrey of Mandeville 'went
across the sea in the King's service' (130b2); to the day of
William Malet's death, or 'when he went in the marsh', or on
the King's service, or was 'taken by the Danes' (II.189, 133b,
247); to 'the division of land between the King and Earl Ralf'
(II.150); to 'the time of Ralf the Staller' (377b2) slain in
1069/70.

Possibly appeal was made to the jurors of Hundred and shire
only where there was a conflict of evidence, or the facts were
not clear. In a great many instances we are told of evidence
adduced by men other than these jurors, and which perhaps
upon occasion enabled the Commissioners to make a decision.
Where a claimant could produce an authenticated charter or
writ, there would be small need to pursue the matter further,
except to require the local jury to state whether they had heard
it read in open court or not. But often enough, it is clear, a
claimant did not rely entirely on the jury. Evidence is adduced

---

[1] Bettisfield (264a2), Wenlock (252bi), Downton (65b2).

by 'the men of this vill' (II.285b), 'the villeins of the manor' (II.393), or by the 'men' of the claimant (II.407b), or by 'the reeve himself' (II.287b). The *ministri* of an Abbey are noted as giving their testimony (II.360b), and when we read of evidence furnished by an ecclesiastical dignitary, this may well imply no more than that monks or servants of the house provided it. Many such witnesses would hardly be regarded as 'the best men of the shire', and it is usually when their testimony is in question that we hear that the authorities required that they should be prepared to back it by undergoing the ordeal. An Englishman whose views were contradicted by the whole Hundred was willing to offer trial by battle or ordeal in support of them. Villeins were apparently prepared to back their statements 'by all manner of proof', which implies subjection to ordeal: this might indeed be offered by a woman.[1] Picot was prepared to back his claim to Charford (44b2) 'by the oath or ordeal of villeins and common folk and reeves', but we are not told that this was required, and from the fact that the manor appears in the fief of Hugh de Port, the oaths of 'the best and oldest men of the shire and Hundred' supporting *his* possession, may have made it unnecessary for Picot's witnesses actually to testify.

An equally compelling, perhaps indeed preferable, method of establishing a claim to an estate was to produce the testimony of the man who had actually put the claimant in possession of it; who had given him 'livery and seizin'. Swegen, the former sheriff of Essex, was asked by Hagebert to state that he had delivered part of the manor of Lawford to him (II.6b). The possessor of Nutley 'called the King himself to warranty' about legality of possession (II.59b): this is not uncommon, but it can hardly mean more than that the occupant claimed to hold by the King's gift. One of his *milites* summoned Earl Eustace 'to his defence' (*ad defensionem*) of his right to possession. The term used varies; we find *saisitor, tutor, protector* – this last rather suggests that the claimant was commended to the man concerned; and in one passage Bishop Odo is appealed to as *protector et liberator vel dator* of the estate. The implication is

---

[1] Instances will be found under Tasburgh (II.190), Branfort (II.393), Matlask II.146b), and on II.166, 190, 213, 277b, etc.

indeed carried back to pre-Conquest days, for Roger Bigot is spoken of as being 'such a *guarantor* as any sheriff might rightly have been in King Edward's time', showing that often it was the sheriff who was called upon to organise the King's gifts of land.[1]

But sometimes such evidence did not favour the claimant. Leodmar had 'invaded' land at Braintree and was holding it as of Richard fitzGilbert's fee, but Richard would not bear witness for his man.[2] Leofwine claimed to hold Flecknoe of Bishop Wulfstan, but the Bishop 'failed him in plea'; whereby Leofwine was 'at the King's mercy' – liable to forfeiture and fine (244bi).

Sometimes, too, evidence was lacking. Westminster Abbey could produce neither the King's writ nor a royal servant empowered to give her livery of Kelvedon; only one man 'out of the assembly of the whole shire' knew anything about the matter: this would hardly be convincing evidence. Ælfric of Thatcham was the only one of the Hundred (-jury?) who had seen a writ giving an estate to a former sheriff's wife. The jurors were compelled to admit that they 'knew nothing' about a claim to part of Witham; that they did not know that Oakhanger was bought from King William by Edwin. Indeed, of one difficulty, 'they do not know how to tell the truth of it'.[3]

Despite the vast number of claims brought before the notice of the Commissioners, we receive only rare notification of the decisions they made. It is quite common to find an estate listed in one man's fief claimed by another, and the claim supported by the evidence of witnesses, but no indication that the Commissioners had found for the claimant. The construction and language of DB very strongly suggest either that it was inscribed before the King's men had time to make decisions, or that much of the text was put together before judgment was delivered. For land, save in the instances of duplicate or parallel entries, is usually listed under the heading of the *de facto*, not the *de jure*, holder. The results would be most confusing

---

[1] See, e.g., fols. II.31b, 208ai, II.103, 2ai, II. 290b.

[2] II.101b: *non est sibi tutor*. In a second entry (II.102b), it is Richard's 'men' who did not testify in the claimant's favour.

[3] II.14b; 57b2 (Hendred); II.1; 49b2; II.338 (Hemingstone).

to future users of DB, but it would be equally confusing to list the claims and decisions by means of a series of appendixes.

Yet appendixes, for six shires, are exactly what we find. To the texts for Huntingdonshire, Lincolnshire, and Yorkshire are appended sections entitled *clamores*. Their position may make us think that they represent a stage late in the Inquest proceedings, but it may be that they were kept separate from the main text (which they rarely duplicate), because to include the matter within would add to the already considerable confusion. From the heading to those of the South Riding of Lindsey, 'Claims and agreement about them according to the men who gave sworn evidence' (*Clamores et concordia eorum per homines qui iuraverunt*), it looks as if the Commissioners did give judgment, based on the witnesses' testimony (375ai). These appendices, it is true, do not include all the points in dispute; e.g. the royal claim to soke over Orton (203bi) does not appear among them. Indeed, since here and in some other shires the existence of a dispute is indicated marginally, by *k* or *kal* (*kalumpnia, calumnia* = claim), they just possibly might be disagreements consideration of which was delayed until late in the Inquest proceedings. They seem to have been derived from hundredal returns or sessions, for the order of Hundreds and wapentakes is fairly consistent, though within each the grouping is often by the individual landholder.

The *invasiones* of the eastern counties are arranged by sections according to the person responsible for each illegality. On the whole, what they contain is absent from the feudal *breves*, and usually, where a dispute is recorded in these, it does not appear among the *invasiones* also. Some Essex Hundreds, indeed, are absent, despite their record of illegalities noted in the body of DB, from the *invasiones* altogether. But the Essex and Suffolk sections are each said to be *invasiones super regem*, and it may be that only those which affected the King's interests, or were in direct conflict with his orders, were here recorded. Ely Abbey had lost a good deal of her Essex land, but none of it is noted among the *invasiones*.

Their principles seem to have been generally adopted throughout the country, for included in the LE are folios, for three counties, headed *Terrae Occupatae*. They contain condensed notes of alterations in the structure of manors, succession to lands not those of the tenant's *antecessor*, and failure to discharge customary dues and obligations.[1] Again the structure is clearly hundredal, though at times entries concerning the individual landholder have been brought together. They contain, also, a little matter absent from the Exeter Domesday, again demonstrating how much disclosed by the Inquest is now unavailable to us; e.g. Chaffcombe, part of the manor of Crediton, is mentioned, but is not in the Exeter Domesday (*499, 117*).

The Inquest and the boroughs

It does seem as if some of the information about the boroughs, or testimony where there was a conflict of opinion, was obtained in much the same way as it was for the rural manors, and at some kind of moot, possibly the shire-moot. The Wallingford burgesses testify that Nigel had a haw or house of Henry as heir of 'Soarding', but that he (Soarding) never had it. The burgesses – they seem to be a King's reeve and another – claim two houses and a garden at Hertford (132ai) 'because they were unjustly taken away from them'. The Nottingham burgesses complain that they used to fish in the Trent and are now forbidden to do so. Those of Lincoln swear that the King had toll and forfeiture over the thirty houses of Tochi Outison, but Ulviet the priest is ready to submit to the ordeal that it was not so. The men of the boroughs of Dover and of Sandwich, and the York and Bristol burgesses, are similarly found proffering their evidence.

The impression is given, too, of evidence of title having been given just as it was in the cases affecting rural holdings. The possessors of Dover houses from which the King has lost his customary dues call to witness Odo of Bayeux as their 'protector and deliverer and donor' (1ai); Ralph of Columbiers does the same regarding the Canterbury houses he has obtained. Odo, presumably in his position as Earl of Kent, is said to have received the borough of Dover; it was to him, too, that a

[1] Verbs such as *occupare, capere*, etc., frequent here, seem to imply in DB illegal action. Possibly the combining of a number of former manors into a single manor was regarded, if unsanctioned by authority, as illegal, even though the owner held them all rightfully.

certain Herbert appealed, saying that the Bishop had permitted his uncle to construct a tide-mill at the entrance to Dover harbour, about which there is complaint that it 'breaks almost all the ships by reason of its great disturbance of the sea and does the greatest disservice to' the King and the men of the borough.[1]

The idea seems to be to set down the position as it was in King Edward's day, so that there shall be record of what privileges and profits King, Earl, sheriff, and other 'inheritors' should be enjoying in the cities and towns. Thus we are frequently told that owners of property had had sake and soke and toll and theam over the lessees of their houses (e.g. at Lincoln and Huntingdon). The King has soke over those owned by Robert of Mortain at Northampton; but the Stamford sokemen were 'so free that they could seek what lord they would', and the King had only their tolls and heriots and the fines paid for their misdeeds; Merleswegen and others had had Lincoln houses 'free of all customary dues' and Earl Hugh has landgavel from two of his houses.[2] Mundret had held Chester from Earl Edwin, for which he paid a farm of £50 and a mark of gold but received the profit of the pleas of the shire and Hundreds except those of Inglefield. In many places, e.g. Stafford, the King had two-thirds and the Earl one-third of the customary renders of the borough. To this aspect of burghal profits and immunities we shall later be returning (Chapter XV).

---

[1] Odo had infringed many of the privileges of the archbishopric of Canterbury and of the monks: twice we have indication of the suit Lanfranc brought against him at Penenden Heath (2ai, 5a2). There is a striking passage telling how Brumann, a former reeve of Canterbury, had illegally taken tolls from foreign merchants where the churches of Holy Trinity and St. Augustine should have received them, and had to admit it.

[2] 'Landgavel' implies *gablum* or rent for land.

CHAPTER IV

The Making of Domesday Book

[Much of this chapter, though in an extended form, appeared as Chapter VI of the author's *The Domesday Inquest and the Making of Domesday Book*.]

WE really have very little idea as to just how the information elicited by the Inquest was written down by the clerks in the forms in which its records have been preserved for us. Despite the strong possibility of individual returns for some of the various fiefs, it is improbable that the bulk of the information was presented to the authorities of shires and Hundreds in written form. It is equally doubtful if even a copy of what we should call 'original returns' has survived, for it is not really very likely that the ICC is more than a partial reconstruction of them. What we have to think of as 'original returns' were perhaps constructed by clerks, possibly largely in the form of rough contracted notes, as the representatives of manors and vills – and perhaps fiefs – gave them the information demanded and made their answers to the necessary questions. From these, successive drafts, culminating in the Exchequer and 'Little' Domesday, seem to have been prepared. Of two things we can be reasonably certain: first, the clerks worked from material which was at some stage or in some form self-contained for each Hundred; secondly, it was predetermined that these putative hundredal returns should be re-cast in terms of the individual fief.

The Exeter Domesday

But for the survival of the Exeter Domesday, almost certainly an example of the earliest process of re-casting Inquest material, we should know very much less of the possibilities than we do. Unfortunately, it is incomplete. We have only a solitary entry remaining to represent the Wiltshire material, and the account of twelve Dorset fiefs and of that county's four boroughs for what seems to have been – for Inquest purposes – a sub-section of the south-west.[1] Some of the Devon material has also disappeared. The record was inscribed in loose 'gatherings' or booklets of varying composition and number of leaves, the majority of which are of four leaves or a multiple thereof. We do not know if originally it was intended that these should be arranged in any particular order, for they include only a partial and disordered index of fiefs. The text is in single column, and suggests that it was inscribed hastily and under pressure, for a very large number of errors were made, many of which were deleted, underscored to indicate deletion, or corrected by the writer or a supervisor. Apart from the suggestion of checking which these alterations furnish, there appear at the foot of certain folios the words *consummatum est*, which may indicate the points the checking operation reached at various times. But equally these could represent the stages reached by copyists.[2]

But it must not be thought that the work was done haphazardly. Examination of its structure suggests that the clerks had a reasonably accurate conception of how many lines a fief would occupy, and planned the volume of each booklet so that where possible each included the material for a single fief or a number of small fiefs. This would not have been difficult if they had full rough notes, and perhaps also a rough index of the holdings within a Hundred, showing the owner of each manor, and comparatively easy if they had feudal returns to guide them. It is possible that they themselves made rough indexes of the properties within each Hundred.[3]

The clerks certainly did not include all the matter available to them. Details for what had formerly been separate manors,

---

[1] Entries for both shires appear on the same folio (*47*), and the folios concerned (*11b–12, 25–62b*) contain none for the other three counties, which occupy fols. *83–494b*.

[2] Detailed information about the aspects indicated in the above paragraph, and about what follows here, will be found in R. Welldon Finn: 'The Construction of the Exeter Domesday' (*Bulletin of the John Rylands Library*, vol. xli, No. 2, pp. 360–87).

[3] The Exchequer Domesday contains one for Yorkshire (fols. 379a1–82a2), arranged wapentake by wapentake, giving names of manors and their assessments, with the owner's name written over each. It could be an imperfect abstract copy of a geld-register. It includes matter not in the Yorkshire text, but omits some entries found therein. It is usually known as 'the Summary'.

but which by 1086 had been absorbed in another manor, must often, if not invariably, have been available, but were commonly ignored (see p. 112). This fact is, however, more clearly seen by collating DB with the ICC and IE, for there is much in both of the latter which was not included in the former. (In much lesser degree, the reverse is true also.) Many duplicate entries also show that there was often information available additional to that which the clerks set down. It has already been noted that some manors were omitted from DB.

None the less, the Exeter Domesday shows distinct signs of an efficient organisation at work. In each shire and each fief, the Hundreds appear in an order which is very largely a consistent one, and in geographical groups which may themselves have been Inquest units. Unfortunately, the Hundred in which a manor lay is not indicated, but it is possible, by collation with the geld accounts and using information of later date, to reconstruct the Domesday Hundreds of 1086 with very fair completeness and accuracy. We find, for example, thirty-two consecutive entries on fols. *125–9b* all for holdings in the Hundred of Braunton-with-Shirwell; twenty-seven from Cannington Hundred appear consecutively on fols. *423–6*. Every appropriate Devon fief begins – as does *Terrae Occupatae* – with the entries for South Tawton, Lifton, Black Torrington, Hartland, Shebbear, Fremington, and North Tawton Hundreds, and only two or three times does the order of appearance of the Hundreds vary within a fief. This order forms a circuit clockwise through the area, of which the chief settlement might be said to be Okehampton, the sheriff's personal headquarters, and this might have been a centre for the holding of the Inquest. Tavistock, with its abbey, is here another potential centre. These same Hundreds, if North and South Tawton are treated as one, open the second list of Hundreds on fol. *63*, and appear in the same order, and five of the six begin the geld accounts.[1]

The order of appearance and sequence of Hundreds are, however, occasionally imperfect, and the manors within a

[1] For further details regarding the order of appearance of Hundreds and their groupings, see R. Welldon Finn, 'The Making of the Devonshire Domesdays' (*Trans. Dev. Assn.*, vol. lxxxix, pp. 93–123), 'The Making of the Somerset Domesdays' (*Proc. Som. Nat. Hist. & Arch. Soc.*, vols. xcix–c, pp. 21–37, and 'The Making of the Dorset Domesday' (*Proc. Dorset Nat. Hist. & Arch. Soc.*, vol. lxxxi, pp. 150–7.)

Hundred do not invariably, in each fief, appear as a single consecutive block of entries. This might be the result of human fallibility, of failure to notice and inscribe all the relevant manors in a single operation; equally it might be because the clerk was obliged to postpone inscription of an entry because the whole of the required information was not available. It is by no means easy to determine just how the organisation worked and how the material was inscribed, for it is often difficult to isolate the different scripts, and illogicalities of order and inscription produce many perhaps insoluble problems.

It looks as if round about a dozen clerks in all were employed on its construction. The work of some is not difficult to identify, for the manner of formation of certain letters, and the employment of distinctive contractions and formulae, help to identify their entries. Several of these seem to have contributed to the account of each shire; some appear in but two or three counties; one inscribed certain Cornish material only. In the articles referred to above, the work of each has been assigned a capital letter: two scribes (styled G and A) seem to have written more than the others, and perhaps had positions of special responsibility.

On what system they worked we do not know, nor is a possible method of construction easy to deduce. That most economical of time would have been for one, or a pair of clerks, to concentrate on a single fief or pair of fiefs simultaneously, picking out the appropriate manors from hundredal returns, or for each clerk to be responsible for inscribing the record of one or more Hundreds, passing from booklet to booklet. But neither seems to have been the method employed. The varying handwritings appear and disappear in accordance with no obvious principle; indeed, not only is the account of the relevant portion of the Hundred in the individual fief often produced by more than one clerk, but some entries were written by two different clerks.[1]

---

[1] e.g. Raddon (*316*), Spettisbury (*47b*). If such changes of script were confined to *marginalia* or interlineations, this, in view of the fact that numerous corrections and underscorings show that the text was checked, would be intelligible. But they are not. They could be due to interruptions of the work, to the need to re-consult witnesses or the Hundred-jury, or to material temporarily missing.

For example, clerk A wrote the Devon entries on fols. *121–1b* which were in Lifton Hundred. Clerk G follows with six Black Torrington entries, and then clerk S writes one for Black Torrington, one for Hartland, and one for Shebbear. Clerk T writes three more Shebbear entries, followed by A again, with five for Fremington, and then G, with three more for that Hundred. A continues with a North Tawton manor, and G contributes two further North Tawton entries. There is no rhythm here.

The explanation early suggested as to why the order and sequence of Hundreds in any shire are imperfect was that the material was dictated to the inscribing clerks, that there were at least two pairs involved, and that as one Hundred was finished with for the individual fief by one pair, the material was exchanged for that which the other pair had been using.[1] Now dictation, the presumption of which was pressed into service to account for the variant spellings of Hundred- and place-names, might seem to be an incomparably inconvenient method of executing the work, and inevitably productive of far more errors than we find. The irregular sequence of the various clerks' work, too, hardly suggests that dictation was the method used. It is hard to believe that if the matter was dictated, one clerk only would use the *hyda* spelling, and in only a small, geographically fairly compact, proportion of the entries he made, or one fairly consistently use an *-ix* instead of an *-ic* termination to names such as 'Brictric'. On Ballard's principle, too, the occurrences of Hundreds should alternate, not, as they do in the south-west, come in largely consistent order.

From the above it does rather look as if the continuity of the individual clerk's work suffered frequent interruption, and that it was entirely fortuitous which of his fellows would make the entry following that at which he temporarily ceased work. There is a curious feature of the ms. displayed by the symbols which as a rule indicate the start of a new entry (not all the entries begin a fresh line, though where they do not, there is rarely an obvious reason why they should not have done so). Each

[1] This is the view taken by Ballard, *Dom. Inq.*, p. 17, and which Reichel seems to have shared (*VCH: Devon*, vol. I, p. 379).

clerk has a characteristic form of these (though there are frequent irregularities); often, one clerk inscribed the symbol to start a new line, but a different clerk made the entry. This rather suggests that the first clerk did not know he had completed a section of the work.[1] If the bulk of the information was furnished at 'back-room' sessions distinct from the formal ones, this would help to account for eccentricities of order and breaks in continuity.

Now if the changes of script occurred always at the close of entries for a Hundred or group of Hundreds, we might think that one clerk handed over the booklet concerned to a different clerk for continuation, or passed his work and its source to another clerk for checking, and proceeded with a fresh fief in a different booklet by means of the record of other Hundreds. But the changes do not occur at such regular intervals, and this hypothesis is unsatisfactory, especially as we can form no idea of the order in which the booklets were inscribed. We must allow for the possibility that hundredal were checked against feudal records, which certainly would interrupt ordered sequence. What would give rise to continual, and irregular, interruptions of a clerk's work would be the need, because there was some dispute about the title to a holding or the composition of a manor (which would govern the fief in which the entry was to appear), to appeal to a higher authority for directions as to how to proceed, or to wait for the decision about a dispute. If, as seems certain, the work had to be done as rapidly as possible, it was essential for it to go on from the point of the stoppage without interruption, and if so, illogicalities of order, unexpected changes of handwriting, and fairly frequent postscripts, would be inevitable. And this is just what we find.

For the great majority of the postscriptal entries are concerned with changes in manorial structure, disputes about ownership, and illegal occupation – indeed, whatever would inevitably be the subject of special investigation and the calling of evidence. It is surely significant that after the Bishop of Exeter produced his charters to establish his title

---

[1] Here and there, e.g. on fol. *262b*, a symbol was inscribed, and a space of a couple of lines or so left blank, but never filled.

to Newton St. Cyres, the *clamat* already inscribed in the manuscript was altered to *habet*. A holding called *Beurda* (*126*) had had a complex and chequered history, being at one time part of, and at another distinct from the royal manor of Braunton. It was claimed by the Bishop of Coutances, but the thegns of the shire said that they did not know in what manner its pre-Conquest owner had held it. It is entered in the Bishop's fief, but is written vertically in the margin. Marginally, too, was inscribed the addition, with doubtful legality, of the manor of Barlington to that of Roborough (*124b*). Other striking examples of marginal additions are the wrongful inclusion of Nymet in the manor of Molland (*95*), the detachment of Pendavy from the royal manor of Blisland (*Glustona*, *101b*), the taking of Keinton Mandeville out of the manor of Barton St. David since the Conquest (*434b*, *480*), the retention of customary dues from Axminster (*84b*), and the transference of moor and meadow and coppice from Seavington to the royal manor of South Petherton (*265b*). A number are concerned with illegal divorcement of holdings from fiefs and manors, always a subject of complaint by the aggrieved at the Inquest – they include separation of the Tavistock thegns with their inalienable land from the Abbey (*177*), the twenty-two holdings taken by Robert of Mortain from the King's manor of Winnianton (*225b–6*), a hide at Ditcheat which 'could not separate from' Glastonbury lordship (*170*). Significantly, this last is marginal on fol. *519* of *Terrae Occupatae* also. This feature, we shall see, recurs throughout the Domesday documents, and it must suggest the possibility that the Exeter Domesday was constructed, not from completed material, but while the Inquest was in progress.

The Exeter Domesday is just what we would expect to be produced by a group of clerks converting hundredal returns into feudal *breves* at a time when many differences of opinion about legitimate ownership of a holding were undetermined. A large number of entries appear twice in the record, especially when title to an estate was the subject of argument; e.g. the Glastonbury thegnlands, many of which appear in the account of the Abbey lands as well as among the fiefs of those who probably claimed that Glastonbury

had now no rights over them. Such duplicate entries would
be inevitable if both parties included their material in feudal
returns.[1]

Recorded in the Bishop of Coutances's Somerset fief is the
manor of *Millescota* (*147b*), held of him for 5½ hides by 'Ass-
celinus', and before him by two thegns 'who could not separate
from the church of Glastonbury'. In the account of Glastonbury's manor of *Mulla* (Mells, *168*), within which the modern
equivalent of *Millescota* lay, 'Ascelin' is said to hold 5½ hides
of the Bishop, *de rege*, and the two thegns and their inability
to leave Glastonbury lordship are also mentioned. These
produced two corresponding entries in *Terrae Occupatae* (*519b*,
520), which suggests that Glastonbury had argued that the
King could not legitimately transfer this sub-tenancy. Unless
the Glastonbury return mentioned *Millescota* by name, it looks
as if the passages emanated from two different returns, not one
for the Hundred of Frome. Roger of Courseulles's ablation of
part of Long Sutton from Athelney Abbey is mentioned twice
in each of the accounts of the fiefs concerned, and three times
in *Terrae Occupatae*.[2] This does not suggest that the clerks drew
their material from a single source only, or that they meticu-
lously noted in purely hundredal returns which items had
already been dealt with.

The most illuminating series of duplicate entries is for the
twenty-two manors taken by Robert of Mortain from the
royal manor of Winnianton (*99–100b*, *224b–7*). The order in
which the manors occur differs, and so do place- and proper
names. We find *Cariahoil* (*99b*), *Cariorgel* (*224b*); *Brixius* (*99b*)
and *Birihtsius* (*226*), and a number of other variants. Moreover,
the discrepancies in the two sets of accounts are considerable.
Roscarnon is in one said to be held by Grifin (*100*), by Grifin of
Jovin in the other (*224*). Five manorial values differ, often
appreciably; e.g. we have 5*s.* and 10*s.* for the same place, and
xxx den. against *ii sol.* The fiscal details vary still more greatly.

---

[1] It was at first thought that the clerks were careful to include the material in
the fief of each disputant. But it is extremely doubtful if all the duplicates are
deliberate ones. 'Duplicate' is here a somewhat misleading expression, the entries
are often obviously of quite independent origin, not from a single source.

[2] Fols. *191*, *191b*, *435b*; *515*, *524b*, *525b*.

Except in the case of the initial entry, we are told in the entries under *Terra Regis* that each manor gelded for so many geld-hides, -virgates, and -acres, but on turning to those in the Mortain fief find that these quantities are really those of total assessments, and that the number of hides for which each holding actually gelds – a different and smaller quantity – is given also. Surely all this implies independent returns; the one for the whole complex royal manor of Winnianton, an artificial agglomeration of small settlements scattered over at least fourteen parishes, and one for each of the constituents abstracted by the King's half-brother, which seem by 1086 to have acquired the status of independent manors.

Wherever duplicate entries occur in the Cornish material, collation almost always displays discrepancies, which argue that a single source did not produce them. From the royal manor of *Lannohoo* (*101*) Robert of Mortain has taken away two manors, *Podestot* and *Sainguinas*, which have twelve plough-lands and were worth £3 when received. There are entries for each of these in Robert's fief, but there they are *Pondestoca* and *Sanguinas*, taken from *Lantloho*, have sixteen ploughlands, and had been worth £2.[1]

The copying of the Exeter Domesday

Though many early commentators denied that there was any direct connection between the texts of the Exeter and Exchequer Domesdays, it was apparent long ago to some that the first of these was copied, and a copy used for construction of the Exchequer version for the south-western counties. As early as 1884 the Palaeographical Society decided that a copy must have been made of the Exeter text, basing its judgments on the character and style of some marginal additions to it.[2] The relationship between Exeter and Exchequer Domesdays was examined a quarter of a century later by F. H. Baring, who produced compelling evidence that the Exeter version was

---

[1] Fols. *238*, *238b*. These appear twice in *Terrae Occupatae* (*507*, *507b*), and the name-forms vary in each entry and more or less correspond in turn with each of the variants of the Exeter Domesday.

[2] 2nd series of reproductions of ancient MSS., vol. II, part i, II, plates 70, 71.

the source of the Exchequer text.[1] Further proof of this relationship has recently been given and discussed.[2]

The arguments for derivation include the failure of the Exchequer clerks to supply information absent from the Exeter Domesday, their exact reproduction of significant words and phrases (e.g. 'iiii virgates' instead of the more usual 'one hide'), the order of entries in both texts, the unnecessary repetition of duplicated material, and the copying of obvious errors.

But the Exchequer Domesday includes a few pieces of information which are not in the surviving Exeter version, and the inference must be that this was copied and slightly improved, and the revised copy used by the Exchequer clerks.

For example, the Exchequer account of Spettisbury says that the pasture 'in another place' (*in alio loco*) is 'by the water' (*super aquam*) which the Exeter text does not (82ai, *47b*). It mentions the mint at Taunton, absent from the Exeter Domesday (87bi, *173b–5b*), and a team it records at St. Keverne (*Lannachebran*) is also absent from the Exeter Domesday (121a2, *205b*). It is equally plain that additions were made to the surviving Exeter Domesday, presumably after it was copied, which were not reproduced in the manuscript from which the Exchequer version was made or in the Exchequer Domesday itself. There are a substantial quantity of these; for example, Exchequer gives the value of Great Torrington as £20, Exeter, over an erasure, as £15 (116bi, *376b*). Sometimes a difference in the ink, or the colour thereof, shows an addition to the Exeter material, not reproduced in Exchequer; e.g. an obviously postscriptal *i* which makes the ploughlands of Modbury 24 in Exeter, not 23 in number as in Exchequer (*217b*, 104b2).

In 1942 Professor Galbraith suggested that the sources of the Exchequer text were a collection of what he styled 'provincial Domesdays', similar in form and content to the Exeter Domesday.[3] The counties included in each probably represent

[1] F. H. Baring: 'The Exeter Domesday' (*EHR*, vol. xxvii. p. 309).

[2] R. Welldon Finn: 'The Immediate Sources of the Exchequer Domesday' (*Bull. of the John Rylands Library*, vol. 40, no. 1, pp. 47–8).

[3] V. H. Galbraith: 'The Making of Domesday Book' (*EHR*, vol. lvii, p. 161).

their grouping in 'circuits', and the various 'provincial Domesdays' are distinguishable by their differences of formulae, absence of customary information, etc. (see pp. 38–40).

The conversion of 'provincial Domesdays' into Exchequer form

If the Exchequer clerks were working, perhaps at Winchester, away from the local sources of information, and with nothing but the bare texts of 'provincial Domesdays' to guide them, the reasons for the kinds of errors their texts display would be readily intelligible. But, as will later be demonstrated, it is highly probable that the Exchequer Domesday was inscribed in the provinces. It seems as if, wherever the surviving Exeter Domesday may have been compiled, Exchequer clerks were present during its making. For there are within it three passages (fols. *153b, 436b bis*) in the handwriting, and using the formulae and contractions, of an Exchequer Domesday clerk.[1] It does not seem likely that it was the surviving copy of the Exeter Domesday which went to Winchester for the making of the Exchequer version and was sent back to Exeter; if it was, we can only think that these two fiefs had not been inscribed in it, and that this missing information was obtained from Somerset and filled in by an Exchequer clerk before the manuscript was sent back to Exeter, which again seems improbable.

None of the handwritings of the Exeter Domesday in any way resembles the set and stylised hand of the staff of the royal secretariat. The formulae and vocabulary of the two versions are altogether different. For example, the opening of an Exeter entry is almost invariably 'Y holds one manor which is called Z', that of the Exchequer parallel 'Y holds Z'; what is the contraction for 'in the time of King Edward' in Exchequer is normally (but not invariably) 'on the day when King Edward was alive and dead' in Exeter. Woodland, again, is usually *silva* to Exchequer clerks, *nemus* to those of the Exeter Domesday.[2]

---

[1] Discussed and reproduced in R. Welldon Finn: 'The Evolution of Successive Versions of Domesday Book' (*EHR*, vol. lxvi, p. 561).

[2] Further examples are given in Baring: *art. cit.*, and in the prefatory matter to the Record Commission's *Additamenta*, vol. IV (pp. xii–xiv), which includes the Exeter Domesday.

Many of the demonstrable errors made by those who inscribed the Exchequer Domesday are just such as could easily occur when using a collection of documents such as the Exeter Domesday – and it must always be remembered that there is every suggestion that the Exchequer text too is hurried work.

Since, in the Exeter Domesday, it is not uncommon for more than one fief to be contained within a single booklet (and presumably this occurred in other groups of shires also), it could well happen that an Exchequer clerk might at first miss a small fief from the interior of one of these, and have to add it postscriptally. Fief no. XXVI, in the Surrey section, which is confined to a single manor, is marginal (36a2); no. LI in the Wiltshire Domesday is written at the foot of fol. 73a right across both columns. Baldwin of Exeter's solitary Dorset manor was at first omitted, and inserted by itself on the front of a leaf (81) which was slipped into an Exchequer gathering. It should have been on 82bi, which must have been completed before its absence was discovered. The number of similar postscripts is not small.

Also, it would be easy for the Exchequer clerk to miss a cross-head, and so ascribe land to the wrong county. The only indication in the Exeter Domesday that the Glastonbury land in Devon is finished, and the estates in Somerset starting, are the words *In Sumerseta*, marginally in two lines, and easily missed (*161*). At times a cross-head indicating a change of county, or of fief, may have been omitted or missed altogether. Earl Aubrey's manor in Dorset, *Gessic*, was incorrectly inscribed at the end of the section for his lands in the Wiltshire Domesday (69ai). The Northamptonshire Domesday includes the Oxfordshire manors of the Bishop of Coutances, the Staffordshire manors of St. Remy at Rheims, bearing the rubric of a Staffordshire Hundred, and Staffordshire and Warwickshire manors of six other fiefs.

This failure to discover the record of a fief at the right moment probably accounts for many of the misplacements of the Exchequer text, and suggests that most provincial redraftings were not indexed: the LE includes, on fols. *532, 532b*, only a fragmentary and disordered list of sections. That

the Exchequer clerks had no indexes to copy is suggested by
the gross imperfections of those they compiled. It may seem an
easy enough task to make a contents list of fiefs, but probably
Professor Galbraith is right in thinking that the indexes of the
Exchequer Domesday were inscribed before the text had
been dealt with, and that all the clerk had to guide him (if the
LE is representative of all the 'provincial drafts') were a
muddled and ill-arranged collection of booklets, with the
lands of several men under a single heading.[1] In consequence,
there is in almost every county a lack of harmony between
Index and titling and order of fiefs; e.g. Alfred d'Epaignes
was missed out of the Dorset index, throwing out the number-
ing, and to restore the congruence, Iseldis, no. LV in the index,
was given no heading or number in the text. Earl Hugh of
Chester should everywhere come early; though he is no. XIII
in the Leicestershire index, his fief is 43rd in the text. The
Kent index is on 2a2, as though the matter preceding it were
already written. In Dorset the clerks left insufficient room
for even a two-column index, with the result that from the
52nd entry the numbers and names spread right across 75a.
The Berkshire index (56ai) is very much cramped, which would
be unnecessary if it were not the result of trying to avoid
running over to a new folio; so is that for Warwickshire
(238ai), which overflows into the second column.

The Exchequer text is so formulistic that any departures
from the norm are intriguing. Many are of such character
that their origin would seem to lie in inadvertent reproduction
of the formulae or information of the appropriate 'provincial
Domesday'. The inclusion of demesne livestock has already
been mentioned (p. 10); these should not have appeared,
according to the Exchequer scheme of omissions. The Exchequer clerks usually converted the *quando recepit* of the Exeter
text before a value to a simple *valebat* or *valuit* or *olim*, but
(e.g., on 96bi–7ai) there are a number of instances of the
Exeter formula. They have the Exeter *mansio* for their customary *manerium* (69b2), the *quod vocatur* which there prefaces
a place-name (e.g. 4ai, 9b2, 90b2, 106bi, 120bi), the *ea die
qua rex E. fuit vivus et mortuus* formula in place of the usual

[1] Galbraith: *MoDB*, pp. 190–3, 199.

abbreviation for *tempore regis Edwardi* (e.g. 48b2, 211ai).
Instead of associating the *servi* with the demesne teams, as is
their normal practice in this and other groups of counties,
they frequently place them immediately after *villani* and
bordarii, as the Exeter clerks did (e.g. 83b2, 90a2, 112bi).

Domesday Book for the Eastern Counties

It was again Professor Galbraith (*art. cit.*) who suggested that
this, which in form and content so greatly differs from the
Exchequer Domesday, was a fair copy of a 'provincial Domesday'. It bears many resemblances to the Exeter Domesday; it is
in single column, written by a number of clerks whose scripts
are unprofessional compared with those of the Exchequer text
and official royal documents, and it makes use of formulae and
terms which are not those of the Exchequer Domesday. For some
reason – perhaps because the work had progressed no further
than this revision when a time-limit for delivery to the King
was reached – it was never converted into 'Exchequer' form.

An excellent description of what is known as vol. II of DB,
or 'Little Domesday', is given in *Domesday Re-Bound*.[1] The text
occupies 451 folios, written on both sides, in single column,
with many blanks, and is made up of 57 gatherings, all but nine
of which are neat quaternions of four doubled leaves, which are
conveniently referred to as 'booklets'. The number of clerks
contributing would seem to be considerable, and to be of 'a
school following a less elegant model' than that of the Exchequer Domesday clerks, 'engaged in a routine task of copying
and making no great attempt at Calligraphy' (*DRB*, p. 45).
They may have been drawn from local monastic *scriptoria*, or
from the official permanent staff of the shire concerned.

The material from which it was constructed – the original
'provincial Domesday' – was probably also in the form of loose
booklets similar to those of the Exeter Domesday. For on some
folios are deleted lists of fiefs, perhaps unthinkingly copied by
the transcriber from the original 'provincial Domesday' in
which, if on an outside leaf, they would serve to indicate the
contents of a booklet. It is suggestive of this form that the first
list covers the contents of eight leaves. They became unneces-

[1] H.M.S.O. (1954): hereinafter referred to as *DRB*.

sary because for each county a general index was inscribed on its first leaf.

That vol. II is a fair copy is obvious. Postscripts, *marginalia*, and interlineations (other than for words or figures at first inadvertently omitted from the text) are remarkably few. In the Essex section there are only about forty interlineations in all. The copyists, however, did occasionally stray. Twice, for Essex, sheets had to be inserted in the quaternions because of omissions and errors, thrice in Norfolk, and twice in Suffolk. The sheet which now forms fol. 35 displays a change in the handwriting from that which precedes it, and so shows the lack of continuity of execution of the existing ms. A second insertion is on fol. 103, which completes the *invasiones*, and thus may be late material.

The aim appears to have been the production of a fair copy and nothing more. There is small evidence of systematic checking of the text, and the placing of some lay tenants-in-chief before the ecclesiastical lands in Norfolk and Suffolk suggests that the clerk collecting the booklets did not trouble to place and index them in the appropriate order. In the Exchequer Domesday, a systematic order for the fiefs is apparent, the royal estates are followed by those of the chief ecclesiastics, these by the Earls' lands, and so on in descending order of importance. Yet, presumably to facilitate consultation, the name of the county was put on the verso of leaves, and an indication of fiefs on the recto.

It might be expected that when a long document such as this, presumably in loose booklets, had to be copied, the work, if complete when copying began, would be divided more or less equally between the clerks available, in which case large consecutive sections ought all to be in the same handwriting. But this is exactly what we do not find. In Essex obvious changes in the script are not very numerous, but the individuality of the hand which produced the account of Colchester (104–7b) is most noticeable, and it is doubtful if this script appears elsewhere in the Essex section. Often it looks as if the script changes, e.g. on fol. 5, where entries for a fresh Hundred begin, and on fols. 48, where Maldon Hundred changes to Tendring, and 99 (sections LXXXIX–XC, which are quite unlike LXXXIV–VIII on 98b). For Norfolk and Suffolk changes of handwriting seem to be rather more frequent and distinctive.

One feature of vol. II is the amount of space commonly left between the end of one fief and the beginning of the next. It is not invariable (e.g. fols. 12b, 19b, 20b, 93), but is often very marked; e.g. the end of fief XXIV occupied only seven of the twenty-five lines of fol. 48b, but fief XXV was made to begin a new folio, 49; though this does not begin a new booklet. Fol. 429b ended with only a couple of lines to spare, and fief XLV was not begun at the top of 430, but with its first four lines unoccupied. With the beginning of the booklets which start with fols. 157, 173, 191, 209, and 235, for example, the handwriting changes, and a fresh fief begins each of these booklets (nos. VII, IX, X, XIV, XXII). Some of these spaces may have been left because a different clerk was or had been at work on the booklet which follows them.

Now it might be expected that if the clerks were copying a manuscript, they need not have left such extensive spaces (except where it was reasonable to open a new booklet), since they should have known from their original when the account of a fief was complete. But it is possible that they did not know whether it was complete or not, and left spaces into which any necessary matter could be inserted postscriptally. For one explanation of the character of much of the postscriptal matter would be that the work of the Inquest was unfinished when they were making their copy, and indeed, it may still have been proceeding when their original was being written. Much of the postscriptal matter has to do with claims and disputes, which may not have been investigated until late in the Inquest, and indeed after the first draft had been made and partly copied. It is clear that the note about the invasion by Ingelric of the manor of Newland Hall, and the Hundred's testimony that it had lain in Writtle, is a postscript, for most of it had to be inserted between lines 21 and 22 (II.31). The claim of the Abbot of Ely to a Roding manor is probably not in the same handwriting as that of the rest of the entry, and overflows into the margin; nor is that which the Ely monks make to Fambridge (II.97b), but for this adequate space already existed. Most of the Suffolk *marginalia* and interlineations look like genuine copying omissions repaired; e.g. on fol. 333.

The accounts of the three shires look as if both they and their sources were largely independent productions, though the texts for Norfolk and Suffolk are highly similar in character, and probably some clerks worked on both shires. Many of the Essex scripts do not resemble those to be found in the Norfolk and Suffolk folios. This suggests, as do the details of the Exeter Domesday, that the original draft for any shire was made independently of its fellows, and that, while for the shires within a 'provincial Domesday' there was a scheme of inscription common to them all, there were differences of treatment within each county both at the inscription of the first draft and at its copying. The treatment of the boroughs follows no general plan: the account of Colchester concludes the Essex folios, and the character of the information is quite different from that for the towns of the two other shires. Norwich, Thetford, Yarmouth and Ipswich appear within *Terrae Regis*. Apparently it was no part of the supervisors' task to convert the burghal returns to a set form or follow a pre-ordained scheme in obtaining and inscribing information about them. There is nothing, in the accounts of the Norfolk and Suffolk towns, like the long list of individual house and other property included for Colchester.

The Exchequer Domesday

Here, again, there is copious evidence of independent treatment of each shire, whether original or ultimate, and marked similarities in the accounts of those which presumably composed the individual 'provincial Domesday'. It is only in certain east midland counties, for example, that we find information regarding the actual holdings of villeins and bordars, while except for the Huntingdonshire manors of the Abbey of Ely, and then only in IE, the dimensions of manors as a whole are never given in counties south of the Trent.

The Exchequer Domesday is a far more professional achievement than are the other Domesday texts. Evidence of careful planning of the form it was to take is patent.[1] Yet things did go wrong with its making, and a careful scheme was not

---

[1] Summarised on pp. 35–8 of *DRB*. This makes it clear (pp. 23–4) that the authors do not think the Exchequer clerks worked from the start with a complete fair copy of the provincial drafts available.

strictly adhered to; accordingly it is not altogether profitless to speculate why certain errors should have occurred. Not only was it necessary to include matter overlooked, but, moreover, a great deal of postscriptal material had to be added marginally or at the foot of the page. Some of these postscripts certainly read as though they are concerned simply with matter inadvertently omitted during the inscription of the relevant folio or column. Some are obviously very late additions, unrubricated, and interrupting matter already inscribed. But there are also an appreciable number which suggest very strongly that they are additions made late because the material was not available, or in a state permitting inscription, when the rest of the text was written. We have seen above how many passages concerned with disputes and illegalities are postscriptal in LE and vol. II; many of the Exchequer postscripts are of similar character. One of these is the illegal addition of Barlington to Roborough (102a2), postscriptal in the Exeter text also (*124b*). The obviously postscriptal passage at the end of fief IX on 175bi, since the evidence of the shire was required for it, may not have been available when the rest of the column was written, nor that on 252ai which gives the statement and complaint of the English burgesses of Shrewsbury.

It is of course possible that DB is the work of a single scribe, but this does not seem likely. To estimate how long it would take one man to compile it from 'provincial Domesdays' is no easy matter, and Mr. Fairbank's suggestion of 240 days has to assume that the writer began work in February, 1086.[1] Difficult though it is to distinguish the possible work of one clerk from that of another, the ms. does not suggest that even the bulk of it is one man's work, and what we must suspect was the maximum time available for its construction, and the obvious need for haste, make it improbable that the work would be entrusted to one man only. It seems, too, somewhat unlikely that if such was the case, he would have been at such pains to plan how many sheets, and how gathered, a shire would occupy, and to begin all but four of the counties with the inception of a gathering. The suggestion that is thrust upon us is that, while one clerk may have written the account of more than one shire,

[1] *DRB*, p. 34

the construction of each county record was an independent operation.

The accounts of very few counties appear to me to be a single writer's work. To suggest reasons why a portion of a column should be in a script apparently quite different from the rest is, however, not easy, unless it is considered that the material could not always be written in the order in which it appears in the text.

If the material was in the form of the Exeter text, two counties from a group forming a 'provincial Domesday' could not be dealt with simultaneously, unless one writer was to deal with fiefs in booklets other than those which a colleague was using. It looks, from the fairly consistent order of fiefs for each shire, and the employment of a vaguely alphabetical principle in determining in what order the lay tenants-in-chief below the rank of earl or sheriff should come, as if the order of appearance of fiefs was pre-determined, but that always to inscribe them in this order would often be impossible or un-economic of time. So the clerks seem sometimes to have been forced to calculate the space to be left for the ultimate inscrip-tion of a fief or fiefs, and sometimes, it is plain, they miscal-culated. It would be no easy matter to estimate quantities, even though they could see their bulk in their source-material, for much of this was to be omitted, compressed, or presented by means of different formulae. It is perhaps because of this difficulty that often a fief was made to begin a new page or column, even though ultimately this left a large blank space at the end of the previous fief.

Such blanks occur more frequently in the second half of DB than they do in the first. This might suggest that a solitary writer wisely adopted this principle after discovering how many marginal or inadequately spaced additions he had had to make in his earlier folios. But equally it could be a charac-teristic of the clerk or clerks converting certain 'provincial Domesdays', and we can never be sure how often, in the first part of DB, blanks were at first left and later scientifically filled.

Certainly blank spaces were left either because the material was not available, or because it was considered injudicious to condense it at that moment. The whole of 37ai,2 and 37bi was surely reserved for the account of the city of Winchester; almost all of both sides of 126 for one of London. In the Exeter Domesday, the accounts of boroughs and of burghal property or responsibilities not attached to a rural manor come as a rule at the end of a fief, and it is quite conceivable that the principal towns were not dealt with by the Inquest until the Hundreds were completed. It is possible, then, that the accounts of many boroughs were not available when a clerk began inscribing the record of a shire, and that he left room for them and perhaps for an Index before beginning *Terra Regis*. A prefatory space, never filled, was left for six out of the first eleven counties, and since the order of inscription of the shires seems to be much the same as their order of appearance in the bound volume, the burghal material may have been unavailable when these were being written, but for other counties it was at least at hand before the rest of the matter was completed.

There are a considerable number of instances where it looks as if a space was left and later filled in a hand other than that of the writer or writers immediately above or below it, often showing signs of compression of material, with less space between lines than occurs in the remainder of the column. A notable example is that of the account of Woodchester on 164a2, the more significant because this Gloucestershire manor had been unjustly made part of the *feorm* of Wiltshire, of which holding no account was given to the Commissioners, and from which no one came to the *descriptio*. Obviously postscriptal, too, is the account of Alveston on 238bi, and this is an entry about the circumstances of which evidence had been required (see p. 34), and which may not have been available when the draft for Warwickshire was written. Other striking instances of unexpected changes of handwriting or of obviously postscriptal matter are to be seen, for example, on fols. 1a2 (15 lines from foot), 1bi (Canons of St. Martin's land), 2ai (nine lines from foot), part of fief XXX on 159ai, fiefs IV–VII on 174a2, 238b2, the final four fiefs on 239ai and XII and XIII on 239a2, 253ai (St. Juliana: postscriptal), 298ai, 299bi.[1]

---

[1] Is it possible that at least some marginal uses of *f, n, n.f.*, etc. mentioned on p. 54 were not inspired by the provision or absence of a feudal return, but by whether the fief could or could not be inscribed with the material as it was at that moment?

Within small compass we can frequently see signs of the inadvertent initial omission of a whole fief, of the leaving of insufficient space for its inclusion and that of a cross-head later, of the addition of entries at first overlooked. Fief VI on 66a2 had to be squeezed into inadequate space, and IX on 67a2 looks as if it is postscriptal to the rest of the column; fief LI on 83a2 certainly is. Melcombe, which was not rightly the King's, but which should have gone back to Shaftesbury Abbey, as fol. 78b2 tells us, is an obvious postscript to 75b2; the accounts of the Shaftesbury estates on 78b2 themselves necessitated postscriptal work. The rest of 75b2 was written before Melcombe was inscribed, for the other omitted entry for *Terra Regis* had to be written on a sheet, 76, inserted into the gathering: surely, then, 77a was already complete when this addition was made. Neither of these entries has survived in their Exeter Domesday form, and must have been in a booklet – itself perhaps postscriptal – other than that which contained the Dorset *Terra Regis.*

Where and when was the Exchequer text produced?

It has generally been assumed that the Exchequer Domesday was inscribed at Winchester, the home of the Treasury, and it has been suggested that it may not have been completed until long after 1087. I am strongly inclined to think that it is far more probable that it was produced in the provinces, county by county, or by groups of shires, as soon as each 'provincial Domesday' was in a condition to enable the work to be begun.[1] If so, the 'writings' brought to King William were surely the Exchequer text, and perhaps vol. II also. Moreover, I believe it was begun before the Inquest was over. Many passages in DB, the positioning of a number of entries, their character, and certain *marginalia* and other postscriptal additions, are in this way most easily explained.

Of obvious significance is the positioning of the entry for Werrington. Now the legitimate ownership of this manor was determined by the *barones regis*, and if disputes were not always

[1] Three of the sections which do not begin gatherings are for Cornwall (closely associated with Devonshire), Rutland ('which belongs to the sheriffdom of Nottingham'), and Lincolnshire, which completes vol. I.

decided until the later stages of the Inquest, it could be that much of the text was already inscribed before judgment was given. In the Exeter Domesday, it forms the very last entry of *Terra Regis* (*98*), and the note describing Tavistock's loss of it comes at the end of the Abbey's Devon *breve*. Its proper place in the Exchequer text was on 101ai. Obviously the column was complete before the clerk could include it, which he did late on 101a2. It looks very much as if the Inquest was still in progress when the Exchequer clerk was writing the Devon folios, or that he began them before information could be forwarded from Exeter or Okehampton or Tavistock to Winchester. But was it forwarded to Winchester? Is it not rather improbable that he had there a draft before him warning him that ownership was as yet undetermined? If so, the draft must later have been brought up to date. It is far more likely that he was writing where he would have immediate knowledge of the need for caution. He knew 101a2 was not the proper place, for he made a mark against the entry to direct attention to that on 101ai showing where it should have come. Moreover, an ablation by Robert of Mortain from Werrington, which seems to have caused trouble to the geld auditors for the Hundred of Black Torrington and was the subject of dispute (fol. *508*), is a marginal entry beside it. There is hardly a county in which, if we study the facsimile text (though this, of course, does not show the rulings, nor a good deal else besides), we do not receive an impression of inconsecutive work. A most suggestive entry is that for Itchen Abbas (48a2). It is credited to Hugh fitzBaldric, a former Yorkshire sheriff who died during the Inquest, but is claimed by St. Mary's Abbey, and the claim is backed by the whole Hundred and shire. In the margin is inscribed 'King William gave it back to the same Church'. This does look as if the Exchequer clerk knew (and if he knew, surely his provincial predecessor knew also) that there was a dispute about the manor. Either could do one of three things: ascribe it to the fief of Hugh, the *de facto* holder; leave a blank space for it, and await further instructions; or omit it temporarily and insert it when required in a convenient space or, less probably, on an inserted sheet. We seem to have seen clerks using each of these methods. But after ours has made his entry,

King William decides the case – surely not at the Domesday Inquest, but perhaps when he was at Winchester in August of 1086 – and a marginal note becomes necessary.

It is suggestive, too, that as a rule, where a claim had been advanced, and the witness of the Hundred supports the claimant, that the entry usually is to be found in the fief of the *de facto* holder, as though the clerks had credited it to him before the facts of the case had been determined. In Cambridgeshire, for example, save for those instances of duplicated material, disputed property is always found under the fief of the actual holder.

Occasionally a clerk, confronted with absence of a figure, noted in his margin *rq. quot* (enquire how many); e.g., Tadley (200a2), 'enquire how many villeins'. Quite often the entry is in red, suggesting it is late work, done, perhaps, when rubrication was added, though it may merely be the work of a checking clerk. Opposite *Tingdene* (Finedon, 226ai), *rq. hid. num.* was written, and between the *xx* and the *vii* is a gap suggesting that the *vii* was added later (it could have been obtained by adding up the details given later in the entry). By the *Otritone* entry (Monks Ottery, 104a2), *r.car.* is noted in the margin. Since the information is in the Exeter text (*195*), we can only think it was absent from the copy used by the Exchequer clerk, yet the figures are in the Exchequer text, and presumably were supplied for it later. Almost invariably, despite the frequency of blanks after *Terra est*, there is no suggestion that the number of ploughlands should be sought out. Perhaps, because of this frequency, the clerks thought this would be wasted labour. But whence did a clerk hope to obtain this missing information? If he was writing at Winchester, did he visualise the forwarding of an enquiry to, say, Derby, and the reception of an answer?[1] If he was converting a provincial redrafting, did carelessness or forgetfulness prevent consultation of the original returns or another copy of his material? For by no means all these memoranda were dealt with and the answers added. It is hard to avoid a suspicion that the improbability of obtaining an answer from distant provincial capitals makes it unlikely that they would be noted if the Exchequer text was being

[1] *Rq. precium* is in red in the margin of 273ai—Charley.

compiled at Winchester. Such marginal memoranda do not
appear in the LE or vol. II.

To offer strict proof of the time-sequence of the Domesday
Inquest is an obvious impossibility, but the evidence as detailed
above suggests the following hypothesis. The unfinished
condition of DB – the unfilled blanks, the termination of the
Dorset text in the middle of a sentence, the absence of entries
we know should be within it, the copious initial errors and
omissions in the Exeter Domesday, the remaining in draft
form of the material for the eastern counties – must make us
suspect that the King had set a time-limit for its completion,
as the authors of *Domesday Re-Bound* stress (pp. 30–7). Since he
left England for the last time late in 1086, the 'writings' must
have been brought to him before the end of that year, and there
is no real reason to suppose that any part of the Inquest's work
was begun before the 'deep speech' at Gloucester at Christmas
of the previous year. If, however, the 'deep speech' was the
result of reports of the difficulties encountered in the initial
stages of the Inquest, and the cause of the despatch of a second
panel of royal Commissioners, our severely-compressed time-
table seems to possess greater probability.

May we at any rate suppose, then, that instructions went
out at some unknown date to sheriffs, and through them to
local officials, to produce, surely by a given date, the information the King had demanded? Many of the magnates would
know this from their presence at Gloucester, and would
perhaps order feudal officials to prepare statements of claims
and returns for the fief. How long the collection of the data
might have taken is indeterminable, but it is probable that all
through the earlier part of 1086 reports of the difficulties
encountered would be reaching the King's Council and officials,
and from his *legati* if they had already been sent into the
shires. It may then have been these which inspired the despatch
of second panels of unprejudiced assessors, and these could
hardly have started work before Easter, perhaps not until
Pentecost.

As soon as the basic information was all gathered, in whatever
form the 'original returns' took, the construction for each

group of shires of collections of feudal *breves*, of the type disclosed by the Exeter Domesday, could begin. This would probably be a matter of weeks, if not months; meanwhile, the Commissioners would be investigating claims and hearing evidence, and as their decisions were given, the results were added to the uncompleted drafts. As soon as these drafts were substantially complete – but not before Exchequer officials present in the provinces could calculate how much space the record of the individual shire should occupy – the work of framing and inscribing the Exchequer Domesday could start. But still the Commissioners were, it seems, dealing with doubtful cases, and as they settled them, clerks added the results to vol. I as and where they could.[1] The provincial drafts would be of small use locally and later if they were not added to these also, as we can see they were. We may have to allow not only for the production of Domesday Book, but also of feudal summaries and abstracts of audited geld accounts for every shire, few of which have survived. We can hardly visualise a single clerk writing the Exchequer Domesday with a maximum of 240 days – and probably very much less – in which to perform his task.

The time limit reached, the 'writings', so the chroniclers tell us, were brought to the King, with the record of each county still separate from its fellows. Perhaps the occasion was that of the Lammas gathering at Salisbury, when 'all the land-owning men of any account in England, no matter whose men they were', did the King homage and swore fealty to him.

It may be that the provincial *juratores*, the 'men who have sworn', were called upon to accept on oath at the shire-moot what the clerks had finally set down, and that at Salisbury their superiors, in addition to taking their oath of fealty, were required also to accept on oath the record of their rightful possessions and duties and those of other men.

The record of the great Inquest was, however, still incomplete, as we can see from what remains of it. One province, the eastern shires, apparently failed to reach its target. That 'region of notoriously intricate tenures' defeated officials and

---

[1] There may have been delays while essential witnesses were summoned to attend a meeting in the shire-town or other local centre.

clerks, and all they could offer the King at the appointed time was a fair copy of their first draft.

So the King left England for the last time with the most notable monument of his reign unfinished. We may think that for safety's sake it was not long before the loose gatherings were secured within bindings long since perished. Apparently nothing more was done towards the settlement of the still outstanding disputes, or towards completing the imperfect record – none without the Conqueror's power behind him would court the unpopularity further enquiry would engender. But, as Professor Galbraith has said, 'the really astonishing thing is that his Inquest did not die with him'.[1]

[1] Galbraith: *Stud. Pub. Rec.*, p. 89.

CHAPTER V

The Subsequent History of Domesday Book

DOMESDAY Book was never completed, never brought up to date, and never edited. Yet, with all its obvious imperfections, it remained of permanent official value, and was never more useful than during those years of the Middle Ages when the system of English government and administration was in process of development.[1] The rebellions and consequent confiscations of William II's reign, the anarchy of Stephen's time, the decline of some of the major families associated with the Conquest, the rise of new men, and major alterations in the composition of fiefs, could easily have caused its potentialities to be lost sight of. But we can see that they never were.

DB was just one spectacular aspect of the change from custom to written law, though it is not, of course, a legal document. It enabled the Exchequer, and those royal agents the sheriffs, to see what a baron's total resources were or could be; with that information available the appropriate – or maximum – sums could be demanded from him. The royal revenue was derived not merely – or, indeed, principally – from taxation, but also from the fees payable at a tenant-in-chief's marriage, on his attaining his majority or succeeding to an ancestor's estates, for the enjoyment of lands and offices, and from the fines resulting for every act adjudged to be an offence against the King.

For these reasons effort was subsequently made, not so much to bring DB up to date, but to use it as a basis for somewhat similar surveys. Even though, from the time of Henry II, the unit of taxation gradually changed from the 'geldable hide' or 'carucate for geld' to the knight's fee, official interest in

[1] Not very much has been written about the place of DB in English history after the Conqueror's death. The two best sources of information are Galbraith: *Stud. Pub. Rec.*, pp. 104–21, and *DRB*, pp. 47–51.

liability on the basis of the old assessment long remained keen. Early in Henry II's reign a copy of the Herefordshire Domesday was made, and the *marginalia* show how it was annotated to indicate who was in 1160/70 holding the estates as they had been in 1086, and that annotation was not confined to a single period.[1] There survive also Surveys for Worcestershire, Lindsey, Leicestershire, and Northamptonshire which were dated by Round as belonging respectively to the years 1108/18, 1115/18, 1124/29, and the reign of Henry I (with additions during that of Henry II).[2] These too record the names of the new tenants and the number of hides each held in each place. Despite the abolition of the Danegeld in the early years of Henry II, it was thought worth while to copy an abbreviated edition of DB now lost, but made probably in the reign of Henry I, and this is not the only abbreviated text which survives. The full details of DB for each manor are reduced to the name, the holder, the hides, and any information regarding tithes and churches. Two survive among the Public Records, known as the *Abbreviatio* and the *Breviate*; a third is among the Arundel MSS. in the British Museum.[3]

But DB was from its inception not of official interest only. The English bishoprics and religious foundations, as we can see from the text of DB, were at enormous pains to have recorded therein both the fact that they had possessed their lands before the Conquest and the rights they enjoyed in them. It would be prudent for such institutions to obtain and preserve a copy of DB in so far as this was concerned with their own estates, and to include this in their cartularies. One survives among the Bath Abbey records, tallying closely with the account in the Exeter Domesday of that house's possessions.[4] The handwriting

[1] V. H. Galbraith and J. Tait: *Herefordshire Domesday* (Pipe Roll Soc., New Series, vol. xxv; 1950).

[2] Each was considered and discussed in Round: *FE*, pp. 169–224. That for Lindsey was edited by Foster and Longley: *op. cit.* See also C. F. Slade: *The Leicestershire Survey* (University College, Leicester; 1956).

[3] The two last come from the Welsh religious houses of Strata Florida and Margam respectively: the original of the *Breviate*, written in the Exchequer, seems to have been little used. There are not very satisfactory accounts of all in Birch: *Domesday Book*, pp. 29–40. See also Galbraith: *MoDB*, pp. 213–4.

[4] Discussed by R. Lennard: 'A Neglected Domesday Satellite' (*EHR*, vol. viii, pp. 32–41).

is quite possibly that of one of the clerks who inscribed a large proportion of the Exeter Domesday: if so, this suggests that the staff of monastic *scriptoria* helped to compile the 'provincial Domesdays', and perhaps then copied for their houses the relevant portions. The source of the IE was surely, if in part only, the appropriate 'provincial Domesdays'. From their surviving records, we can be sure that Bury St. Edmunds, Abingdon, Evesham, Peterborough, and both St. Augustine's and Christ Church, Canterbury, at some time possessed a copy of those portions of DB of moment to them. Professor Galbraith believes that 'a very slight amount of research would show that a copy of the relevant extracts from Domesday occurs somewhere in the extant cartularies of most religious houses'.[1] Of the *Domesday Monachorum*, though it contains a large amount of material absent from DB, Professor Douglas has said that 'nothing in the Christ Church survey is, however, inconsistent with the hypothesis that there may have existed a preliminary draft of the whole Kentish Domesday'; its basis may have been either the house's return to the Inquest or a 'provincial Domesday' for Kent or the south-east.[2]

DB, as Professor Galbraith pointed out, was as important to the holders of fiefs and their tenants as it was to the government of the country: 'it was at once the basis of all claims, and the defence against all usurpations'.[3] Bury St. Edmunds Abbey surely secured a copy of DB so far as her lands were concerned. The information DB furnished, supplemented by private local information, was set out in a 'book of enfeoffments' by Hundreds and manors, with the holdings of the individual military tenants in a self-contained section. It was so useful that it was re-copied at the close of the twelfth century, and a little later another book was compiled which recorded the military tenants and traced the descent of the holdings and tenures by means of a series of documents to the 'book of enfeoffments' and then to DB.[4]

---

[1] Galbraith: *Stud. Pub. Rec.*, pp. 117–8.
[2] D. C. Douglas: *The* Domesday Monachorum *of Christ Church, Canterbury;* 1944.
[3] Galbraith: *Stud. Pub. Rec.*, p. 119.
[4] The 'Feudal Book of Abbot Baldwin' (a contemporary of the Conqueror) is discussed in D. C. Douglas: *Feudal Documents from the Abbey of Bury St. Edmunds;* 1931.

Appeals in connection with lawsuits to the authority of DB began to be made within a short space after its inscription; one was made in a suit before the Treasury at Winchester in 1108/13. Before long such appeals engendered writs ordering DB to be searched to establish the facts of a case, and such writs, and returns to them which include the certified relevant extract from DB, are still preserved among the Public Records. Private persons, too, quite apart from legal necessity or business in the Courts of the realm, obtained *exemplifications* or Letters Patent which consisted of an official extract from DB.

With the reorganisation of the Exchequer late in the twelfth century its usefulness to officials became even more apparent. It was used for checking certain portions of the annual returns of local officials, embodied in the Pipe Rolls.

Official use of DB throughout the Middle Ages is disclosed by numerous references to it. The author of the 'Dialogue of the Exchequer' (*Dialogus de Scaccario*) tells us that it was daily referred to during Exchequer sessions in the reign of Henry II. In Edward I's reign it was accompanying the Exchequer to the provinces; we know it was used in 1300 at York, and sent thence to Lincoln. In his grandson's time it was in frequent official use; during the fourteenth century there are records of lists being made of the towns which in DB appeared among *Terrae Regis* so that the levy upon them known as tallage could be assessed.

Inclusion among the manors which had been Crown property at King Edward's death conferred upon both owners and tenants considerable privileges, and DB was the one document which showed the extent of royal possessions before the Conquest. DB, from the end of the thirteenth century, was preferred to the evidence of a local jury as a means of determining whether lands were of the 'Ancient Demesne' and establishment of the fact that they had been upon it protected tenants within them against the imposition of increased services by a new lord of the manor, and against ejection, provided the customary services they owed were performed.

Certified extracts from DB could upon occasion be valuable to those who found in them evidence of their rights; the burgesses of Norwich paid to have one supplied in 1398, and landowners had appropriate passages copied to demonstrate the extent of a predecessor's fief. The record was used to determine the boundaries of Forests, to settle disputes about tithes, and in connection with the advowsons of churches. Much later, persons engaged in tracing their pedigrees, and the antiquarian, began to find it a valuable source of information.

Domesday Book, indeed, was throughout the ages so well known and so highly respected that it became common to apply its title to local records which possessed especial standing and authority. There survive, for example, a 'Domesday' of Chester and of St. Paul's Cathedral in London. The title has been variously applied since: we have a 'Domesday of Inclosures' and a 'Domesday of Crown Lands' among historical publications. If a firm of estate agents, or the writers of guidebooks, wish to draw attention to the antiquity of some estate or village, they are inclined to pronounce that it is 'mentioned in the Domesday Book', overlooking the fact that so are some thousands of other places, most of which boast an antiquity far greater than that of 1086. The habit displays, however, the Englishman's appreciation that in Domesday Book he has something which is unique, and of which everyone has heard, even though he might be hard put to it to explain how and why it was made, or what he might expect to find therein.

Part Two

THE LAND AND THE PEOPLE

CHAPTER VI

The Hide, the Ploughland, and the Plough-team

The hide

THE Inquest officials were instructed to report 'how many hides are there'. This was done in order that the total liability of the holding for any kind of land-tax might be an integral feature of DB. It might be expected that they would be told to report the existence of any immunity from liability also, but this, we shall see, was not done systematically, and there is no indication in the preface to the IE that this was required of them. Obviously, however, landholders would use the Inquest as a means of establishing the validity of documentary or customary right to such immunity.

The 'hide' is a notion we meet with very early in the history of pre-Conquest England. The social organisation of the early English period was clearly dependent on the agricultural holding of the peasant household, the *terra unius familiae* which is the Latin equivalent of the *hid* or *hiwisc*.[1] The hide, indeed, is something which is never defined for us, though it is clear that quite early responsibility for public service, and for taxation, was proportional to the number of hides held. It seems, too, to be common form that in the districts conquered early the amount of land which was reckoned as capable of maintaining the average household was 120 of those units known as 'acres' which represent a forenoon's ploughing, though this is no hard and fast equation.[2]

The hide, indeed, seems to have varied in size according to local standards of living and probably also according to soil

---

[1] The 'family' implied was probably one consisting of several generations.

[2] The origin of English land-measures (all of which have a practical basis; e.g. twelve thumbs or 'inches' are roughly the length of a man's foot, the furlong is the length of the average furrow in the ploughed field) is immensely complicated. See Maitland: *DBB*, pp. 362-99.

variations and to the amount of land available. It is unlikely that there were fundamental changes in its composition between the English and the Norman Conquests. It was divided into four quarters, known as virgates, from *virga*, a rod or 'rood'. We have, for most of England, little evidence of the acreage, real or arithmetical, of the hide. In the eleventh century it was undoubtedly reckoned as being composed of 120 acres in Cambridgeshire, and probably throughout eastern England. Very often, in these districts, we are given the total assessment of a vill or manor and also the figures for its component parts, and the required totals can be obtained only if the equation 120 acres=one hide is used.[1] A hide of 120 acres would be, as Maitland pointed out, a most convenient quantity: it factorises readily, and goes well for accounting purposes with a pound containing 240 pence. A 48-acre western hide might indeed be connected with the fact that there were five pence to the West Saxon shilling ($5 \times 48 = 240$). That in Gloucestershire, too, the hide contained a large number of acres is suggested by a passage in Domesday Book which says that 'in this hide there are only 64 acres when it is ploughed' (165a2). But in Wiltshire and Dorset we get equations which are soluble only if there are at times 40, at others 48 acres to the hide. The fairly frequent incidence of quantities of one-third and of two-thirds of a virgate may suggest that the south-western hide did not have a decimal basis, but rather a duo-decimal one, but it happens that in different copies of a geld account for Calne Hundred we find 3 acres in two of them equated with one-third of a virgate in the other, and 7 acres with two-thirds. Mathematically one must be wrong, and the probability is that frequently approximations were used to express small quantities. Eyton based all his calculations on a 48-acre hide, but never gave the evidence for his belief in this relationship.[2] Unfortunately we can discover also the most improbable equations, and all we can say is that it looks as if here the hide represented a much smaller area than it did in the east.

---

[1] See, especially, Round: *FE*, pp. 36–44. An instance is here given on p. 244.

[2] See J. H. Tait: 'Large Hides and Small Hides' (*EHR*, vol. xvii, pp. 280–2), and *VCH: Wiltshire*, vol. II, pp. 182–3.

In Somerset, Devon, and Cornwall, and occasionally elsewhere, we find frequent mention of the fourth part of the
virgate, the ferding or ferling or ferting ('fourthing'). In the
last county, too, DB expresses quantities in terms of an acre
which is not the acre of other shires. This acre is shown by
certain passages (e.g., *Tretlant, 100, 227*) to equal one-third of
the virgate, but it is a unit of accounting, not of area, and
seems to correspond to 64 customary acres. For in the infertile
west the *terra unius familiae* would need to be of considerable
extent to feed the average household.

The hide, especially because it varied so in extent, became
in time a mere measure of accounting; the unit of responsibilities and of taxation. No doubt, though, when shires and villages
were first assessed, a realistic basis was employed, and the
number of hides allotted in some measure corresponded with
the number of households. Its capacity and reality were none
the less still appreciated by the witnesses in 1086, for we read of
'a hide of pasture' (Corsham, 68ai), and of 'the two best hides'
of a manor (Horton, 78bi).

Carucates and Sulungs

Elsewhere, in the core of what was Danish England, we
find, long before the Norman came, the carucate and not the
hide as the unit, and the carucate is certainly the land for one
caruca or plough-team of eight oxen, and of 120 acres, real or
conceptional. In Kent, too, the earliest of all English conquests,
which long preserved its individuality, we find a unit known
as the sulung, a term which also implies a ploughland, and the
fourth part of which was the yoke or *jugum*, derived from the
pair of oxen which made up a quarter of the normal plough-
team, just as the bovate, the eighth of a carucate, derives from
the eight oxen or *boves* of the standard plough-team. The sulung
was still the unit of assessment in Kent when DB was compiled,
and, in theory at least, seems to have had a capacity double
that of the hide.

The Ploughland and the Plough-team

According to the list of questions included in the IE, a statement about the amount of land for which there were teams

available, reckoning, so it is thought, eight oxen to the plough-team, was not required by those responsible for conducting the Domesday Inquest. Yet, from the fact that this appears so regularly in the record of many shires, it looks as if information about it was commonly demanded. No other item in the accounts of manors seems to have engendered the difficulties that this one did, and the number of entries which include the words *Terra est* followed by a blank is very large. Rarely, where a blank was at first left for the number, do we find this to have been filled later.[1]

In the eastern counties the information is consistently miss-ing, and the carucates here recorded, since their sub-divisions are so many acres, not bovates or yokes, probably have to do with assessment, not arable land. In the west midlands, ploughlands are very rarely recorded: they occur only about half a dozen times. Once *terra est v carucis* is interlined (Ham-brook, 165ai,2); twice Worcestershire ploughlands appear, but in both instances the land was waste, so that these may be estimates of potential capacity or of assessment. In Hereford-shire, in what is the Bishopstone portion of Mansell (182bi), we are told of one demesne ploughland and another unused (*ociosa*). The ploughlands of the Northamptonshire Domesday are not ploughlands at all, but represent the figures of an older assessment in hides (p. 245). This may be true of other counties also, of which Leicestershire may be one. Here we have no uniformity of formula, as we do in most shires, but information is given by means of four phrases: (a) 'there can be *n* teams', (b) 'there is land for *n* teams', (c) 'in the time of King Edward there were *n* teams', (d) 'there were *n* teams'. But the use of a particular formula seems to depend on the fief in which it appears; the accounts of some fiefs use one phrase, others an alternative.[2] For the King's land ploughlands are not recorded at all, save for a postscriptal entry, and this happens for other

---

[1] In the margin of fol. 104a2 is written *rq.*, 'enquire'. The number of plough-lands (or teams) must have been at the time blank in the source: it is now filled in. Marginally on fol. 360b2, where there is a blank for the number of plough-lands, is *rq. de terra arabilis* – 'enquire about the arable land'.

[2] The table in the *Domesday Geography of England*, vol. II (p. 325) shows the sequence of formulae and absence of information, but not, unfortunately, the division by fiefs.

fiefs also. In Shropshire, fols. 252–7 use one formula, and (with slight interruptions) the rest of the text a different one, and since the first does not mention, but only implies, plough-lands, this may be the result of the caprice of an Inquest official who reckoned the ploughlands in terms of the potential teams, for we are given the number of teams and told that there 'could be' so many more.

The artificiality of the ploughland figures

The artificial character of the number of ploughlands given in certain sections of DB is most marked. Those of Rutland are a particularly obvious instance. We are told that in Alstoe wapentake (293bi) there are 24 carucates and land for 48 ploughs, which seems symmetrical enough, but when they are counted, the ploughlands recorded add up to 84, and while each of the 'hundreds' of twelve 'carucates for geld' has 42 ploughlands, the teams at work come to 43 and 58½ respectively. Martinsley wapentake (293bi) is said to have 12 carucates and 48 ploughlands, divided equally between the three manors, but there were 120 teams at work, and these were not all there could be; e.g. at Oakham (293b2) there were 39 teams for the 16 ploughlands, and there 'could be' four more teams. In the land of Albert the clerk (294ai) 'there can be eight ploughs, but nevertheless sixteen teams plough there'. The figures for the ploughlands are obviously 'conventional quantities, connected with an obsolete fiscal system which was based on a duodecimal system of rating'.[1] The ploughlands of the Soke of Peterborough, too, have an obvious duodecimal basis, and their figures are arbitrary and artificial. In Leicestershire the ploughlands fall into three groups: in one the ploughlands equal the carucates, in another they are half the number of carucates, in another two-thirds. In Lincolnshire, the assessment in carucates and the number of ploughlands is often equal, but just as often the ploughlands are double the number of carucates. It may be that we are being told that the assessment, having regard to the arable in use, is equitable, or only half of what it should be. Kelsby (371ai), for instance, is said to have land for four oxen, and justly is rated at four 'bovates for geld'. But in point of fact

[1] Sir F. M. Stenton: *VCH: Rutland*, vol. I, p. 126.

'it is waste, except for three villeins with six oxen', yet its value has remained constant. Canon Taylor thought that in Yorkshire (and so perhaps elsewhere) the authorities estimated the ploughlands by means of the assessment to the geld; if two carucates seemed to be a fair rating, they said there was land for two teams; if the holding was assessed at four carucates, and this seemed too high (Yorkshire had been cruelly ravaged), they said that here too there was 'land for two teams'.[1] But these are not the only proportions of carucates for geld to ploughlands; we find also 3:2 and 4:3. Another instance of artificiality is apparent in the Golden Valley (*in Valle Stradleie*, 187ai): 112 teams can plough the land, and over this is interlined '56 hides'. The frequency of 3, 6, 9, 12, 24 ploughlands in Yorkshire entries is such that there must lie behind it some artificial duodecimal conception.

The treatment of teams

The common method of reckoning the ploughlands was to say that there was land for *n* teams. The formula varies: we find, for example 'ten teams can plough the whole manor' (North Newnton, 67b2). As Professor Darlington has said, 'the teamlands of Wiltshire are a rough estimate of the number of plough-teams of eight oxen which could be employed on the estate if it was being fully exploited': the statement would apply to many other counties also.[2] Over and over again we find entries which suggest that to the officials' minds there should be as many teams as there are ploughlands, or ploughlands equal in number to the teams: 'this', it is said of Alfardisworthy (*399*), 'one team can till, and it (the team) is there'. At Chedglow (71a2), there is land for six oxen, which are ploughing there. It is, after all, a poor economy which maintains teams for which there is no land. When there is inequality, the clerk, in a large number of instances, stresses the fact: there is land for *n* teams, but (or 'however' – *sed, tamen*) there are more (or less). 'There is land for two teams', he wrote of

[1] For Canon Taylor's arguments, and his theory of the meaning of the 'carucate for geld' see his 'The Ploughland and the Plough' in *Domesday Studies*, vol. II, pp. 143–86; also Round: *FE*, p. 87, and Maitland: *DBB*, p. 426.

[2] In *VCH: Wiltshire*, vol. II, p. 49.

Wolfhamcote (241ai) 'and yet there are three teams there'. But we find also numerous entries where there are ploughlands and no teams, and in which there are teams but no ploughlands. Some of these, no doubt, are the result of clerical error. But some must have a different significance. We are indeed told that there were no beasts at Uffington (366b2), but that it is tilled by means of the teams at, and belonging to, the manor of Belmesthorpe (346a2). Again, at Barley (139ai), 'the villeins work with their own teams from Newsellsbury'. Abbot Thorold of Peterborough 'holds the land of Colegrim and ploughs it with his own demesne' (Houghton, 370bi); that is, he uses the demesne teams from one of his manors there. In many places where there were ploughlands but no teams, teams from a neighbouring holding must have been used to turn the soil. Tamarland (114bi) has more teams than recorded inhabitants (and two men are needed to drive the plough and guide the oxen); probably they were employed also at Peek (114b2), a neighbouring manor of the owner of Tamarland, which had no teams.

Also, many holdings could not muster a full team, and it is doubtful whether, even in the most favourable of soils, men struggled to plough with less than a full team. Plumstead (II.224b) 'was always ploughed with two oxen', but this surely implies that its owner contributed two oxen and neighbours the rest of a team or teams: this, too, must be the interpretation of 'one villein ploughing with two oxen' (Whitacre, 242a2). Not a few holdings can muster but a single ox (e.g. Fernhill, *332*), and expressions such as 'he has one beast (*animal*) in a team' (*in carrucam*), can only mean that the owner contributes one ox to a syndicate (Coleridge, *329*).[1] At Stanford (218b2) there was land for half an ox – that is, one-sixteenth of the extent of the normal plough-team – *et ibi est semibos*. Some inhabitant must have shared possession of an ox with another, or else his ox had to do duty on this and another holding, half time on each.

Eight oxen, we have said, made the full team. So collation of entries would suggest: e.g. what in DB are four oxen at Babraham are half a team in the ICC (202a2; 95b); this

[1] We are told that at Grimsby (360b2), 'four villeins have one ox in a team'.

equation recurs throughout IE and ICC, and is present in LE also. Maitland had no doubt this was so, pointing out that if the relationship between a team and the number of its oxen varied, many Domesday phrases would be useless to anyone who wished to use it officially.[1] Expressions such as 'five teams less 2 oxen' (North Thoresby, 342b2) mean nothing unless the number of oxen in a team is known. To be a balanced team there must be an even number of oxen; if there are eight to the team there are at Thoresby 38, if six 28 – a wide difference, complicated still more if some of the five are teams of six and some of eight.

This, however, was not the current view. Mr. Seebohm, his belief strengthened by the fact that documents some forty years and more later than DB give a variable number of oxen to the team, (often only four to a peasant team) thought that the Domesday *caruca* did not necessarily imply eight oxen.[2] Fairly recently Mr. Lennard has also had doubts about the invariability of the equation. He noticed that the number of oxen stated in the Exeter Domesday is often in the Exchequer text given in terms of a team or fraction of a team, and that frequently the relationship is other than that of eight oxen to the team.[3] He has pointed out that what in the Exeter Domesday are seven oxen (Bulkworthy, *211*) are in the Exchequer text given as a team (104b1), and that a team and five oxen (Appledore, *295b*) are by the Exchequer clerk set down as a team and a half; there are numerous other instances of apparent inconsistency.

He has been answered by Dr. Finberg, who quotes a number of passages in which the Exchequer clerks approximate, converting fractions to the nearest whole number, which is probably what they did in the above passages. Quite frequently, too, they ignore a small number of oxen; where the Exeter text gives two oxen (e.g. Hele, *128*), these are not mentioned at all in the Exchequer version (102b2).[4] The

---

[1] *DBB*, p. 414. See also Round: *FE*, p. 36.

[2] F. Seebohm: *The English Village Community* (Cambridge, 1883).

[3] R. W. Lennard: 'The Domesday Plough-team: the south-western evidence' (*EHR*, vol. lx).

[4] H. P. R. Finberg: 'The Domesday Plough-team' (*EHR*, vol. lxvi).

balance of probability must make us think that to the Inquest clerks a 'team', however composed, implied eight oxen. While we do indeed hear of 'nine oxen in a plough-team' (Cropwell Butler, 291a2), this may only be the equivalent of 'two priests with one team and one ox' (Orston, 281b2). When we get fractions of a ploughland, and the number of teams equals the number of ploughlands, we can hardly visualise, say, one-sixth of a team of eight, but that the clerk is telling us there are sufficient oxen for the land (e.g. at Chaddesden, 275a2).

Teams and teamlands

But this approximating or ignoring of fractions of teams by the Exchequer clerks implies that they also did so in regions other than the south-west, and therefore that we cannot elsewhere obtain a satisfactory conception of the proportion of teams to teamlands. It is indeed doubtful if we can arrive at one anywhere. The enormous scattered manor of Crediton (101b2) is said to have 185 teams and 185 ploughlands. The suspicion immediately arises that the number of ploughlands has been arrived at by adding up the teams. It is enhanced by examination of, e.g., large and complex manors in Wiltshire. Each contains numerous sub-tenancies, the teams on which are stated, and when we add them up, we find their total is the number of the ploughlands: Ramsbury (66ai), for example, has 54 of each. Some figures are surely artificial. At Westbury (65a2, 74bi; *3, 9, 16*) there are 40 hides and 7 non-gelding carucates, 47 ploughlands, 40 + 7 teams, and $4 + 3 = 7$ teams in the sub-tenancy, leaving 40 ploughlands and teams for the royal manor. Sometimes we may, if we add up all the figures for a county, count ploughlands or teams twice. *Millescota* (88b2) was part of the manor of Mells (90bi), but is the subject of an entry separate from that of Mells, and its five teams seem to be included in the $11\frac{1}{2}$ at Mells.

While indeed one might say that the authorities felt there should be a team for each teamland, or the reverse, we find wide discrepancies, and what seem to be approximations as to the number of teamlands. Did the dispersed episcopal manors of Taunton and Wells (87bi, 89a2) really have 100 and 50 ploughlands, or were there about this figure? North Molton

(100b2) is said to have 100 ploughlands, but there are only 47 teams to till these; the triple royal manor of Carhampton, Williton, and Cannington (86bi) had 48½ teams for the same round figure of 100 ploughlands. Yet at Otterton (104b2) there are 46 teams, but only 25 ploughlands for these to till, and we cannot think that 21 teams were maintained in idleness, or as reserves. Derby (280a2) is said to possess twelve carucates which eight teams can plough; these, we may think, are carucates smaller than the common ploughland.

Of such strange figures there are three possible explanations. First, the hundred ploughlands may represent, not 12,000 acres of arable land, but the whole land of the manor – land which is tilled, meadow, pasture, wood and some, if not all, of the waste and rough moorland or downland pasture. Secondly, in regions where the soil is poor and thin (and the above are largely Exmoor and Quantock manors), there may be 'land for one hundred teams', but in any one year only one-half or one-third is being ploughed; the rest is recovering from former crop-bearing or has not yet been broken.[1] Thirdly, it looks very much as if, in complex manors, we are given the teams for all the holdings, including the often quite numerous sub-tenancies, but the ploughlands for the unleased portions of the manor which are not sub-infeudated. At Crondal (41a2), where there were six sub-tenancies in villages nearby, there are 29 ploughlands, and the same number of teams on the Crondal demesne and *terra villanorum*. But there are also 16½ teams in the sub-tenancies, for which no ploughlands are mentioned. In the first two cases we shall have a marked preponderance of ploughlands over teams; in the third, a surplus of teams for which apparently there is no land to till. At Dadsley (319ai) and its satellites there are 33½ teams on the land which is said to be for eight teams; the teams must have been employed elsewhere besides on these eight ploughlands. Some expressions are highly nebulous: 'the villeins have more ploughs than the land needs' (Preston on Wye, 181bi); 'there were more teams then than there are now' (Wellington, 187a2). There is a classic instance in which the entry says 'there is land for 15 or 30 teams' (Ludgvan, 122b2). But the Exeter version (*260*)

---

[1] A document from Wells refers to the periodical ploughing of land on Quantock.

shows that the formula was written down twice, and into one transcription the wrong figure was copied.

Indeed, many entries suggest that the number of teams is below what it might be. The normal procedure is to give separately the number of teams which are the lord's personal property, said to be 'in demesne', and which presumably did not work (unless rented) on the *terra villanorum*, and those of the *villani*.[1] (Sometimes, though, when DB says that the *villani* have so many teams, we find no villeins recorded for the manor, only bordars or lesser men.)[2] But over and over again we are told that there could be so many more demesne, or villeins', teams than there are. The statement may be given in its simplest form: 'there are four teams; there could be more' (Eyton, 266b2) or as 'there are four teams, and there could be six more' (Naunton, 165b2). In some entries the existing plus the potential teams do add up to the number of ploughlands; e.g. at Cheveley (189bi), there were twelve ploughlands, tilled by two demesne and eight villagers' teams, but it is said that both demesne and *terra villanorum* could each employ another team. Sometimes the formula is that extra teams could be 'made' (*fieri*). It seems as if the writer is trying to indicate one of two things; either that there is land potentially arable but which in 1086 could not be cultivated because there were insufficient teams, or that there were at one time more teams (and therefore, presumably, cultivable land for them) than there are, and that economic tragedy has stricken the holding.

Economic disaster was never far distant from the medieval village. Pestilence must frequently have deprived lord and villagers of their working capital: DB mentions 'the loss of the beasts' at Essex settlements in the times when Swegen and Baynard were sheriffs.[3] The passage of an army, the circumstances of a revolt, though ephemeral in many of their effects, would often involve the loss of oxen, as army rations, as

---

[1] Sometimes the teams are said to be possessed between the lord and his villeins (e.g. Exford, *430 – inter se et suos homines*).

[2] At Petherham (*424b*) 4 bordars have the team.

[3] Witham, Hatfield Broad Oak (II.1, 2). It might have been due to war or theft, not pestilence.

I.D.B.

punishment for complicity in rebellion or from lack of food for the beasts or their owners. Substantial differences between the number of ploughlands and teams may often indicate that because of the above causes there are now far fewer oxen than there had been; too few to keep all the arable land available cultivated. It is significant that we find this phrase about additional potential teams in those shires which certainly saw rebellion and punitive expeditions or border warfare – Cambridgeshire, East Anglia, the west midlands.[1] The formula may be absent from the south-east, which certainly suffered severely during the Conqueror's initial compaign, because it was not the practice of those in charge of this circuit to include the information: here we deduce former losses from the falls in value between 1066 and the nebulous 'afterwards' (*post*).[2] Staffordshire, we can see from the DB text, was harshly treated after the revolt of 1068, and some phrases may reflect this. The teams at Burton (248bi) fell from twelve to four between 1066 and 1086. At Weston and some other places (250bi) there were at some unspecified date eleven teams (though only five ploughlands are recorded); in 1086 there are five only. So wasted may the land have been that the jurors did not know how many ploughlands there might have been formerly or could be: on fol. 246b2 it had several times to be noted there was land for one team or, interlined, two; at Wootton under Weever 'or three' is interlined over 'there is land for two teams'. Other instances of our being told of a decrease of teams are given in entries such as that for Cropredy (155a2): there are 30 teams in all, and the Bishop 'found' 35; that is, when he took over the manor from his predecessor. But a further reason for disparity between ploughlands and teams may be the creation of new demesne farms, or of major estates which were also geographical units. It should not be assumed that the creation of new demesne was accompanied by the cultivation of new land. In most cases, the new home farm must have arisen on the ancient arable. Its establishment meant the employment of new teams without any corresponding increase

---

[1] The formula may owe its appearance to use by some, but not all, of the circuits.

[2] See p. 234.

in the number of village teamlands.[1] Maitland pointed out that when the small estates of free men came 'into the hands of lords who held large and compact estates, the number of plough-teams would be reduced'.[2]

The exotic information about ploughlands and teams is naturally sparse. Sometimes 'arable land' is specifically mentioned, largely in Lincolnshire, where the phrase *terra arabilis* recurs; even so small a quantity as nine acres is recorded (Wood Enderby, 363bi). Sometimes the dimensions are given: the arable was 22 × 7½ furlongs at Cranwell (355ai), and two leagues by one at Rolleston (248bi), but as much as 5 × 3 leagues at Southwell (283ai). Occasionally we hear of reclamation of the waste: Little Grimsby (340b2) 'was waste; it is now cultivated'. How low some estates had fallen is indicated by an entry such as that for Higham (II.78b): 'he found only one ox, and one acre sown'. One team is specifically mentioned as having a duty other than that of ploughing: it 'drew stone to the church' – from quarries for the benefit of the Evesham monks (Offenham, 175b2).

---

[1] Sir F. M. Stenton: in C. W. Foster and T. Longley: *The Lincolnshire Domesday and the Lindsey Survey*, p. xix.

[2] Maitland: *DBB*, pp. 428–9.

CHAPTER VII

The Peasantry

Problems presented by the statistics

DESPITE the wealth of human statistics DB provides, it is not possible to make a really close estimate of the total population of eleventh-century England. The figures suggest a 'recorded population' of something over a quarter of a million, which, allowing for a reasonable average family and survival rate, has been estimated to indicate a total of some five times that number. But such figures could be appreciably distant from the truth. We have no idea how many people may have lived in those places undescribed in DB – Northumbria, London, Winchester, and other towns – or in the holdings for which the population is not given. We have no clue to what must have been the considerable number of monks and monastic servants, to those forming royal and baronial households, or to the numbers of garrisons. We do not know if the figures for slaves represent individuals, or merely the fathers of families: it is highly probable that the former was the basis of the count.

In a quite considerable number of entries, we are not given any figures. We are not, for example, told how many heads of households and slaves there were at Fulbourn (197ai). We are told that at Ashley (199bi) 'the villeins have two teams', but not how many villeins there were. Sometimes we are merely told of the holder of an estate 'with his men' (e.g. Berkeley, 163a2; Cerney, 168b2) without their number being specified, or of an unknown quantity of persons 'holding there' (Bodney, II.273a). At Eastnor (182ai) there are two bordars, but there are also 'certain other men' whose number is not given. In East Anglia, it is common for the accounts of holdings to end 'others hold there', *alii* (or *plures*, 'many') *ibi tenent*, and this may imply not that more than one man has a share of the village, but that there are people who are otherwise unrecorded living on each of the holdings where this phrase appears.

Some persons we know to be unrecorded, apart from those entries in which no inhabitants are mentioned. In that for Almeley (182b2) it is noted that 'the men of another vill work in this vill', and the unnamed vill is known to be Upcote, for which there is no entry in DB.[1] The imperfections of DB are numerous: an instance such as the following is of small account, but it is unsatisfactory when we find $3\frac{1}{2}$ villeins mentioned at *Sudtone* (359b2), but no trace of the other half-villein. The phrase must imply a man who had duties in two distinct manors. By contrast, some men may be reckoned more than once, because they are concerned with more than one manor or recur in several entries. A sokeman or free man may have had several small holdings.

Sometimes, too, we are not told how many people of a certain status there are, or a single figure is given for persons of unequal status or of opposite sexes. We are informed that there are eight 'between the free men and villeins' (Sutton, 252b2), or that there are twenty-eight 'between the male and female slaves' (Stanton Lacy, 260bi). Again, we hear of two widows (Besford, 259ai), but are not told their husbands' status.

Nor can we always allot persons to a particular holding. We are told of five villeins who are attached to the lands of the Abbey of St. Mary of Lyre (52bi), but also that they are 'in several manors', and we do not know which these were.

Any estimates, any comparison of factors of eleventh-century population, must then be somewhat unsatisfactory. We can only guess at the size of the average village household, or whether the term 'villeins', for example, includes all male adults, and whether unmarried though mature sons are excluded. The figures may exclude those too old to work in the fields; we do not know at what age a youth was considered old enough to be reckoned in the count. We can, by means of the maps in the *Domesday Geography of England*, see which districts were more densely populated than others, and how prosperous

---

[1] We should not know this had there not survived a copy of the Herefordshire Domesday, made about 1160–70, with the aim of recording the tenancies as they were at that date.

East Anglia compares with infertile Cornwall, or ravaged Staffordshire with wealthy Kent, but this is all. We can compare the proportion of, e.g., villeins to total recorded population in one province with that in another, but little more.

Fortunately DB gives us more than its authors were asked to provide. The quantities of free men, sokemen, villeins, bordars, and slaves only were required: a rough classification sufficient for Norman needs. But those responsible for the statistics recognised more delicate gradings than this, and often enough returned the population of the manor in a larger number of groups. Also, they sometimes listed by occupation or responsibility persons who to them did not seem necessarily to fall into any of the above groups – smiths, potters, fishermen, rentpayers, reeves, for example. But, for all the order and method of the Inquest, nothing was done uniformly within the province or shire. Some counties hardly diverge at all from those named major categories. Others, from the accident of the individual report outside the general pattern, give us information now quite useless. It is of small profit to find a solitary female slave recorded for Devonshire and for Staffordshire. In other counties, the female slaves who must have existed are not mentioned at all. There must have been far more smiths than are noted; presumably only a few manors thought fit to mention them by occupation, while most lumped them with the villeins. Of the names, and, as a rule, of the crafts practised by the lesser folk, we are told nothing.

Servi

At the lowest end of the social scale come the slaves, who, though styled 'serfs' in many works, are better thought of as slaves, and as in no sense free men. Their position in the manorial economy is indicated by that which they occupy in the entries; either they come at the very end of the categorised population, or they are coupled with the demesne teams. 'In demesne', say the entries for a number of counties, 'are *n* teams and *y* slaves': they are men who, unlike the villeins and some lesser men, have normally no share in the village teams or its land. They are the men who did the bulk of the work on the lord's demesne, aided by the *ancillae* or female slaves who

must have existed in every part of England, though in some
shires they go unrecorded in DB.

The slave was the mere chattel of his master, whose value was
reckoned at round about twenty shillings, and whose market
value was the only compensation exacted from the man who
slew him. The Church might frown and demand a penance if
a man killed or grossly maltreated his slave, but the law gave
the slave no redress and inflicted no punishment on his owner.

But the slave seems to have possessed some minor privileges.
A small amount of free time was permitted him, and he was
allowed to labour for pay during his leisure hours. The fact
that occasionally he was allowed to purchase his freedom shows
that he cannot have been altogether without property. Indeed,
the codes of law of Anglo-Saxon England ordain that the male
and female slave shall each receive certain annual provisions.
The man had corn, a couple of sheep, a cow (and a pig if he
was a swineherd), and a food-allowance at major religious
festivals; the woman eight hundredweight of corn, a sheep,
and beans. It looks as if it was common for a slave to possess a
plough-acre of his own.

Whether slaves possessed hovels of their own, or were maintained in communal barracks, we are not told, but a few seem
to have some degree of independence. Here and there, as at
Kenn (88a2), which was not a manor, we read of a slave who,
with his putative family, lives alone. For in certain manors the
slave may have had special duties: he may have lived a solitary
life as guardian of a flock in some distant outpost of a manor;
certainly he often acted as a swineherd, while the female
slave must often have done the work of the dairy. But his main
task was probably to act as ploughman. It took two men,
however, to manage the team, and it is rare to find a quantity
of slaves double that of the teams. In some counties (e.g. on
the Welsh border) we find considerable numbers of 'oxmen',
bovarii, presumably concerned primarily with ploughing. That
these were of slave status is perhaps indicated by the fact that
once we are told of a *liber bovarius* (Upton Cresset, 255a2).[1]

---

[1] 'Free oxmen' might be enfranchised slaves: a number are mentioned in the
west. Tait (*Cheshire Domesday*, pp. 69–70) did not agree with Round's contention
that *bovarii* were slaves (*VCH*: *Worcs.*, vol. I, pp. 274–5; *Shropshire*, vol. I, pp. 302–3).

The total number of slaves recorded is well over 25,000, and unless they were reckoned as individuals, and not as the senior males of a family, they represent some 10% of the total recorded population.[1] Some sections of DB suggest that under the newcomers' régime their numbers were falling: in Essex, for example, there seem to be far fewer than there were before the Conquest. At Theydon and at Wimbush, for example, where in 1066 there had been four and six slaves respectively (II.47b, 96b), in 1086 there were none. To free a slave was ever considered to be a good and pious action, and the manumissions noted in many a gospel book bear witness to the tendency.[2] In DB itself we hear of twelve slaves whom William Leofric made free (Hailes, 167bi). But a more powerful motive was probably sound economy: the elderly or ailing slave was nothing but a liability, and in many a manor it was probably more profitable to emancipate a certain number of slaves and furnish them with the means of subsistence rather than maintain them. They would still have to perform their heavy and varied labour on the demesne.

In the east, the percentage of slaves to total population is comparatively small; there are less than a thousand in each of the thickly populated East Anglian shires, whereas Devon and Somerset have well over five times that number between them. The percentage in the shires of the west and south-west, indeed, varies from 20–25. Very few are recorded in Derbyshire and Nottinghamshire, and none in Yorkshire, Lincolnshire, and Huntingdonshire. It has been suggested that in these Danish-influenced counties slavery had ceased to exist, but the IE shows slaves existing in the Ely manors in Huntingdonshire where DB records none, and to the extent of about 10% of their total population. It is probable, then, that the other northern counties also had their slaves, but that for some reason these were omitted from DB. We cannot but be suspicious when we find 13 out of the only 20 slaves recorded for Derbyshire in a single fief, and those of Nottinghamshire

---

[1] 'Serfs may have been recorded as individuals, and not as heads of households': on this assumption some of the maps in the *Domesday Geography of England* have been constructed; see vol. I, p. 360.

[2] Examples of records of manumissions are given in *Eng. Hist. Docts.*, vol. II.

appearing in three fiefs only. This again makes a true estimate of total population impossible.

The lack of uniformity in the proportion of slaves to total recorded population is well marked. Any such figures have to be treated with reserve, for the statistics of DB could well be misleading, but those we have give us:

East Anglia	$4\frac{1}{4}$%	(Norfolk, Suffolk)
South-eastern counties	8 %	(Kent, Sussex, Surrey, Middx)
East Midland counties	$11\frac{1}{2}$%	(Essex, Cambs, Beds, Herts, Northants)
Central Midland "	14 %	(Bucks, Oxon, Warwicks)
West Midland counties	$17\frac{1}{4}$%	(Herefordshire, Worcs, Salop)
South-western counties	$18\frac{1}{2}$%	(Berks, Hants, Dorset, Wilts Glos, Somerset, Devon, Cornwall)

From these it is plain that the percentage of slaves was high where the manors were frequently large and demesne land extensive, and in the less progressive portions of the kingdom.[1]

We might expect to find the Church maintaining only a small proportion of slaves, but we do not. Her broad demesnes needed considerable slave labour. Indeed, we find figures as high as 28% of the recorded population on the Buckfast Abbey lands in Devonshire, and in those in Somerset of Bath Abbey, and this figure is approached by 24% in the Devon manors which had been the late Queen's. On the royal manors in these counties there were 10–$12\frac{1}{2}$%, yet in Wiltshire the figure is more like 25%, whereas in that county it is under 6% on the Bishop of Salisbury's estates, and no more than 11% on those of Glastonbury Abbey. Tradition, convenience, and availability no doubt had much to do with proportions, and the east and north had less of an uninterrupted tradition of servitude than the south. Traffic in slaves was still functioning in King Edward's day, though the Church had forbidden their sale to foreigners or to heathen: the toll on the sale of a man was 4*d*. (Lewes, 26ai).

---

[1] The northern counties have been omitted, since in them slaves are so rarely mentioned. Omitted, too, are Leics. and Rutland, where the figures cannot be trusted, and Hunts. It is impossible to think that in the last there were slaves only on the Ely manors; surely they existed on, e.g., the Ramsey demesnes also.

Within a comparatively brief interval, slavery as such was
unknown in England. It is true that the disappearance of
slavery was part of a process which 'merged slave and free
peasant alike in a condition of serfdom' and made *villanus*
and serf synonymous terms.[1] But this is to look forward too far
beyond the England of 1086.

Coliberti

These seem to have been former slaves enfranchised in a group,
and who were probably given small plots of land by which to
sustain themselves. They are most numerous in Wessex and
western Mercia, though the number is never large, except on
the individual manor. Only in Hampshire do we obtain
indication of their potentialities: two at Kingsclere (39a2)
rendered 13s., eight at Cosham (38a2) owned four teams and
rendered 49s. 4d. This suggests comparative prosperity: at
Barton Stacey (38bi) they certainly hold and had held land.
But it is noteworthy that however long they had been freed,
DB, by the use of the term *coliberti*, records their former servitude, and where they are mentioned does not equate them with
a higher social class of peasant.[2]

Thrice they are equated with 'boors', but they can hardly be
the *gebúrs* of pre-Conquest documents, who must have been
well superior to them in social and economic standing. *Bures* is
interlined above *coliberti* in the entry for Powick (174b2),
vel bures at Wallop (38b2). The Cosham entry has *viii burs i
coliberti*, and the *i* may be a badly written *l* (for *vel*), or a contraction for *id est*.

Coceti, Cotarii, Bordarii

The Normans recognised no clear-cut divisions of the peasantry
with which they could equate the gradations of Anglo-Danish
rural society, and took little interest in the implications of the
latter. The social and economic classes indicated by the various
surviving codes of English law were to them of small moment,
as is demonstrated by their separation of the population for

[1] Lennard: *Rural Eng.*, p. 389.
[2] There may well have been a number elsewhere who do not happen to have
been styled *coliberti* in DB.

Inquest purposes into five sections only. But they appreciated the existence of a non-servile element inferior in status and possessions to the *villanus*, the *túnesman*, the 'man of the village', and in the instructions covered this under the general heading of *bordarii*.

Lowest in the scale come the *coceti*, the coscets (the form of the word varies in DB).[1] They are unrepresented in some counties, and their place is not easy to define. It can hardly be said that they are not dwellers in the village, but rather that they live in hamlets and outlying settlements on the fringe of the wild, for at times we find them as the sole class on a holding. The *miles* or soldier who lived at a Hartham settlement (68b2) had with him only three coscets and two slaves, no villeins or bordars – there is no one above the rank of coscet on any of the five holdings here; at the two Horningsham holdings there were in one four bordars, in the other a solitary teamless coscet (68bi, 70bi). Thickwood (69bi), a detached part of the manor of Bremhill, was inhabited only by six coscets, and these have no plough-team.

To the organisers the coscet may have seemed for practical purposes indistinguishable from the *cotarius*. Wiltshire and Dorset are full of the former, but he is unrepresented in Hampshire; in some Wiltshire Hundreds we find *cotarii* but no *coceti*, in others the reverse. In Somerset the coscet appears only in eastern Hundreds, especially in those of the south-east.

The *cotarius*, the cottager, is virtually indistinguishable from the *bordarius*, though the two may appear in the same entry; e.g. at Meldreth (IE 42b2). The Inquest clerks often did not trouble to distinguish between them, for what in one place are described as cottars are in another styled bordars. In the Summaries included in both the LE and IE, the *cotarii* of the individual entry are counted as *bordarii* in the totals given, and what are cottars in IE are frequently bordars in DB, and *vice versa*.[2] In some counties not only do cottars and bordars

---

[1] Maitland (*DBB*, p. 39) thought they were superior to cottars and bordars because they often come earlier in the entries. But so, frequently, do the slaves.

[2] e.g. Soham and Waddon (190b2, 191a2; IE 39a2, 42a2). Any second set of folio references in this chapter, except where an alternative source is given, is to the IE.

never appear in the same entry, but while some Hundreds have cottars, and no bordars are recorded, the reverse is also true.[1] In Devon, it is rare to find a cottar mentioned except in the south of the county. In some places they represented a substantial element in the population; at Upton Snodsbury (174b2) 21 out of the 57 recorded inhabitants were cottars. We read, too, of female cottars – there were nine at Stokesay (260b2) – but what their duties can have been is indeterminable.

In the accounts of a few shires DB gives us the actual holdings of the peasantry, as do the IE and ICC. At Harrow (127ai) there were two cottars, with thirteen acres between them, and at *Stibenhede* (127a2) forty-six had a hide and paid 30s. a year. The holding of a cottar seems rarely to have been in excess of five acres, and a good many of this class had appreciably less. On the Ely lands the average holding of a cottar is only a single acre. An appreciable proportion appear to have been without any land whatever, and some had nothing but what are described as their 'gardens' (*orti*). But at Westminster the forty-one cottars could pay 40s. 'for their gardens', and here another cottar had as much as five acres (128a2).

It is clear that a high proportion of the cottars had no beasts of the plough of their own. But DB tells us of some who had oxen. The eight 'coscets' at Ludgershall (69a2) had a team between them, and the same proportion of oxen to coscets occurs elsewhere also; at Codford (71b2) two have an entire team. We can be sure that the economic position of the cottar, as with other classes of the peasantry, varied appreciably, and it is quite impossible to arrive at a norm. The eleven cottars at Ardington (62a2) had only half a team between them; the eighteen at Ditchampton (66a2) two teams.

The *bordarius* is surely the *kotsetla* of earlier documents, and also a 'cottager', though often it is suggested that his status was not insignificant. We obtain some idea of the position and duties of certain socio-economic classes from a pre-Conquest document known as the *Rectitudines Singularum Personarum*, and in this it seems to be expected that the ancestor of the Domesday

---

[1] This is particularly marked in Surrey; the south-eastern Cambridgeshire Hundreds have no cottars recorded.

bordar shall have a share in the village fields, and that this shall not be less than five acres. Free man though he was deemed to be, he was apparently bound to work every Monday on his lord's land, and at least three days a week in August at harvest-time, and to reap an acre and a half in the day, for which he was to receive a sheaf of oats or corn.[1] The description of those bordars at Tewkesbury (163a2) as *circa aulam* suggests their connection with work on the demesne, as does that of the Evesham bordars as *servientes curiam* (175bi).

In some counties we are told how much land some of the bordars had. A Middlesex bordar might hold as much as half a virgate (Hampton, 130a2; Stepney, 130bi). The normal holding of the bordar seems to have been five acres, but again variation in the extent of his holding must have been appreciable. At Sawbridgeworth (139b2) there were forty-six bordars who each possessed eight acres and two who had ten between them. Harewell (130a2) contained seven bordars each with five acres, but another had three only; the three cottars are not said to have any land.

Some contributed oxen to the village teams: at Owersby (352ai) there were two bordars 'ploughing with two oxen'. At Baverstock (68a2) four bordars possessed two teams, and at Cadenham (69ai) eight had a single team. But these are probably extraordinary quantities, and it is doubtful if the average bordar could contribute more than a single ox to the villagers' plough-beasts. Often he must have had none; an entry such as that for Corscumbe (84b2), which reads 'there is a villein with one team, and four bordars', probably means just what it says.

But we find also bordars without arable land (e.g. at *Perestela*, II.75b). In the south-west, that countryside of hamlets as well as nucleated villages, we find a bordar at Avill (*359*) with twelve acres, and another at Treborough (*463b*) with ten; at Petherham (*424b*) the bordars have a quarter of the hide at which the holding is rated, and can pay ninety pence to its owner. We may doubt, however, if these are in any sense the

---

[1] The smallness of the holdings of the lesser peasantry means that they cannot have found employment thereon for all the remaining five working days of the week.

equivalent of an equal number of acres in more prosperous East Anglia or the east midlands. The three bordars at Sharnford (*231b*) possess six *animalia*, which suggests they had six plough-oxen between them. But we hear also of 'poor bordars' (Suckley, 180b2), and of a bordar 'who has nothing' (*Hatete*, 177b2). Unless *bord.* is a mistake for *burg.* (burgesses), twenty had plots of land within the small town of Bowcombe (52a2). Some must have fallen, as a result of the Conquest, from their previous estate: we hear of two bordars with a quarter of a virgate which T.R.E. they had held freely (84b2). About 89,000 bordars and cottars are recorded.

Villani

Since it was an enquiry on a national basis, the services due from the peasantry to its lords was no concern of the inquisitors, and only occasionally do we obtain a hint of the duties and responsibilities of the villeins. What is plain, however, is that *villanus* is an elastic term, and that there was wide variation in both their property and commitments. In many places persons were recorded as *villani* who elsewhere might have been given an alternative classification, and they seem to have the characteristics of those who in older documents are styled *geneat* and *gebúr*.[1] For the *villanus* is simply the villager, the backbone of manorial economy, a man who cannot be equated with one who, however humble, has a named estate which in some sense is his alone, and which he exploits as he pleases. Over 108,000 are recorded, and in most shires they form the largest element in the population.

The standing and duties of the villeins quite possibly varied from village to village, and those of one villein may have differed appreciably from those of another. We can obtain some idea of what these may have been from those ascribed to their apparent predecessors in the *Rectitudines*. The *geneat*, among other responsibilities, had to do guard and escort duty and carry and lead his lord's loads; he had to reap and mow on his lord's land in harvest-time; he had to furnish a swine by way of pasture-rent. Among the obligations of the *gebúr* were working

---

[1] Quite often (e.g. at Dean, 210a2) the 'villeins' are said to have teams, but no villeins are recorded: at Dean, besides two slaves, there were only eight bordars.

on the demesne two days a week, and three in time of harvest, with extra duties at Candlemas and Easter, ploughing an acre a week of his lord's arable, and eight acres in the year by way of pasture-rent, paying rent for his own holding, and furnishing boon-work. He had to act as watchman, pay a money-rent, furnish 23 sesters of barley or wheat to his lord's stock, and a couple of hens or a young sheep. We know also what the duties of the *ceorls* of the manor of Hurstbourne Priors were before the Conquest, and the *ceorl* too seems to have been the ancestor of the Domesday villein. They had to pay a rent of 40*d.* per hide held, work on the demesne three days a week for forty-nine weeks in the year, plough three acres and mow a half-acre, and sow this area with seed they themselves provided, wash and shear the lord's sheep, and split and carry timber.[1]

DB naturally mentions the specific duties of villeins only rarely, but those of Leominster (180ai) had to plough and sow 140 acres of their lord's land with their own seed, while at Marcle (179bi) they had to plough and sow 80 acres of wheat and 71 of oats. At Grafton (175ai) even the free men had to mow for one day in the meadow, and perform other services also; other notices of the peasants' duties can be found under, e.g. Bricklehampton (174bi) and neighbouring entries and Deerhurst (166a2). But sometimes the statements are altogether nebulous; at Luffenham (219a2) 'the men labour at the King's work as the reeve shall command'. We may be sure that the sum of their obligations was varied and extensive, and that when we read of villeins 'who do not plough' (Addle-thorp, Friskney, 370b2), this does not imply that the lord got no work from them. They might have to work on a holding other than that under which they are recorded; of Broadholm (291bi) it is written that 'the land lies in Newark' in Nottinghamshire, but the service (*opus*) of the villeins belongs to Saxby in Lincolnshire.

None the less, there were villeins of some substance, even though land and tools may have been only leased to them. It does seem to have been regarded that except for just cause the lord had no right to alienate the villeins' land, the *terra villan-*

---

[1] The *Rectitudines* and the customs of the manors of Tidenham and Hurstbourne Priors are given in *Eng. Hist. Docts.*, vol. II, pp. 813, 816–17.

orum, for if a sub-tenancy has been created therefrom, or the land taken into the demesne, the passage recording it always reads as though this was unfair.[1] When, too, we find recorded 'the widows of four villeins lately deceased' (Hidcote Bartrim, 166ai), it looks as if the family share in the village fields had not been taken from them.

Five villeins at Fulham (127bi) possessed as much as a hide each, and 34 a half-virgate each, while 22 cottars had half a hide and 8 merely their 'garden plots' (*orti*). At East Pennard (*166b*) four had one hide which earlier had been thegnland, leased to a Glastonbury dependant. At Kelshall (IE 49b2), two villeins had half a hide, and a further ten five virgates, while nine bordars possessed between them a virgate. At Hadham (IE 49bi) one villein had a whole virgate, and fourteen others a half-virgate each, while seven cottars had a half-virgate.[2] These, so far as plain figures go, are holdings larger than some of the East Anglian free men and sokemen are said to be enjoying.

Examination of the information for Middlesex shows that here the villeins' holdings conformed to standards which gave the individual a hide or a virgate or a moiety of these quantities. The normal amount would seem to be the virgate or half-virgate; this is borne out by entries such as that for Sawbridge-worth (139b2), where each of fourteen villeins has a virgate and each of a further thirty-five a half-virgate. These, too, must surely be 'real' as opposed to 'geld' acres, for often, if we add up all the given holdings, they come to more than the total assessment of the manor.[3]

Even in the less free south-west, the villeins have appreciable quantities of land, unrewarding though this may be. A villein at an estate added to *Madescama* (*404*) has all its land, rated to the geld at half a virgate, including one ploughland, and worth 30*d*. But how, at Lessland (39b2), the four villeins can have a team and a half in demesne is a mystery, for the essence of the demesne and its teams is that they are the lord's.

---

[1] 'Now he has in demesne five hides of the land of the villeins' (Norton, 158b2).

[2] DB often omitted the quantities, which are now available only in the IE.

[3] For information about peasant holdings, see Lennard: *Rural Eng.*, p. 339 *et seq.*

Yet villeins could hold the whole of an estate without the intervention of a sub-tenant between them and the lord whose land it ultimately was. Both Alverstoke and Millbrook (41bi,2) 'were and are held by villeins': in the second instance we are further told 'there is no hall there', and it must have been merely an outlying berewick of a manor of the Winchester monks. But it is significant that they are said to 'hold' these villages, though presumably they were merely renting the land.

Some, too, could afford quite appreciable rents. At Lympstone (*460*) the ten villeins (there were also six bordars and two slaves) paid £8 by way of *feorm* to the holder of the sub-infeudated manor, and six held 1½ hides at *Herstanahaia* (*398*) at farm for 10s.

According to the *Rectitudines*, the holder of a virgate should have been the owner of a yoke of oxen. It is doubtful if the villein of DB often possessed more, but all we can do is to strike not very satisfactory averages, for normally DB does not tell us how many oxen the individual possessed. All we are told is that so many villeins possessed a certain number of teams; frequently there is the complication that y villeins and z bordars – and often other categories of the inhabitants also, e.g. the priest or a *miles* or some 'Frenchmen' – are said to have the teams, without indication as to who had oxen, or how many, and who had none. We have to remember, too, that the demesne teams were usually insufficient to plough the demesne land of themselves, and accordingly the villagers' oxen were not employed solely on the *terra villanorum*. The villagers' teams may have contributed as much as one-third of the ploughing of the demesne.

All we can say is that the figures suggest that few *villani* possessed as many as four oxen, and that while the average is nearly three, there must, especially in the less wealthy parts of the country, have been many who at most had an ox or two. But we ought to calculate on the basis of how many teams DB says there should be, not by how many there are. If we assumed that all the villagers' teams in Devonshire were owned by villeins, they would have just about half a team apiece, but we must allow for some oxen belonging to bordars and cottars and others, which would materially reduce the villein average. When we find three teams between the demesne and three inhabitants at Owlacombe (*407b*), and a solitary ox between two bordars at Coleridge (*329*) in the same county, we begin to see that averages are deceptive, especially as they can take no account of soil variations or temporary disaster or population changes. In a great many entries no villeins' teams whatever are recorded, and it is improbable that the wording invariably implies that where teams are recorded these are in part demesne teams and in part the villeins'. Some entries make it clear by describing the teams as *inter se et suos*, or *inter omnes*.

Sometimes they seem to have possessed a share of the manorial appurtenances in their own right. We find them with fisheries in the Severn (164ai), and with woodland at Rothley (230ai); these are noted as *piscariae, silva villanorum*. They rented the five fisheries at Ruyton and elsewhere (257b2). But normally they must have had to pay some sort of due for use of what was not village common land; e.g. in Sussex one pig out of every seven pastured had to be handed over to the lord as herbage-due or 'pannage' (16bi).

We hear indeed of 'free villeins', *liberi villani* (Barford, II.145), but it seems possible that these are former *liberi homines*, free men, who have been reduced to holding by villein tenure. There must have been a large number of the villeins recorded in DB whose ancestors had owned their land, and who were 'personally free but in economic dependence'.[1] We do indeed hear of a former free man at Benfleet (II.1b) 'who has been made one of the villeins'. Equally, in many places former villeins seem to have been reduced to the status of a bordar. Maitland instanced five Essex villages in which the number of villeins had in the score of years following the Conquest fallen from 139 to 130, whereas that of the bordars had increased from 56 to 202. In these, too, the number of slaves had declined from 36 to 27.[2] It may be that in such instances we are seeing the inception of the process which made the peasantry to be regarded as 'either free or servile', without gradations of status. But even before the Conquest men had held estates 'as though they were villeins', *quasi villanus*; e.g. on Alvric's three-

[1] *VCH: Wiltshire*, vol. II, p. 54. [2] *DBB*, p. 363.

virgate sub-tenancy at Crondall (41a2) or the reeves' two hides
at Chilbolton (41ai).

DB tells us so little of the villagers' equipment and responsibilities that we are obliged to depend for the picture on post-
Conquest documents and estate surveys which fortunately are
close enough to the time of the Inquest to ensure that the
conditions they indicate are not greatly different from those of
1086. These surveys come from widely separated parts of the
country and cover the lands of Burton, Peterborough, Shaftesbury and Caen abbeys. They speak of villeins and 'half villeins'
– those with a virgate and those with only a half-virgate – and
show us the villeins working for their lord three days a week
until harvest-time and then daily until Michaelmas, and the
cottagers one day a week but for two in August. They have to
lend their plough-teams three times at both the winter and
spring ploughings, and for harrowing, and reap and cart what
they sow. They have payments to make at Christmas and
Easter and on the Feast of St. Peter, hens to supply at Christmas
and eggs at Easter. The amount of work demanded and the
renders required vary from place to place and with the status
of the peasant. The duties include thrashing, malt-making and
cutting the wood to dry the grain, washing and shearing the
sheep, and the renders occasional sheep and cows, loaves,
butter, and cloth. Probably the peasant's 'rights of common'
were restricted; he could turn out into the unenclosed pasture
and waste only a number of beasts proportional to his holding,
and for the privilege, as of using a strip in the meadow to grow
his hay, and for feeding his swine in the woodland, he had to
pay the due known as 'pannage'.

Some of these surveys tell us of holdings possessed in consideration of the services done to the manorial lord, and also of
holdings which were rented. But what might appear to be the
commutation of services for money-payments does not necessarily imply a total absence of obligation, for we find rent-
payers who also did 'week-work' (the regular labour on the
demesne so many days a week) and 'boon-work' (service on
special occasions, such as of ploughing or harrowing). Rents
varied appreciably; a shilling or eighteenpence for fifteen
acres frequently appear.

Miscellaneous inhabitants

In addition to the above, we hear in DB of some dozens of minor categories of population, many of whom could probably have been classed with one of its principal divisions. Collation of texts enables us to say, for example, that in some instances those who are styled merely 'men' (*homines*) in DB are elsewhere called *villani*. Numbers are rarely large, but would no doubt be much greater if witnesses and clerks had recorded some by means of their special occupation, instead of classing them as villeins or bordars. This must apply in particular to the smiths and iron-workers, who must have existed in large quantities, though in most shires only a few are mentioned. In lesser degree this must be true of swineherds also, for it is only in occasional counties that they are more than infrequently mentioned. The rents or swine-renders these have to pay are sometimes noted, but where the information recurs, as in Somerset or Devon, there is no consistency about the figures. At North Cadbury (97bi) one had to pay a dozen swine; at Bruton (86bi) another paid five only; while at Cutcombe (95b2) six swineherds furnished 31 swine, and in the manor of Taunton seventeen paid £7 10s. It must be true, too, of such categories as bee-keepers, carpenters, fishermen, masons, millers, potters, and salt-workers, who appear in the accounts of some, but not all, counties, but irregularly and often without any indication of their numbers.

DB is frequently altogether vague about the status or function of some of those it mentions. It includes people who are described merely as 'countrymen' (*rustici*), who may have been villeins of the less prosperous type, as 'Englishmen' or 'Frenchmen' (the latter, however, may have been free retainers of continental ancestry), Flemings or Welshmen, as rent-payers (*censores* or *gablatores*). It mentions reeves and bailiffs and beadles, but never delimits their spheres of authority, and only incidentally and occasionally their duties. From the manner in which all these are frequently brigaded with the villeins and bordars, it is probable that for the most part they had no superior status. We may think so the more when we see that though a certain Wulfric had held Haddington (173bi), he had done so *sic rusticus serviens*; he had been rendering villein services. But then it is not unknown for men of classes which elsewhere we find as holding or renting their own estates – men described as free men, sokemen, thegns, customary tenants, *milites* – also to be brigaded with the villeins and bordars.

Some of the rural inhabitants mentioned above are best considered when we come to concern ourselves with the appurtenances of the manor with which they were chiefly concerned (pp. 184–203). So are those who, though often they rendered services which were also the duty of the villein, were on the whole of superior status. But there are a few categories which are conveniently considered at this point.

Priests

In many an entry the priest is mentioned in such fashion as to make us think he was often of villein status, though it is problematical whether he was indeed regarded as one of the villeins. In a large number of counties the text frequently tells us that there are so many villeins and bordars 'with the priest' who have *n* teams; sometimes the formula is 'between them all they have *n* teams'. In some similar entries the mention of the priest precedes that of villeins and bordars, but still the general impression is that the village priest, while owning a ploughbeast or two, is not socially to be distinguished from the peasantry. At times, it is true, the priest is linked positionally in the entry with the lower middle classes, with reeves and radmen and French settlers, but it is clear that the ordinary village priest was of humble status. Some priests had no oxen, but that does not necessarily imply that they had no land: the villagers' oxen may have ploughed their holdings. It is significant that the priest is not infrequently described as 'the priest of the manor' (e.g. Bedminster, 86bi), almost as though he were considered to be part of it: he is also described as being 'the priest of the vill' (e.g. Windsor, 56bi), while it is common to read of 'the church of the manor' (e.g. Morville, 253ai). For the church of the manor, as we shall later see (p. 193), was among its profitable assets.

In a great number of entries, especially where the priest is linked with the villeins, there is no indication of his possessing any land. But an appreciable number of entries do specify the priest's holding, which varies considerably in magnitude, and which – in Norfolk and Suffolk at any rate – represents the church glebe-land. We find it recorded at as little as an acre (Barsham, II.168b), and as extensive as two whole carucates (Long Melford, II.359). We find churches to which, so far as the text of DB indicates, no land was attached, and when we come to consider the churches as a whole, we shall find many respectably endowed. But the great majority seem to have possessed no more than did the average villein, and there are plenty which have no more than the five-acre holding of bordar or cottar.

From the general tenour of the record, it is plain that, while not all villages included churches or chapels, the existence of a church implied the presence of a priest, and *vice versa*. Once, in Huntingdonshire, where the formula usually tells us no more than that 'there is a church and a priest', it is noted that there is a church, but no priest, and this seems to be an abnormal state of affairs (Houghton, 204bi). Sometimes it seems as if a priest had to serve more than one church (e.g. at Hartford, 203bi) one of which must have been at a village unnamed, and once we hear of 'a priest and his deacon' (Market Bosworth, 233ai).

The record for some counties virtually ignores the priests, and often the churches also. In Cornwall we are told only of the collegiate churches, and village churches and priests go unmentioned. Both in Oxfordshire and in Cambridgeshire we hear little of either.

Hospites

The status of these is never indicated, the term merely denoting that they had been invited to settle on newly-won or reclaimed lands on the Welsh border. They may have been the economically surplus, and especially the younger adults, of the relevant lord's villages elsewhere. Silence suggests that their duties were not heavy ones: it would have been inequitable if, among the hazards of March life and on new ground, they had been further handicapped. We hear even of some who 'have nothing' (Hampton, 264ai).

Welshmen

The number of Welshmen concerned is given in very few entries, and it is probable that in some which do not specify the nature of the inhabitants, these were Welsh; e.g. the men of the district of Archenfield (181ai), who lived under Welsh law and custom, as did those living within the jurisdiction of the castle of Caerleon (185bi). Naturally they are mentioned in the accounts of the four border counties only.

CHAPTER VIII

The Lower Middle Classes

Pre-Conquest tenures

DOMESDAY Book is frequently altogether vague about the status of many of those who had been holding land in King Edward's day. Often it does not give their names, but simply says that one or more thegns, or men of some other category, held the land. It is indeed quite impossible to furnish simple definitions of the various categories mentioned, and while the structure of tenancies in the highly manorialised parts of England is usually clear enough, in the east and north the position of free men and sokemen is often a highly complex one.

DB constantly informs us as to the manner in which the minor pre-Conquest landholders had enjoyed their estates. Men held them as *alodiarii*, or it is said that the estate was 'not an *alod*'. *Alodiarii*, DB makes clear, held their lands by a particular form of tenure, but allodial tenure is something very difficult to define, though in the south-east it seems to have been of some importance to record whether an estate had been so held.[1] Men held their lands *pro manerio* (which, it has earlier been suggested, implies that the payment of the geld due from them was their own responsibility and that the holding was an independent unit); they held them *libere* or freely (which, roughly, may imply that while the holder might be the 'man' of someone greater than himself, he was not legally dependent on a particular individual); they held them *in paragio*. The last expression has been held to imply that several heirs had equally shared and divided an ancestor's property, or that they were deemed to be the equals, the 'peers' of men holding freely and perhaps of thegnly status. If we collate the various drafts of DB we shall receive the impression that the clerks saw small

---

[1] See Maitland: *DBB*, pp. 153–4.

difference between *pro manerio* or *libere* or *in paragio*, for the
terms seem to be virtually interchangeable. But until this
question has received a good deal more study than it has so
far received, definite opinions are unwise. For this is normally
all we are told about them, but about some other tenancies we
are sometimes given more information.

Liberi homines and soc(he)manni

To distinguish between the free men and the sokemen of DB is
not an easy matter, especially as there are passages in which
the two terms seem to be regarded as interchangeable. We are
told that at *Nordberia* (II.353) 'one free man was wholly a
sokeman'; at Fordham and at Hilgay those who in DB are
sokemen are free men in the IE (II.136, 276; IE 55ai, 54b2),
and we find a similar apparent equation at Bawdsey (II.387b;
IE 64a2, 69b2). Yet the instructions prefacing the IE obviously
regard them as distinct. The Summaries of the IE keep the
lands of sokemen and of free men separated from the demesne
and thegnland, yet here we are told of the total lands only of
sokemen in Norfolk, of free men in Suffolk (48bi). Much of the
most useful information about these people is obtained from the
records of the eastern counties, where we have the IE and ICC
to supplement DB. Sokemen are recorded in certain counties
only, mostly in the north and east, and it is plain that whereas
T.R.E. they had been fairly numerous in some counties, in
many, by the time of the Inquest, they or their descendants
were not classed as such. In the highly manorialised south and
west they make no appearance, and it is possible that as a class
their survival and importance depended largely on the degree
of manorialisation in a district.

The ICC and IE, like DB for the relevant shires, and many
passages from DB for other counties, constantly distinguish
between those men who could sell their land without a superior's
leave, and those who could not. The formula varies; the latter
class cannot 'recede' from, or leave their lord, or 'go with their
land' to a different lord, or give or sell it, or they are said to be
'always in the abbacy', or 'episcopate'. Very frequently, when
we are told that a man could do any of the above, we are further
told that if he did so, his soke remained his lord's, and we are

usually told, in passages where the above does not apply, who had soke over a man. At Melbourn (200ai; IE 43ai; ICC 105a2) Edric had held $2\frac{1}{2}$ hides of King Edward, and could sell or bequeath them to whom he pleased. There were also eight named sokemen who were men of the Abbot of Ely, with $2\frac{5}{8}$ hides, who had the same power, but if they exercised it, the Abbot retained soke-right over them. Whether the soke-right was over the land or the man is not always certain. But retaining soke over a person would be essential if he merely transferred his commendation from one lord to another.

Thegnland

It is clear from DB, and still more so from the IE and ICC, that the holders of thegnlands could not sell the land they occupied. Some of these thegnlands at least must have been created out of demesne land, and some were no doubt granted to those who served the ecclesiastical organisations – the principal creators of thegnland – in an official capacity. But we find also what can only be leases of portions of the demesne, and sales of land which were to be operative for a limited time only.

Thegnland could also be created in instances where a minor landholder sought the patronage of one more powerful than himself, which he might receive in respect of the performance of definite services. At Starston (II.186; IE 56ai) a free man commended himself in such fashion to Ely Abbey that, having done so, he could no longer sell his land: here and in certain other instances can be seen the conversion of a holding held freely into one in which the occupier was the dependant of another.

The services rendered by the holders of thegnlands must have varied widely in character: those of the holder of a few acres only may have been not so very different from those exacted from the villeins, but we find also King's thegns and priests holding thegnland, and the services in respect of which they held their land could vary from military service to acting in the capacity of steward.[1] The post-Conquest holder of

---

[1] Quite often, in the south-west, it is a *miles* who holds thegnland. For a priest's tenure of it, see Bridgham (II.213b, IE 53ai).

ecclesiastical thegnland is frequently described as a *miles* or trained soldier, and it may be that pre-Conquest holders too served the lords of their land in times of trouble.

Many holders of thegnland were certainly 'thegns', but equally we find thegnland which is very small in extent and held by somebody quite unimportant. It was not the possession of thegnland which made a man a thegn: the thegn had a legal status and was commonly free to dispose of his land as he would. The lessee of thegnland could not dispose of the land he occupied, though often there seems to have been continuity of tenure: it is not uncommon to read of thegnland being granted for 'three lives'; that is, for the space of existence of the lessee, his son, and his grandson.

The disturbances of the Conquest, as has been indicated earlier (p. 28), caused bishoprics and abbacies to lose substantial portions of their thegnlands. But its inalienability is clearly shown by the Conqueror's orders that those who had usurped the Ely thegnlands should hold them 'under' or 'of' the Abbot, and render him the accustomed service for them.[1]

'Thegnland' we meet frequently in the counties covered by the IE, and in the south-west. The Abbot of Glastonbury sold three hides of the manor of Hannington (66bi) to a thegn in King Edward's day, for the lives of three men, during which period the Abbot was to have the service from them, and at the end of the period they were to return to the Abbey demesne land. Such an entry shows that the holders 'stood outside the fundamental arrangement of the manor and were only connected with it by special services', and that thegnland was inalienable from the manor out of which it had been created.[2] We find Edward the Sheriff holding a hide at Langford (66bi) which by right belongs to the thegnland of the same Abbey. Three Englishmen held Durnford (67b2) T.R.E., and they could not be separated from the nunnery of Wilton. Two of them paid 5*s*., and the third 'rendered such services as are due

---

[1] Harston (191a2, 200a2), Hauxton (198ai): see also the Cambridgeshire Summaries in the IE (48a2 and succeeding folios).

[2] Vinogradoff: *English Society in the Eleventh Century*, pp. 370–1. Vinogradoff seems to have had no doubt that the service was primarily military service, but some of his views and quotations are not always acceptable.

from a thegn'. Such service may well on occasion have been military service. Two Englishmen hold part of Potterne (66ai); one of them, who was nephew to the former Bishop of Salisbury, Herman, is a *miles* (knight or soldier) by the King's command. Whatever the pre-Conquest conditions for the holding of thegnland, the tenants in 1086 must often have had the duty of furnishing the armed knights that the great lords had to provide towards the royal host.

The freedom demonstrated often seems to be quite extraordinary. A certain Tostig bought land at Highway (72a2) 'for three lives' from Malmesbury Abbey, but he was not obliged to commend himself to Malmesbury; indeed, during the term of his lease he 'could go with the land to what lord he pleased'.

Free men

'Thegn', for all the pre-Conquest documents defining thegnly status, is a somewhat meaningless word. Some of the King's thegns were well-endowed and influential men; probably they acknowledged no lord but the King, and the land they held may well have been an adjunct of the royal demesne. But some, from the number who individually or conjointly possessed quite small estates, were little or in no way superior to the *liber homo* or sokeman of DB. Indeed, when, as we often are, we are told that a man held his manor *libere*, freely, T.R.E., it may only mean that he held it independent of any lord and a lord's manor, though he may have been commended to some man greater than himself. We hear little of commendation in the south-west, but that does not say that the practice did not exist there. Many landholders are said to be the 'men' of some great ecclesiastical institution.

To define the *liber homo* of DB is obviously a most difficult matter. Those who organised and recorded the Inquest obviously differentiated him from the sokeman, but it is impossible to be precise and to define just what the difference was. He cannot be equated with the thegn in every instance and respect, for though often the free man of the eastern counties could sell his land, we find him also obliged to perform agricultural services, and the amount of land he holds is often very small. It can hardly be implied that the *liber homo* of these counties is more 'free' than was the sokeman, for the holder of thegnland is normally a free man, but he cannot sell his land, whereas the sokeman may do so. It is not true, either, to say that the free man has the power of commending himself while the sokeman has not; nor is it true that the free man was the justiciable of no man but the King. It is not necessarily true that the free man's ancestry was more distinguished than that of the sokeman, but probably it is true that the economic independence of the sokeman gave him some status in legal affairs.

Sokemen

It is the essence of the sokeman of the IE and ICC, whence we derive much of our knowledge of him, that usually he can sell his land, but that if he does so, soke over him does not pass to the buyer. But still it is not always altogether clear whether soke-right was over the person of the man who might sell his land, or whether it was over the land which he sold, implying an obligation to be discharged by the purchaser. Some passages certainly imply that soke-right was over the man: they speak of 'his soke (*socha eius*) remaining in the Church of St. Audrey'.[1] Equally there appear to be passages which suggest that soke-right was inherent in the land. Soke-right often followed commendation, though the latter had not necessarily anything to do with tenurial relationship, nor did commending oneself transfer soke-right.

As Mr. Miller has said, really in some cases sokeland was being turned into thegnland. Of $1\frac{1}{2}$ hides 6 acres at Shelford which were of the Abbot's soke, only three virgates could T.R.E. be sold without leave.[2] If they were sold, the Abbot still had soke over them. But we find instances, too, where a man could sell his soke with his land (Standon, 142b2). Soke-right could, we may think, given favourable circumstances, easily develop from soke over the individual to soke over the land. Judicial rights could be extended to men 'let them live wherever they lived and work wherever they worked', as a

[1] Harston (191a2, 200a2): ICC 98b2: IE 41b2.

[2] E. Miller: *The Abbey and Bishopric of Ely*, p. 56. Pp. 49–65 of this book contain much useful material regarding thegnland and sokeland. As well as the Shelford instance (IE 42ai) he quotes that of Meldreth (DB 199b2, IE 42b2).

writ of the Confessor's states: 'wheresoever they do wrong, the abbot will have the forfeiture', as it is said in the IE (MS. C, 211a) in the passages dealing with the results of the Ely enquiry. When the Conqueror confirmed Ely's privileges, the writ included the statement that she was to have 'all other penalties for which a money amendment can be made'. Much of what we find in these writs is concerned with the fines for breaches of law and custom, but in time the privilege of receiving the profits of justice inevitably added to itself the actual right of doing justice which earlier had been the function of the appropriate Hundred-court.

Soke-right, indeed, might be obtained because a man lived or worked in a manor or Hundred where this had been bestowed on a local lord. Ely obtained the whole soke of Mitford Hundred, which was worth 60*s.*, and of five and a half Suffolk Hundreds.[1] Mention is occasionally made of the 'six forfeitures'; of those powers of exacting the penalties for the commission of six specified crimes, the profits from which, normally the King's, were reserved to him on whom they had been bestowed. In the manor of Hanworth (II.179b) Withri, a free man, had sake and soke, but the King and the Anglian Earl the six forfeitures; in Kenninghall, a royal manor (II.223), lay 'the soke of the six forfeitures'. Bury St. Edmunds had sake and soke, and 'all custom' besides its six forfeitures (II.413b, 384b); but of twenty-four men at Tunstead (II.244) it had three forfeitures only.[2]

In the northern counties we commonly find an entry describing some obviously important manor, after which come brief accounts of other holdings (often appreciably distant from the head of the manor) which are headed 'Soke of the manor'. These were the places whose holders' fines for trespasses, though there was not necessarily held a manor court to do justice upon them when the tenants erred, went to the lord of the manor. It is not difficult to see how, the sokemen being on the whole impoverished and of scant influence, these

---

[1] Bury St. Edmunds had soke over an extensive district: the names of, e.g. the Soke of Peterborough (Abbey), and of Thorpe-le-Soken, part of the great Essex manor of Eadwulfsness, have persisted till to-day.

[2] For the type of crime involved, see p. 268 *et seq.*

holdings would often in course of time become part of the manor. The free man might involuntarily find himself without power to 'go where he would with his land' or to 'sell it outside the manor'.

Commendation and soke

We cannot, moreover, necessarily equate the *liber homo* with the man who has the power of 'commending' himself to some more powerful man. Commendation, indeed, is often spoken of as though it is the slightest of bonds between lord and man – 'of this man Osmund his predecessor had only the commendation' (Anmer, II.261b) – but the real implication of the telegraphic Domesday text may be that whereas possession of the commendation of and soke over a man so frequently go together, the lord had only the commendation, not the soke also. This is frequently stressed: e.g. at Benham (II.213b; IE 53ai), there were three free men of whom the Abbot of Ely had only the commendation; their soke lay in the royal manor of Kenninghall. At Drinkstone (II.291; IE 56bi) the free men were commended to Ely Abbey, but their soke belonged to that of Bury St. Edmunds. In the Anmer example, we are not told who had the man's soke. Though many men commended to one more powerful than themselves could still sell their land, it was not uncommon that they should both commend themselves and simultaneously lose the power to sell.[1] A man, too, could commend himself to two lords simultaneously, so that we find tenants-in-chief each apparently in possession of half a man. There was a freeman at Alverston (II.376b), one-sixth of whose commendation had belonged to a man who himself was under commendation to the predecessor of Robert Malet, while five-sixths were Saxo's. 'Rannulf brother of Ilger' is said to have half a free man at (*I*)*Sduetona* (part of Nacton: II.406b; IE 57a2); he had half his commendation, while Ely had the other half, and his sake and soke. Equally it was possible to have a man's whole commendation, but only half his soke (Barham, II.352; IE 57b2). Hence we hear of 'whole' and of

---

[1] A priest obtained land from his wife on his marriage and made an arrangement by which on his death Ely Abbey was to have it (Brandeston, II.431b, IE 60a2).

'half' free men (*integri, dimidii*), as at Campsea Ash (II.293b;
IE 58bi). Commendation, except for the fact that to commend
himself a man must have his own holding, and be of above
villein status, does not enable us to differentiate between free
man and sokeman, for either is said to be commended to some
lord.

Where both classes occur, we might expect to find the proportion of one to the other reasonably constant. But while this
is true of Norfolk, in Suffolk there are more than eight times
as many free men recorded as there are sokemen. Lincolnshire
and Huntingdonshire have large numbers of sokemen, but
none styled free men. It looks as if here the witnesses saw no
real distinction between the two; it may be that the free man of
the eastern counties is merely someone whose origins were
higher in the social scale than those of the sokeman, but that
in 1086 each man was often no more than the peasant pro-
prietor of a small semi-independent estate. But some, it is
true, hold quite a substantial amount of land.

The holdings of free men and sokemen

The one thing DB shows clearly about the sokemen is, first,
how very small the holdings of many of them were and had
been, and secondly, how the effects of the Conquest had
reduced the status of many of them. We find two free men
sharing $1\frac{1}{2}$ acres (Wacton, II.189b) and one with a single
acre (Westhope, II.371); three with no more than five acres
between them; one with a solitary acre (Moulton, Aslacton,
II.190). Eighteen sokemen at Islington (II.213, IE 52a2) had
only $17\frac{1}{2}$ acres between them, and half a team, and their land
was worth only 16s.; a free man at Melton (II.388, IE 65a2)
had only two acres.[1] While, if we interpret DB literally, we
find sokemen and free men who seem to have possessed no
oxen at all (e.g. at Rushmere, II.386b), we find also that if we
can trust average figures they had more oxen than the *villanus*.
In this connection it must be remembered that the villeins'
oxen had also to plough the demesne land. But there were, of
course, still free men and sokemen of some substance, and
before the Conquest there must have been many who were of

---

[1] These, presumably, are geld-, not areal acres.

no small local importance. At pre-Conquest Sawbridgeworth
(140ai) a sokeman had had a couple of hides, but he was the
'man' of Asgar and could not sell his land. There were four
other sokemen also, two of whom had a virgate apiece and
could dispose of their holdings, while the other two shared
half a hide and also could sell their land. They or their successors were still there in 1086, and had seven cottars under them.
We find in DB sokemen of, e.g., 15 and 12 acres (Hardwick,
Stratton; II.215, IE 56bi,2) who had four bordars under and
helping them. It is possible that the tendency to limit the
freedom of the sokemen is to be seen in the quite numerous
instances in which sokemen who T.R.E. had had many
different lords are at the time of the Inquest to be found all
under the same superior; e.g. at Hatley (ICC 101b) – the
situation at Wymondham (II.137b) is equally suggestive.
Cambridgeshire seems to have known 900 sokemen; DB
records only about 200. What can have happened to the
missing 700 or their heirs? They cannot all have died, at
Stamford Bridge or at Hastings with Harold, or in and after
the troubles of the early years of the reign. The answer must
be that they, or at least many of them, lost their independence,
and sunk to villein status or worse. Once we are told of a
free man 'who has been made one of the villeins'; he was surely
not the only one to suffer such degradation.[1] In 1066 there
were fifteen sokemen with $3\frac{1}{4}$ hides between them at Meldreth
(199b2; IE 42bi; ICC 104bi); in 1086 there are none, but
there are fifteen bordars and three cottars: either these represent the former sokemen, or the sokemen and their families
are gone and the descendants of lesser men, who may be unmentioned and helped the sokemen on their lands, have come
into the picture.

The depression of small peasant proprietors

The reduction in status of free men and sokemen, and the
increase in their services, may in part account for the decline
in the number of slaves noticeable in many entries; it is more
profitable for the lord to have the labour – even part-time
labour – of men he does not have to feed and house and stock

---

[1] Benfleet, II.1b.

than to employ slaves. At Benham (II.213b; IE 53ai) there
had been four slaves; in 1086 there were none: in Essex the
servile population fell heavily during the twenty years following
the Conquest.

Cambridgeshire is merely one of the most striking instances
of a county in which we can see the debasement of the peasant-
farmer. There are few sokemen left in Yorkshire, and still
fewer *liberi homines*, and this may be because the Conqueror's
harrying and the severity of those left to control the rebel
north had caused their economic ruin: they may often have
been reduced to villein status. Some men of sokemen-status
are still to be found in the Buckinghamshire and Hertfordshire
of 1086, and there are many in the north-eastern midlands.
But apparently they have gone altogether from Middlesex and
Surrey, and almost entirely from Kent. We do not find them in
the south, or the west midlands, because these were not largely
a land of small peasant proprietors. But there are here numerous
instances of holdings held jointly by several thegns, held freely
(*libere*), often with the privilege of 'going with their land to
what lord they would,' where in 1086 there is no indication of
anyone above the status of the *villanus*. For here the thegn can
often have been little, if at all, better economically placed than
the sokeman or free man of the far more fertile eastern counties:
where six or eight thegns held two teamlands, or eleven four,
and the needs of inheritance still further sub-divided the land, it
would not be impossible, in the score of years following Hastings,
to reduce all from proprietorship to villein status or below it.[1]

Certainly we find both sokemen and free men, like the
radmen, with services to perform on a lord's land. Long before
the Conquest, it may be, they helped a man more prosperous
than themselves to till his land, but probably by way of private
bargain rather than of enforced duty. Before 1086 some of the
Ely sokemen are said to plough and thresh, others to plough
and weed and reap, cart provisions to the Abbey and lend their
horses.[2] Often, too, we are told of the customary rights a lord
has over such men, and often he is said to have 'all custom', as
though these dues are many and varied. Fold-soke, the right to

---

[1] See, e.g., fol. 83a2 – *terra in tribus locis*.
[2] See Round: *FE*, p. 30; IE fol. 211b (MS. C).

cause a man to shut up his sheep in his lord's fold for the sake of the manure vital to an overworked soil, is one.[1] In Cambridgeshire and Hertfordshire the free peasantry have to do carrying-service for King and sheriff, and provide a guard for the former. From some soke-right the lord seems to have got little: at Somerby (368ai) it was such that 'it used to render nothing', but the sokemen used to 'help in the King's host by land and sea'. There is the occasional suggestion that a man must pay a money-due to his lord, and as Maitland said, the use of *consuetudo* does not suggest this is mere rent for his land.[2] The nineteen sokemen of the manors of East Dereham and Flockthorpe (II.214b; IE 53bi) had to find fifteen pence of geld – the same amount that the demesne and *terra villanorum* had to find.

Maitland quotes, too, instances of heavy increases of customary dues. Ælfric, reeve under Roger Bigot, the sheriff of Suffolk, raised money payments to an alarming extent – from nothing to £15, from twenty to one hundred shillings.[3] As he says, too, if the lord got more out of peasant proprietors and lessees, we may take it he got more work and higher rents out of his villeins also. No wonder that the man who held Marsh Gibbon (148b2) before the Conquest, and now holds it of William fitzAnsculf at farm, is said to do so *graviter et miserabiliter* – it implies heavy burdens which have reduced him to a wretched state of poverty.

DB and its kindred documents tell us, then, so much about the free peasantry and yet so little. It may be that to its authors they were considered to be of small account, and provided enough was said to indicate the lawful descent of the land, and the lord's rights, this was considered to be sufficient.

Sokemen and free men together number some 35,000 – more than the slaves – and the number of sokemen is just about double that of the free men.

Miscellaneous categories

DB mentions by varying titles a number of people who are not easy to classify, and still harder to define. For the most part

---

[1] See, e.g., II.187b (Nayland, Wreningham).
[2] Maitland: *DBB*, pp. 77–8.   [3] II.282b, 284bi.

they seem to be of above peasant status, and yet it is made plain that a great many of them rendered services, though in considerably lesser degree, just as the peasantry did. Rent-payers (*censores* or *gablatores*) may well often have been villeins: equally they may have been close to sokemen and free men in status. 'Frenchmen' seem often to have possessed minor hold-ings of their own: the *franci, franci homines, francigenae*, we can as we please think of as 'Frenchmen', free men, or what later we find as franklins. The *servientes*, to which sometimes *franci-genae* is appended, might be 'servants' or 'sergeants', free or foreign, but what forms their services may have taken, or whether it is implied that they held a small estate by tenure in sergeancy or in service, is not made clear. The *mercennarius* might be a hired servant or a professional mercenary; the merchants (*mercatores*), minor burgesses, small traders, or even pedlars. But it is to be noted that all these are given a classifica-tion, and not numbered with villeins and bordars; on the other hand, it is always worth remembering that there is no uniformity about the DB entries.

Radchenist(r)i, Radmanni

Radmen or 'riding men' are to be found mostly in the west midlands and Hampshire, and seem to be more or less equat-able with the *geneats*. They were regarded as free men, but they had to perform 'riding service' (running errands, escort duty, carrying loads) for their lords, and a limited amount of plough-ing, harrowing, and mowing on their lord's lands – *ad curiam domini* (Berkeley, 163ai; Deerhurst, 166a2). Entries in which they appear suggest that they cultivated their own holdings, the extents of which are sometimes specified, with the help of labourers.

Drengs

Drengs or drenchs appear only in the district which is now South Lancashire, which in 1086 had not yet become a county, and is described as 'between Ribble and Mersey'. It is in a sense a collection of large royal demesne manors, showing strong signs of Scandinavian influence. Composed of six 'Hundreds', each of which is also styled a manor' (270ai), an organisation had developed similar to that of Anglo-Danish England, with six 'carucates' to the 'hide', and we are told that to each manor there belong so many berewicks, which T.R.E. had each been held as a manor. Here 'the ownership of the sovereign precluded . . . changes of any considerable moment in the status of its inhabitants'.[1]

These petty landholders, styled indiscriminately drengs or 'thegns' or *liberi homines*, resemble the free peasantry of the eastern counties. They have been lords of small manors, but now (and perhaps previously) they have services to perform, which vary slightly with the Hundred. They have to 'make the King's house as the villeins do' (construct him a hunting-lodge?), make 'hays' or barriers to confine the deer, send their reapers to cut the King's crops for one day in August, and fish (269b2). In West Derby Hundred, if formerly any man wished to 'withdraw' from the royal land, he could go where he would on payment of 40s. (269b2). They paid a customary rent of two ores (32d.) to the King for each carucate.

A little later we find these drengs, with apparently the status of the minor pre-Conquest thegn, common in the north country, and some idea of their position may be gathered from the fact that while no such category appears in the Kentish Domesday, Archbishop Lanfranc is reported to have made his local drengs knights.

Milites

The *miles* of DB, of frequent occurrence, presents a problem. The term is variously translated 'soldier' or 'knight'; often the former is probably placing him too low, and the latter too high, in the social scale. For we find the *miles* both mentioned in connection with the peasantry and as holding what is often a not inconsiderable portion of a manor, presumably as a sub-tenant. *Milites* at Enford (65b2), two of whom are named, have five, two, and three hides respectively, and the value of their land, coupled with that of the priest's hide, is worth the not inconsiderable sum of £19. As it 'could not be separated from the church' (of Winchester), they seem to be holding thegnlands. Croc the huntsman has North Tidworth (74bi);

[1] See *VCH: Lancs.*, vol. I, p. 275.

three thegns held it T.R.E., and in 1086 it is held in part by Croc and Edward the sheriff has appropriated a virgate (69a2), while a *miles* of Croc's has two out of the three hides. But at Yatesbury (73ai), apart from the slaves, 'there are seven bordars and one *miles* with one plough-team'. While here and there *miles* seems to imply no more than 'armed peasant', the land-holding *miles* is often the professional mounted soldier, and the equivalent of the lesser thegn of pre-Conquest England, his lord's retainer but given the means of support which avoids expensive maintenance of him as a household servant. The *miles* appears in the record of King Edward's reign: e.g. Feckenham (180bi) was held by five thegns who had four *milites* under them 'who were as free as they were'.

The society of pre- and post Conquest England is obviously exceptionally difficult to classify. Often it seems as though free man and sokeman differ but little in status from the villein, and while economically the minor thegn is in a vastly different position from a man styled 'thegn' who had held estates in several shires, he is still not to be equated with what has been styled the 'free peasantry'. To differentiate between 'peasantry' and 'middle classes' is obviously far from satisfactory, yet the line must be drawn somewhere, and the two most obvious places are above the villeins and below the tenants-in-chief.

CHAPTER IX

The Towns and their Inhabitants

A PRIMITIVE agricultural society, such as that from which had evolved the England indicated in the last two chapters, cannot, unless it is to stagnate, long remain altogether self-sufficient. Internal manufacture and trade cannot long lag behind a settlement intended to be permanent, and each implies the growth of the town and the market-place, and of a trustworthy coinage to enable goods and services conveniently to be bought and sold. Of the early development of English towns we know little, but certainly the Scandinavian and Danish invasions gave urban creation and extension a marked impetus. There had been *burhs* or strongholds before the time of Alfred, but the need to fortify new *burhs* to serve as offensive and defensive centres against the enemy vastly increased the number of places where men might in safety store goods, carry on their production, and be sure of constant visits from rural customers and from more sophisticated traders whose business would lead them to the borough.

Even if at first some were no more than small defensible areas, with little more than a garrison in the way of inhabitants, they were towns and not villages. But with the coming of more peaceful times, garrison-duty would not be the prime reason for residence in a borough. It can never have been the only reason, for the garrison needed craftsmen and tradesmen to supply their wants, and the security offered by a well-defended fortified place would encourage traders and merchants to take up residence within a borough. Most of the early boroughs had been founded on what was royal land (the monarch had inevitably obtained from the first those sites which were most favourably situated as regards communications or strategic importance), and land was ever of profit to its owner.

The early English towns naturally mostly grew up in those

sites so favoured by physical circumstance that they had been royal villages retained by a monarch, or the natural sites of headquarters of shires and sees – e.g. Southampton, Wareham, Tamworth, Exeter, Oxford, Worcester. Save, then, by special grant, the profits of urban life were the landowners' – tolls on trade, rent for the occupation of property within the borough, fines for breaches of urban custom, and a host of customary dues which often we find noted, as sources of profit, in DB. For someone had had to find the labour and material for initial fortification, and was entitled to a return on his capital outlay; he was at pains to ensure that the burghers and those who profited by the security and advantages the borough offered kept the King's peace and maintained that security against enemies.

The King could grant plots of land within a borough – the *hagae, ma(n)surae, orti* of DB – to Churchmen and nobles just as he granted manors and franchises, whether from piety or generosity or to encourage their loyal support: the owners of such plots could lease them, or a portion of them, to men who wished to carry on a trade within the borough and reside there. It is certain that individuals and monastic communities had been investing in borough properties. The town began to become a community, and with its inhabitants' diverse interests there would rapidly arise the need for the evolution of a set of customs of the town, and of a code of urban law where that obtaining in rural holdings was inappropriate. For all breaches of law, or failure to discharge obligations imposed, fines would be payable, which would go to the King, to his officers on his behalf, or to anyone to whom he should grant them.

It was not merely the inhabitants of the towns and professional traders who had an interest in them. The borough was the centre for the marketing of surplus rural produce, and the connection between town and country was ever strong throughout the period. This is clearly shown by manorial entries which mention that there are so many burgesses, or so many houses, in a borough which is named, and what these render.

Of the origins of this system, by which town houses and their inhabitants were in some sense attached to rural manors, we

cannot be absolutely certain, but we can without difficulty see
why it should have existed. The creation or development of
many of our earliest towns found inspiration in the need for
defensible strongpoints, in the absence of which, the Danish
onslaught had succeeded so much the more easily. Each needed
its garrison, and it was possibly the duty of each thegn of the
shire to maintain an armed man in residence in the appropriate
borough: there would be an obvious connection between the
borough property and responsibility and the manor whose
owner had installed his representative therein. Perhaps, since
the normal minimum equipment of a man of thegnly rank was
five hides, he was expected to maintain one trained man
within a borough for each five hides he held. Even if this was
so, we should not expect to find perfect agreement in 1086
between the number of borough properties a man possessed
and the multiple of five hides he held: time would bring
fluctuations. It has already been suggested how not only those
whose business it was to defend the town but those who were
responsible for its prosperity obtained a lease, apparently often
an heritable lease, of property within a borough from its original
owner or chief lord, or from a man who, because of his capacity
to organise and share in its defence had been granted one or
more plots within it. The rents payable and the customary
duties demanded from the lessees would conveniently be
attached to the possession and profits of some neighbouring
manor of the lessor.

Such entries are of frequent occurrence; in Wiltshire alone
there are about forty of them. For example, in connection with
the manor of Bishop's Cannings (66ai) one house in Calne is
said to render 20*d.* a year; in the Purton and Netheravon
entries (67a2, 65a2) one burgess in Cricklade renders sixpence
and five burgesses in Wilton 6*s.* respectively. In the account of
Malmesbury we are given the names of those who have property
therein, and the accounts of fifteen manors mention houses or
burgesses of the town. Sometimes it seems as if we can see a
direct connection: Edward the sheriff has three masures (64bi),
and attached to his manor of Great Somerford is one house
paying fifteenpence (69bi), and to that of North Wraxall
(69b2) two burgesses paying 2*s.* That sometimes there is no

arithmetical equation may be due to the fact that a masure often contained more than one house. Humfrey de l'Isle has only one masure in Malmesbury. But he has four burgesses in the town, one of whom pays 1s., one 8d., and two eighteen-pence.[1]

Borough property

The accounts of towns in DB are indeed so diverse that the only standpoint of consideration can be one which argues that if a place is said to contain houses or burgesses it is in some respect different from the ordinary rural manor and holding. We cannot isolate the towns from the villages according to the terms the clerks used for them: Stafford is said to be *civitas* and *burgus* and *villa*, but it cannot be put on a par with eleventh-century 'cities' such as York or Exeter, while many a small vill is also *villa*. Even Lydford (100a2) in Devon, never of anything but minor military importance, is *civitas*.

Some of the small boroughs are indeed only incidentally mentioned or treated as such. The account of Milverton never suggests that it might have burghal status, except that its third penny and its market are mentioned, though the existence of a market does not necessarily imply that a place was a borough. But the account of the manor of Oake (*433*, 94a2) mentions a house 'in the borough of Milverton'. Quatford is referred to only in the Eardington entry (254ai), where it said that 'a new house and (? in) the borough called Quatford render nothing'. No mention is made of the borough of Wigmore (183bi) except for the amount it renders, and the fact that a castle was built there by Earl William fitzOsbern on waste land called Merestone. The only indications of a borough at Bodmin are that in one passage there are said to be 68 houses there, in another the same number of burgesses (120b2, *528b*). Seasalter (5ai) is indeed called a 'small borough', but no burgesses are mentioned in the entry.

Many towns were, however, of such extent that decentralisa-tion of their organisation was inevitable. Distinction is made in DB between the part of Thetford (II.118b) which was the King's

---

[1] Great Somerford, Smithcote (70b2), Castle Combe (71a2). Castle Combe also has a burgess in Wilton, a long way from it.

and in Norfolk, and that on the other side of the river 'towards Suffolk', one-third of which belonged to the local earldom. Cambridge was divided into ten wards; Huntingdon into four *ferlingi* or 'quarters', in two of which none of the numerous *bordarii* recorded is mentioned.[1] York was composed of seven 'shires', one of which was the Archbishop's, and one waste 'because of the castles'. To estimate the total population of any DB town is a difficult matter, for we do not always know how many houses may have stood on any particular masure, or the average size of an urban family, or how many inhabitants there were of whom indication is not necessarily given. Professor Darby thinks that Lincoln may have had 4–5,000 people within it, Norwich perhaps rather more, Shrewsbury over 1,000, Stafford (246ai) some 750, the smaller Suffolk boroughs about 600. In King Edward's day York may have had a population of over 8,000. The estimates, it is agreed, are probably too low rather than too high.

In a number of entries we are given the number of burgesses, but the details for some towns make it clear that these were but one element in a diverse population. We are usually given the number of masures or houses each property-owner possessed, and their values or what they pay in respect of dues, but we can never be sure whether these include the figures for those rural manors to which urban property is attached. We can never be sure, too, just what is implied by the terms used – *masurae*, *mansiones*, *hagae* ('haws' or town-houses) or *domus* – and whether the first two imply a single house or not.[2] It might be thought that a collection of houses is styled a *masura* or *mansio* just as a collection of holdings in single ownership is called a *mansio*, but the occurrence of two or more of the same terms within a single passage seems to make this improbable. We find every term except *mansio* used at Wallingford, (56a2), *masurae* and *domus* at Warwick and Shrewsbury, *mansiones* and *domus* at Gloucester. Sometimes these are described as *hospitatae* or

---

[1] From the IE we know that at Cambridge the second was the 'Bridge Ward' (bruggewarde).

[2] At Nottingham Roger de Busli had three *mansiones* or masures on which there were eleven houses. The same passage mentions 'houses of the knights' (*domus equitorum*) in which merchants dwelt: it looks as if houses previously owned by local thegns had been granted to Norman soldiers and then let out to traders.

inhospitatae – inhabited or uninhabited. References to borough property in manorial entries, too, make use of different terms within the same shire: there are *masurae* and *burgenses* in Shrewsbury in rural manors, *masurae* and *domus* in Warwickshire.[1] We hear too of tofts at Lincoln and of 'the tofts of the sokemen of the thegns' at Grantham (337ai), and also of crofts, and these would seem to be inferior dwellings. *Orti*, or garden closes, are frequently recorded.

Of some parts of towns we have no account whatever. Five of the Stamford wards were in Lincolnshire, but the sixth was 'beyond the bridge, in Northamptonshire' (336b2), and is described in the Domesday of neither county. The description of Worcester (172ai) is almost altogether confined to financial affairs, and the only mention of burgesses and houses is to be found in the accounts of about a dozen rural manors. But at, e.g., Norwich and Colchester, we have long lists of holders of property, both in the form of houses and of agricultural land. It is not always the King who has the largest number of houses; at Leicester (230ai) Hugh de Grentmesnil has about five times as many as the King has, and probably the reason is that such a borough grew up on land which was then largely a Mercian Earl's. Some boroughs, we shall see, are almost altogether in the hands of a foreign magnate; some owe their origins to the newcomers.

The original connection of residence within the town and its defence seems to be echoed by the mention in the account of Oxford (154ai) of mural houses – *mansiones murales* – which were held free because their owners had to repair the city wall if the need arose and the King so ordered; the owners were free of all duties and payments, except, in King Edward's time, 'army service and wall-work', but if they failed to comply with the summons, they were liable to a forty-shilling fine and lost their houses. Even the owner of a house which was 'waste' still had to help repair the wall if the need to do so arose. The necessity of organising the upkeep of the walls is also referred to among the customs of Chester, where each hide in the shire had to send one man to repair the wall when the reeve so ordered. Thirty-one of the Stafford houses are said to be

[1] Emstrey (252bi), Woodcote (256ai), Wolverton (243a2) and Pillesdon (242ai).

'within the wall'; burgesses are often said to be 'inside' or 'outside the city', or 'the circuit' (*ci[r]cuitas*); e.g. at Canterbury (1ai). The implication may be that these lived beyond the shelter of the city wall; at Lincoln and elsewhere there are houses 'outside the wall'.

The townsmen

Of the actual persons who inhabited the boroughs, who carried on their trades, and lived under their special laws and customs, DB tells us practically nothing. The only entry which names numerous classes of residents is that which deals with Bury St. Edmunds (which, incidentally, is not specifically styled a borough). It includes men empowered to give and sell their land, and 'quite poor' freemen and almsmen, each with their bordars; priests, deacons, clerks, nuns, and 'poor people who daily recite prayers for the King and all Christian people'; bakers, ale-brewers, tailors, washerwomen, shoemakers, robemakers, cooks, porters, and agents (? wholesalers), who 'daily wait upon the Saint, the abbot, and the brethren'. Thirteen reeves too are mentioned, and thirty-four French and English trained soldiers.[1] To house all these, who imply a population of 3,000 and more, 342 houses have been built 'on the demesne of the land of St. Edmund which was under the plough in the time of King Edward': under Norman rule the town had apparently more than doubled its previous housing accommodation. But for the most part we are never told just what part the inhabitants play in the life of the community; they are, except for the moneyers and doomsmen, styled merely 'burgesses' or 'men'.

Nor do we know what privileges, what powers within their town, these burgesses possessed. Most of them probably did not own the houses in which they lived, but leased them from the thegns of the shire and the foreign barons who succeeded them, though the lease was probably inheritable.[2] Many, especially in the west and south, had to help to cultivate the

---

[1] These too have their bordars, who presumably cultivated borough property adjacent to the town in their interests.

[2] At Buckingham (143ai) the thegns who had held property, such as Burchard of Shenley and Azor Totison, are mentioned. Leofwine of Nuneham still held his.

demesne land of King or Bishop or Earl where the borough had
arisen on a manor of one of these. The Hereford burgesses
could not sell their burgages without the reeve's consent, and
he received one-third of the price on behalf of his royal master
(179ai). The 'relief', the death-duty, to be paid on the death of
a burgess is often noted, and if it could not be paid, then the
land with the houses upon it had to be surrendered. But in
the east and midlands, where tenures seem to have been more
free, as at Stamford or Norwich or Thetford, and the development of *burhs*, in districts at the material time under Danish
influence, was late, some burgesses held their property 'in
demesne' and could seek what lords they pleased. The land
which lay around the borough and upon which they depended
in part for their subsistence seems sometimes to be held freely,
but it was not every burgess who held such land, and it is
clear that it was not the property of a corporation of burgesses.
Of six carucates of land at Nottingham, which were liable for
geld, we are told that they had been shared by 38 burgesses,
and that the King received 75s. 7d. from the rent of the property
and the burgesses' labours or that of their inferiors; the account
of Derby provides a parallel passage. It is to be presumed that
the other 145 pre-Conquest burgesses had no share in this land.
Community of ownership *may* be implied by some entries, such
as the pasture in common enjoyed by the Oxford burgesses (for
which, however, they paid rent, for it was royal land), or
Canterbury land which burgesses and the 'clerks of the vill'
hold 'in their gild'.[1]

But it is inevitable that the burgesses should aim at obtaining
both freedom from the tolls and services exacted by their
lords and also the power to manage their own affairs. Even
before the Conquest, some of the boroughs were being farmed,
though they were being farmed by the sheriff or the royal
reeve, not by the burgesses. There can be no doubt that the
round sums we find payable to King or Earl or sheriff or reeve
are the results of agreements to pay a fixed sum, and are not
the total of individual liabilities. When we find the burgesses of

---

[1] It is not certain that this implies a gild or association of burgesses, though
there were gilds of thegns before the Conquest: it may imply 'for which possessions
they pay geld'.

Northampton (219ai) paying the sheriff £30 10s. a year which 'belongs to his farm', there can be small doubt that the King is getting less than this sum, while the burgesses are getting more than what they have agreed to pay the sheriff. But DB furnishes few suggestions that the burgesses are as a group buying the right to apportion their joint liabilities, or contracting to pay a fixed sum which is less than they hope to receive from the rights for which payment is made.

The town and the countryside

The majority of the boroughs include property which is connected with a rural manor. In many instances these properties appear, so far as they can be identified, only within the entries which describe the manors concerned. But in the account of Leicester, except for ten burgesses connected with a couple of manors, the inhabitants, and the houses attached to rural manors, are mentioned in the account of the town itself. Occasionally, as in Wiltshire, we can trace the items in both types of entry; e.g. in Berkshire the Bishop of Winchester had 27 houses in Wallingford, which are said to be valued in Brightwell, and the value, though described as from 'the pleas of the land', is recorded again in the account of this manor (58a2). Miles Crispin had 20 houses in this borough, and they are all linked with manors in the countryside: 'all the land belongs to Oxfordshire, but nevertheless it is in Wallingford'. We must be seeing here the enduring results of a system by which a district supported the borough which guarded it, not necessarily a borough within the county in which it lay. This would account for Bishopsworth in Somerset (88a2) having ten houses in Bristol, despite the proximity of Somerset's borough of Bath, where indeed it also has two houses. Twenty-four Yarmouth fishermen belonged to the manor of Gorleston (II.285); many a manor outside Worcestershire had houses in Droitwich which were connected with salt-renders. Reinbald had had a house in Reading (58ai) which he transferred (*trahebat*) to his manor of Earley. Robert of Rhuddlan claimed as thegnland the land on which the church (*templum*) of St. Peter stood, but the county jury said that it had never belonged to a manor outside the city but 'belonged to the borough', and their judgment was supported by the fact that the King and the Earl had received customary dues from it as they had from other property of the burgesses.

The town and its activities extended beyond the walls, and the towns themselves were extending. Colsuen had 36 houses and two churches 'outside the city on the waste land which the King gave him' at Lincoln. Southampton was obviously developing, perhaps because the intensified cross-Channel connection was extending its trade; 65 Frenchmen and 31 Englishmen had settled there since King William's coming. So was Pevensey (20bi), where the number of burgesses rose appreciably after the Conquest. At Chichester (23ai) there were sixty more houses than there had been formerly. A 'new borough' at Norwich is mentioned, and forty burgesses 'in the King's demesne' are said to be in the new borough at Northampton. At Nottingham there were thirteen houses in the new borough which were not there before. These do not necessarily imply separate towns, but rather extensions of the old ones. Probably these were settlements of the newcomers, who would hardly mix happily with the English inhabitants. Possibly, though we are not told so, such building deprived the inhabitants of land vital to them. For the burgesses were not all, or wholly, engaged in the business of trade; outside the built-up area lay fields and pastures which were one of their means of sustenance. Moreover, in most places there seems to be an element which is not composed of townsmen as such, but of those who till the fields and tend the flocks inseparable from any but the largest of communities.[1] When we are told of these, they seem to be mostly rather low in the social scale, and for the most part are said to be 'outside the borough'. In the entry for Coton End (238ai) we read of one hundred bordars, who are associated with the borough of Warwick, 'with their garden plots outside the borough'; there were bordars at Norwich, and at Bury St. Edmunds, 'from whom the Abbot gets little aid'. At Leicester six carucates of land outside the borough belonged to the burgesses 'and their men'.

---

[1] It is as well to remember how small medieval London was. From the town to the fields and woods and pastures was only a short journey; many of those who cultivated them presumably lived 'outside the wall'.

We quite frequently encounter, in the borough entries, mention of the social and economic classes who appear in the accounts of rural manors. These villeins and bordars whom we find in such entries are not, of course, burgesses in the strict sense of the word; they are in the position of those on rural manors, but it would be hard to say from DB who their lords are.

Constantly we are told of these fields, and of other essentials for existence, which lie outside the area the town occupies. There were 600 acres of arable land attached to Stamford; two carucates and forty acres at Huntingdon of which two-thirds were the King's and one-third the Earl's, which the burgesses 'lease and cultivate through the servants of the King and Earl'. The Exeter burgesses had twelve carucates of land 'outside the city', and these had rendered customary dues only to the city (100ai). Even if these were not necessarily land held by a corporation of burgesses, they probably represented land cultivated by villeins and bordars who, though not mentioned here as they are in the accounts of other towns, worked in the interests of certain of the inhabitants. The Nottingham burgesses had six carucates *ad arandum* – ploughlands, not geld-units in terms of the carucate – and twenty bordars and fourteen teams with which to work them. The Archbishop of York had near his city six carucates of land which were neither settled (*hospitatae*) in 1086 nor had been previously, but which were cultivated 'here and there' (*per loca*) by the burgesses.

Meadow and pasture, sometimes 'common pasture', scrub-land, mills and fisheries (not, as a rule, of course, for common enjoyment) are repeatedly mentioned. The burgesses seem to have their own ploughlands, and there can be no doubt that many of those so styled were engaged at least part-time in agriculture. There are 110 burgesses recorded in the account of Totnes, of whom fifteen are said to 'work the land'; this may also be the implication at boroughs such as Lydford (100a2) where we are told that there are 28 burgesses inside the borough, but 41 without. The burgesses belonging to St. Juliana at Shrewsbury 'labour on the land'; the eight Tamworth burgesses connected with the manor of Drayton Bassett (246b2) 'work like the other villeins'; those at Steyning (17a2) 'work at the court like villeins'.

I.D.B.

For side by side with town life went the life of the countryside. The most rudimentary form of borough is indeed, as we
have seen in Wiltshire in the instances of Warminster and
Tilshead, a large and prosperous country manor which is
distinguishable from hundreds of similar properties only by
having some burgesses within it, and in some instances a
division of dues between the King and one of his magnates.
The accounts of a great many 'boroughs' record the ploughlands and the teams, the villeins and bordars and slaves, the
woodland and the meadow and the pasture, the demesne
livestock. Sometimes there seems to be some distinction between
manor and borough, as at Salisbury. On fol. 58ai we are told
first that the King has the manor of Reading in demesne, then,
in a separate entry, that he has 28 *hagae* in the borough of
Reading. But some boroughs seem to be no more than a special
part of the manor; the brief account of the borough of Ax-
bridge is included in that of the manor of Cheddar, as is that of
Langport in that of Somerton (86a2). Of Milborne Port (86bi)
it is said that: 'in this manor are 56 burgesses', and of the
Stafford houses that three 'lie in the hall'; they belonged to a
property which we think was a manor as distinct from the
borough of Stafford. Twynham (38b2, 44ai) was certainly a
mixture of defensible town and agricultural property, for some
of its woodland and arable is said to have been taken into the
New Forest. The Cambridge burgesses had to lend their
plough-teams to the sheriff nine times a year; it shows that they
themselves had need of them to cultivate the lands which lay
outside the borough. Some Sudbury burgesses were *halle
manentes in dominio*; burgesses they may have been, but they
seem none the less to have been closely associated with the
King's manorial demesne (II.286b). The opening of the entries
for many of the small western boroughs is often 'the King has a
manor', not, as elsewhere, 'the King has a borough'. The
burgesses at Wychbold (176b2) who are attached to Droitwich
'mow two days in August and March and do service at the
lord's court'; at Tewkesbury (163a2) there are mentioned
eight Gloucester burgesses 'serving at the hall', and they are
coupled with the sixteen bordars who 'live around the hall'.
Manor and borough, lord of the manor and burgesses, are

intimately connected. Apparently the owner of a number of burghal houses could treat them as, and style them, a manor: Robert d'Oyly had 42 houses within and without the Oxford wall (158a2), and he holds them 'as one manor' (*pro uno manerio*).

The poverty of the burgesses is not infrequently recorded. At Ipswich there are 'poor burgesses' who can contribute only one penny each to the geld; at Dunwich 'poor men' are recorded (II.311b). There were 'minute mansions' at York, and also *mansiones hospitatae* 'between great and small' (this probably refers to size rather than to their owner's status). *Tateshale* (366bi), the modern Pontefract, included sixty *burgenses minuti* – Maitland described these as being 'burgesses in a small way'. Cambridge burgesses mostly 'render nothing' (but this might be a tribute to their freedom rather than their poverty); Derby has 'lesser burgesses', *burgenses minores*. Some townsmen had left Norwich (twenty-two of them moved to Beccles), because they had been ruined by the forfeitures of the rebellious Earl Ralf, fire, the King's geld, and the oppression of the King's reeve Waleran.

Castles

Fire meets us all through history as the frequent destroyer of towns so largely built of wood; the rapacity of the King's and other officials is copiously mentioned in DB; and the inhabitants of the towns had other troubles also. DB tells us in many passages how the construction of a castle could damage the economic life of a town. Over and over again we are told that a high proportion of the houses have been destroyed 'by reason of the building of the castle'. At Gloucester 'sixteen houses are lacking from where the castle now stands'; twenty-seven in one ward at Cambridge were destroyed to make a castle; one of the 'shires' which composed the city of York was 'wasted in making the castles'. There are few large towns in which we do not hear of such losses. We hear intermittently of houses 'in the ditch' (*fossa*) of the city, and upon occasion these were destroyed in its construction or in the interests of military security: at Canterbury twenty-one were 'waste'. The eleventh-century castle, often no more than one of the motte and bailey type with a wooden tower, might itself occupy scant space, but the ground had to be cleared about it in every direction to deny besiegers shelter and deprive them of a tactical and strategic screen. The castle was indeed hardly a part of the old *burh*, though rudimentary fortification may here ong have existed; it was rather an imposition of the newcomers, as is suggested when at Lincoln we find 'waste houses' described as 'outside the castle boundary'. These could hardly have been ruined as a result of the raising of the castle; indeed, we are told that it happened not because of this or of 'the oppression of sheriffs and officers' (*ministri*), but was caused by 'misfortune, poverty, and the ravages of fire'. It can hardly have been the construction of the castle which produced waste houses in all the ten Cambridge wards. It may have been the building of the castle at Cambridge which, by action of the sheriff, cost the burgesses some of their common pasture, but here it was the construction of three mills which 'took up the pasture and destroyed houses'. The foundation of castles is often disclosed to us by DB, and sometimes the effects are indicated by a reduction of assessment which Shrewsbury did not enjoy, for where they stood there would now be no inhabitants or houses to furnish the geld. The manor of Clewer (62b2) had defended itself for five hides, but its assessment had been reduced to $4\frac{1}{2}$, 'because the castle of Windsor is on half a hide'; the assessment of Alvington (52bi) was similarly reduced, 'because the castle' (of Carisbrooke) 'stands on one virgate'.

It was not in the larger towns alone that the King's barons built their castles, though often they must have used the sites of earlier fortifications for new strongholds. Probably we are not told of all those in existence, especially when they were not royal castles.[1] Okehampton was the castle of that Baldwin who was sheriff of Devon and virtually Earl of the shire, and in that same west country William de Mohun, sheriff of Somerset, had built his castle in what in 1086 was the quite unimportant manor of Dunster (91bi). Earl Robert of Mortain, in addition to his two Cornish castles, Trematon (122ai) and Launceston, the latter of which is described, as *Dunhevet* (121b2), indepen-

---

[1] Unless the 'castle of Wareham' (78b2) is that of Corfe, not far from Wareham, Corfe is not mentioned, but was a fortified place (as was Wareham) long before the Conquest.

dently of the manor of the Canons of Launceston, had made for himself above the village of *Bisobestona* the castle which went by the name of Montacute which in time superseded that of the village (93ai). Wigmore we have seen to have been built on waste land, and Clifford, also in the Marches, though 'of the kingdom of England', not within a Welsh principality, 'did not lie in any Hundred', which suggests it too was built where there was no previous settlement (183a2).

Markets

But if the castle destroyed something of the life of the town, it also added to it. Arundel (23ai), obviously a borough, is styled *Castrum Harundel*. While not every borough, not every place over which a castle frowned, is in DB said to have a market, it is improbable that there was none in most of these towns. We are not told of any markets in the whole shire in the account of Essex or Cambridgeshire, Shropshire or Warwickshire, but it is improbable that no market had been licensed for Colchester or Cambridge, Shrewsbury or Warwick, especially as we find markets in comparatively unimportant places such as Melton Mowbray (but not at Leicester hard by), Titchfield, Thornbury and the unidentified *Caramhalla*.[1] It was the protection a castle and its garrison afforded and the special peace engendered within royal property that fostered trade and the existence of a market, and the market dues swelled the revenue of the lord who permitted its establishment. At Tutbury (248bi) 'in the borough round the castle', were 'forty-two men of the market living of themselves' (*suo tantum viventes* – that is, by trade alone). Berkeley (163ai), which probably was fortified, included seventeen men 'who dwelt in the market', and who also must have been merchants and nothing else. We read too of houses 'in the market-place of Worcester'. In some small towns or large villages, which may or may not have had a castle by 1086, 'new' markets had been established, e.g. at Cirencester (162b2) and Bolingbroke (351a2); that at Tewkesbury (163b2) had been established by the late Queen.

But the establishment of a new market could and did harm

---

[1] Fols. 235bi, 39a2, 163b2, II.230. *Caramhalla* might be Kelsale. The words used are *mercatum, forum*: we hear also of a *feria* or fair.

an older franchise. At Hoxne (II.379) there had been a market in King Edward's day which continued to function after the Conquest, and was 'set up' on Saturday. But William Malet made a castle at Eye close by, and 'set up a market in the castle' – rather, in the castellate or precincts of the castle – also on Saturdays, and so spoilt the Hoxne market of which the Bishop of Thetford had the tolls that by 1086 it was of little worth. By the time of the Inquest he had had to try to avoid competition by holding it on Fridays. A market profited not only townsmen and peripatetic traders, but also the lord who granted leave for a market to be held and whose steward collected tolls for the privilege of setting up stalls and trading. We are occasionally told not only on what day a market was held – that of Otterton (*194b*) took place on Sundays – but just where goods were bought and sold; at Abingdon ten merchants were stationed in front of the porch of St. Helen's church at *Bertone* (58bi).

The market dues might not be all in one lord's hands. One-third of those at Haverhill (II.428) are mentioned, but not the other two-thirds; fractional dues appear also where we hear only of a portion of a market, as at, e.g. Dunham (II.137 – one-half), Litcham (II.207b – one-quarter), and Beccles (II.369b, II.283b) – a whole and a quarter-share. Often, when we read of a toll (*theloneum*), it must be a market-toll which is meant, as at Pershore (174bi) or Titchfield (39a2).

Mints

It was too the 'peace' and good order inspired by the existence of the borough that often made it the place where money was coined. King Æthelstan had ordained that this should take place only in a *port*, for supervision was necessary where valuable metal for public use was to be accumulated, and an art which inspired potential fraud and deceit practised. It had not been the largest towns only which enjoyed the privilege; some minting-places, such as Bedwyn or Crewkerne, were never of prime importance. Usually a large sum was exacted for the privilege of coining – £75 at Lincoln, £20 at Gloucester – and a fee was charged for the new dies when the design changed, as it did with each new reign. Each Worcester minter had to pay

20*s.* to London for his dies; the moneyers in the four Dorset boroughs each paid the King a mark of gold, and twenty shillings 'when the money changed'; the seven at Chester £7 to the King and the Earl. Twenty shillings seems to have been the normal payment, but there are variations. The three minters who had been resident at Huntingdon are said no longer to be there, but they had paid only 40*s.* between them. In some cities, such as Exeter and York and Lincoln, we do not hear of mints, though we can be certain they existed. The industry was not confined to those towns in which the King had a major interest or to royal manors: the Bishop of Thetford had a mint at Norwich, and the Bishop of Winchester one at Taunton, a borough and manor which was wholly under his influence. The Bishop of Hereford had one of the seven moneyers in his see-town, and while here each gave 18*s.* for his dies when the pattern of the coinage changed, the King and the Bishop each further received 20*s.* from their respective coiners within the month following.

The above few pages cannot hope to do justice to the picture DB presents to us of the boroughs in the time of King Edward and after King William 'came into England'. A far larger canvas is needed, and even then a true synthesis of the implications and of the unhomogeneous information it saw fit to include is almost impossible of achievement. For the inquisitors were principally concerned merely with what the King, and, in lesser degree, other great men, had a right to expect from the cities and towns of England; urban life in all its other aspects touched them but incidentally.

CHAPTER X

The Appurtenances of the Manor

General Principles

The instructions ordained that there should be recorded 'how much wood, how much meadow, how much pasture, how many mills, how many fisheries' there were in each manor, for each of these could be a source of profit to its owner. There were other aspects of village life which equally could be of financial benefit – marsh and moor, salt-workings, churches, and a host of oddments varying from forges to potteries and from quarries to vineyards – and which were intermittently recorded. But there was an additional reason for noting many of these factors in manorial economy: they were vital to the existence of the inhabitants; they were, as one entry puts it, *ad manerium sustinendum*, 'for the maintenance of the manor'.[1] The woodland provided timber for house-construction and making fences and barns, fuel, and pasturage for the swine; meadow was essential if the livestock were to have hay; pasture of varying kinds was required for their grazing; the cereals grown had to be ground at the mill and converted into flour.

To hope for uniformity, or even a complete record, would have been too much. In certain counties meadow or pasture are never mentioned.[2] The references to churches are in some shires only scant, and far more churches must have existed than are mentioned in DB; there was indeed no real reason to mention a church unless someone was profiting financially by its existence. In some Hundreds the authorities do not seem to have troubled to make a return of certain features: it is highly improbable that there was no woodland in north Berkshire, or

---

[1] Olveston (165a2). Woodland, etc., is frequently described as that 'of the manor'.

[2] Mention of pasture is entirely absent from the record of the northern counties, save for four Derbyshire references and a solitary Cheshire entry; no meadow is mentioned in the Shropshire folios, and no pasture in the west midland 'circuit'.

no pasture (other than, perhaps, common pasture) in seven of the Surrey Hundreds, but that is what the text suggests. If the wood or meadow or pasture of a manor was not returned, the clerks rarely seem to have troubled themselves about its omission. (They must have been supremely bored by their monotonous task of eliciting and inscribing formulistic information, and possibly had difficulty in securing agreement among their informants as to how much wood or pasture there was; they must have been glad to accept any reasonable estimate.)

Certainly the most casual statements were set down. Highnam (165bi) is said to possess 'as much wood as suffices for the manor'. There were meadow and woodland at a group of Gloucestershire holdings (165ai) 'but not much'; at Burrington and Covenhope (183bi) there were respectively 'very little wood' and a 'a very small wood'; at Ruiscop (185b2) 'a great wood'.

Estimates of quantities

No uniformity of unit for the reckoning of amounts seems to have been expected or demanded. A great number of entries give linear dimensions, saying that the woodland or meadow or pasture is so many leagues or furlongs long and so many broad. Obviously the land concerned did not lie in neat rectangular blocks of the given proportions, and whether the witnesses thought in terms of maximum or of average dimension we have no means of knowing. We cannot even be sure of the relationship of the furlong to the league. The league is commonly thought of as containing twelve furlongs, or one and a half miles.[1] But doubt has been expressed as to whether such an equation was constant. Round doubted if it obtained in Worcestershire, since furlongs, when mentioned, never exceed three. Professor Darlington has quoted entries which suggest a Wiltshire league of fifteen furlongs.[2] At times, however, the number of furlongs is so considerable that we cannot help wondering why they were not converted to leagues. Ashill (92ai) had wood said to be forty furlongs long and twenty broad; Shillingstone (83a2) pasture forty-two furlongs by

---

[1] So the twelfth-century Register of Battle Abbey suggests. For the lack of uniformity in antique measures, see Maitland: *DBB*, pp. 368–99.

[2] See *VCH: Worcestershire*, vol. I, pp. 271–2; *VCH: Wiltshire*, vol. II, p. 51.

eight. Also, we are frequently given a single measurement only; and whether 'there are six furlongs of wood' implies the extent of a semi-perimeter, or these leagues and furlongs are 'areal' leagues and furlongs, as some have thought, none can now say.[1] But at times the estimates become extremely detailed. The woodland at Wood Walton (205b2) is said to be 'six furlongs and two roods' (*virgae*) in breadth, and at Folksworth (205bi) 'two furlongs and six perches'. The perch (*pertica*) is of quite common occurrence; at one of the numerous Tarrants (78b2) there were 50 × 40 perches of woodland. The pasture at Poxwell (78ai) was 8 furlongs and 26 roods long and 3 furlongs and 14 perches broad.

Estimates in terms of the acre are extremely common, especially where meadow is concerned. But we find the acre used also as a measure of dimension – perhaps this implies the acre's breadth: the wood at Kingweston (91b2) is three furlongs long and one acre broad, at Abbotskerswell (104ai) 5 furlongs long and 30 acres in breadth. The acre is not the only areal measure used; Edington (74bi) is said to have 'as much meadow and pasture as befits one hide'. Copeland (369bi) has 'five carucates of meadow', and, what is more, they are *ad geldum*.[2] These, however, may reflect assessment-standards rather than area. Woolsthorpe (353a2) had 30 acres of meadow and 'three virgates' – possibly some other category of land was omitted here; at Heckington (370a2) there were 2½ bovates of meadow 'belonging to the inland of the borough' (of Lincoln?) and at Bleesby (352a2) two bovates of woodland; at Holkham (II.264b) one rood of wood. The hide is used also as a measure of woodland; at Cold Norton (II.69) two of its eight hides are said to be wood. One hide, 'between wood and field' (*inter boscum et planum*) was taken away from Abbots Langley (135b2).[3] Occasionally the arpent, a French measure usually reserved in DB for vineyards, is used (e.g. Grafton, 74bi).

[1] See Eyton: *Key to Domesday*, pp. 31–5; C. S. Taylor: *Analysis of the Domesday Survey of Gloucestershire*, p. 59.

[2] This meadow, and some marsh, represent the whole of the entry. The place is not styled a manor, but seems to have been a gelding unit.

[3] This is the equivalent of the expression common in earlier documents, *bi wode and bi felde*. Chedworth (164ai) is said to possess 15 hides 'between wood and field and meadow'.

The extents are sometimes considerable: Corby (344bi, 371ai) included 1,130 acres of woodland in the two manors; Waltham (II.156) had wood for 2,382 swine. There were 1,000 acres of pasture at Litton in the Mendips (89bi); but equally we find very small quantities – Spriddlecombe (105b2) had only half an acre of wood. Quantities of meadow are naturally, on the whole, the smallest, but the quantities in Lincolnshire are large, and may imply in part pasture not truly meadowland. Frequently round numbers of acres, or estimates of quantity or dimension, must have been given.

It has already been pointed out (p. 52) that there is no consistency of employment of the unit within the individual village, and from the curious apparent omissions, it could well be that we are not told of anything like all the woodland, pasture, and meadow in existence. We cannot map its distribution with complete satisfaction, largely owing to this lack of uniformity. In Norfolk, for example, feeding for swine is the normal unit, but acres appear in the Hundred of Clackclose and some other places. Again, if the woodland of the various components of complex manors was individually recorded and added to give a single set of dimensions, the results must often have been very strange. There are instances where the dimensions of the woodland exceed those given for the whole manor.

For quite frequently in the northern counties, but only rarely south of Trent, we are given what would appear to be the dimensions of the manor, or of the manor with its berewicks and sokelands. It is quite impossible to determine their real implications; for example, on fol. 308ai a group of villages is said to extend over an area $2\frac{1}{2} \times 2$ leagues, but then we are told that they include woodland which is 3 leagues by 1 league; at Healaugh (326ai) the woodland seems to occupy half the extent of the manor. We can hardly feel confident that Riccall (302b2) was really half woodland, one-quarter meadow, and one-quarter arable, as the text implies. The district of Yale (*Gal*, 254a2) is said to be $5 \times 1\frac{1}{2}$ leagues in extent, and in the entry for Thorner (373bi) is a reference to both a first and 'the newest' measurement': the vill is said to be within Ilbert de Laci's castellary at the first reckoning and without it at the

second. Had the Inquest twice enquired into the actual extent
of manors and fiefs?

Woodland

The woodland is specified in a surprisingly large number of
ways, the normal term being *silva* or *nemus*. Coppice or under-
wood, described as *nemusculus* or *silva minuta, modica*, is recorded
with considerable frequency. So is the character of the wood:
we hear of oakwood (*quercus*; Shipley, 239a2), ashwood (*frax-
inetus*; Lamport, 226bi), alderwood (*alnetus*; Spalding, 351b2),
thornwood (*runcetus*; Chilmark, 67b2), brushwood (*bruaria* or
broca; Boveridge, 77b2; Gate Burton, 347ai); spinney (*spinetum*;
Harlaxton, 337b2), a small willow plantation (*parvum salictum*;
Toton, 287bi). We hear too of wood for making the fences
(*ad sepes reficiendum, ad clausuram rispalia ad sepes*; Clopton, 197bi;
Holybourne, 38ai; Graveley, 140b2), or for house construction
(*ad domos curiae, ad faciendas domos*; Elsworth, 192bi; Broughton,
38bi,2), or for use as fuel (*ad focum*; Toft, 202bi), or firing
(*ad ignem*; Whittington, 173bi). What is described as a 'grove'
(*lucus, grava*) is occasionally mentioned; there had formerly
been one in the royal manor of Bedwyn which had passed into
other hands (64b2, 72a2) – on its second mention it is merely
silva; the royal reeves had removed one from the Archbishop
of York's manor of Mottisfont (42a). Indeed, the information
about the woodland is more comprehensive than it is for any
other manorial appurtenance. We are told of wood which has
been wasted (Wheatley, II.43), of wood which is useless
(*inutilis*; Littleton, 45b2), or 'of little value' (*vilis*; Ketton,
219a2), of wood 'which does not bear' (*infructuosa*; Lubbes-
thorp, 235a2).[1] Several times the wood is said to be *parva*
(South Tidworth, 46b2), and whether this implies woodland
small in extent or stature cannot be determined; the word
silvula is also used (Tickenhurst, 11bi). At Sunwood (44b2)
there was wood 'the greater part of which has been blown down'.
The renders from woodland are sometimes given for the occasions 'when it bears mast' (*cum oneratur*, Aldwinckle, 22ai;
quando fructificatur, Wrotham, 3a2).

[1] The wood at Canterbury said to be *infructuosa* is in the *Excerpta* described as
silva minuta, which suggests that it was not fully grown.

Woodland, too, we find described not by dimension or area, but by its capacity to provide pasture for swine, or by the rents which have to be paid for swine-pasture within it. There is said to be *silva pastilis*, (rarely *silva pascualis*) 'wood for *n* swine' or 'wood for pannage for *n* swine', or, occasionally, 'as much wood whence *n* swine go out for pannage'. Such expressions are capable of two interpretations: one is that the number of swine specified fed in the wood, the other that the number of pigs stated were paid to the owner of the manor for the privilege of using his woodland. At Bishop's Hatfield (135ai) a number as large as 2,000 obviously implies the total number feedable, and 'wood for fattening ten swine' (Betton, 259a2) is capable of a single interpretation only, but '1½ pigs from the pannage' (*de pasnagio*; Donnington, 17bi) suggests a rent in kind.

We are indeed intermittently told of the swine-rents to be paid. At Pagham (16bi) one pig is to be paid *de herbagio* by each villein who has seven, and a marginal note says 'and likewise throughout Sussex'. But at Bishopstone (16b2), also in Sussex, one pig in three has to be paid, and at Aldingbourne on the same folio one in six, while in Surrey, at Malden (35ai) and Titsey (36bi), the proportion is one in seven. At Battersea (32a2) a villein with ten pigs had to surrender one of them, but none if he owned less, and at Streatham (34b2) one in ten is specified, and this was the quantity required also at Leominster in Herefordshire (180ai). These swine-rents are not infrequently coupled with rents in money, and with wood said to be 'for the fences', etc., and occasionally it is stressed that no due is paid for pannage (or that no pannage-right exists); wood is said to be *non pastilis* (Whiston, etc., 222bi,2) or *sine pasnagio* (Quarley, 39a2). But this may imply that it is unsuitable for pasture.

Woodland, indeed, from its nature, is frequently inseparable from pasture. For in the south-east we hear simultaneously of *pastura* and *herbagium*; e.g. at Fetcham (30bi) six pigs are rendered from 'the pasture and the herbage' – mast-swine and grass-swine.[1] Sometimes wood-dues and herbage-dues are kept separate; at Ferring (16b2) there is 'wood of four swine' and

---

[1] *Pastura* and *herbagium* are never found together in the individual entry in Sussex.

'one pig in seven (is paid) for herbage'; at Tarring (16b2) tenpence is received for the wood, and 20s. and two pigs for pannage. We cannot be sure that *herbagium* or *pasnagium* always relates to the grazing of swine; in a number of entries other beasts, and pasture other than the woodland, may be intended. But on occasion the statement is quite definite: at Kennington (12b2) 40 swine or 54½d. 'go out from the pannage' (i.e. are received by the lord).

It is possible that when we are told of a manor having more than one wood, a difference in the quality of the feeding may be indicated. Many a large and complex manor must of course have possessed several stretches of woodland, and more than one of these may be described, though not by name, in a single entry. Paxton (207ai) has *silva pastilis* and *alia silva*; two woods are mentioned in the account of Cirencester (162b2); Lilstock (98bi) has 20 acres of wood in one place and wood one league long by half a league long in another; Dowlish (87b2) has a wood of 8 × 3 furlongs, 'and 20 acres over and above this'.[1] In a number of entries we are told there is *silva per loca* – here and there – and this may imply woodland scattered within a manor and its components. Where, as at Otley (303bi), which had sixteen berewicks, we hear only of dimensions for single quantities of pasture-wood and coppice, it is probable that some or all of the components had wood, the measurements of which were combined into totals. The entry for Hovingham (327b2), after details of the manor and its fifteen berewicks, ends with lines beginning *Silva, Totum*, and which are otherwise blank. Presumably the individual amounts of woodland were to have been totalled, and then some further information provided.[2] Three of the dispersed components of the manor of Pilton are described on fol. 90bi, and are said to include four acres of wood. But the Exeter Domesday tells us that two acres were at Pylle and two at North Wootton (*166*).

---

[1] Three manors had been added between 1066 and 1086 to the manor of Dowlish; the 20 acres probably lay in one or more of these.

[2] The manor of Amesbury (64b2) had woodland 6 leagues by 4. This cannot have all been in the neighbourhood of the head of the manor on the eastern side of Salisbury Plain: the manor included land in the New Forest and the Isle of Wight. The woodland of South Petherton (86a2) may well have been in what was later Neroche Forest, some distance from the marshland in which the vill lay.

Occasionally the name by which a wood went is furnished. In the manor of Colkirk was 'the wood of *Fangeham*' (Fakenham, II.197b); in that of Hempnall (II.248b) 'the wood called *Schieteshaga*'. 'Haucombe Wood' is mentioned in the Dorset text (75a2); in Leicestershire there was 'a wood of the whole shire called *Hereswode*', four leagues by one (230ai). Chute Wood in Wiltshire (*Cetum*) is mentioned in the account of Collingbourne (65a2), and the third part of the dues was an appurtenance of the manor. In the same county the manors of Wilton nunnery of South Newton and Washern (68ai,2) had each the right to pasture 80 pigs in Melchet Wood, and to draw from it 80 cartloads of wood and whatever was necessary for repairing houses and fences.

It is of a lord's interest in woodland that we frequently read. Snailwell (199a2,bi) was held by Hugh de Port-en-Bessins as of the fief of the Bishop of Bayeux (rightfully it belonged to Ely Abbey), and here two cartloads (of wood) might be taken from the King's wood at Cheveley. Thorney Abbey had 'a customary due of 2s. in the wood of the Abbot of Peterborough' in the manor of Water Newton (205ai), which incidentally was a Thorney manor. But we are told also of *silva villanorum* (Rothley, 230ai) as well as the demesne woodland. Besides a 'wood of 300 swine' the owner of Newport Pagnell (148b2) had 4s. also 'from the men who dwell in the wood', and at Brill (143bi) the King has £12 'of money burnt and assayed' for Forest dues.[1] The woodland at Oakley (149a2) would have accommodated 200 swine were it not 'in the King's park', and this was worthy of record because it decreased the profits of the holding. Woodland was both so essential and so profitable that one of the disputes recorded is in connection with a quarter of the wood at Reepham (II.376b). From numerous passages in DB, the value of a hawk seems to have been not less than £10, and consequently the existence of nests of hawks in a manor was frequently recorded (e.g. Limpsfield, 34ai, where there were three).

It is clear from pre-Domesday documents that some villages (expecially in Kent) 'came to regard certain localities in the Weald, often a long distance away, as their own particular

[1] Consideration of land 'in the Forest' is deferred until the next chapter.

swine pastures, known as denes or denns'.[1] DB records a number, but far from all, of these, and there are references also to ownership by a sub-tenancy in the royal manor of Windsor of one-third of a dene (56b2), and to a Surrey dene (Ewell, 30bi). They are not recorded in Sussex, but there is a strong suggestion that outlying Wealden holdings in the rape of Hastings had been allotted to the lords of estates in the Pevensey district and subsequently colonised. They may have begun as denes, and then the woodland cleared and a small settlement founded: in DB Tiffenden (13b2), with its two villeins and half-team assessed at half a *jugum* and valued at one hundred pence, 'seems to have been only just emerging from a swine pasture'.[2]

As a rule, information in DB about the Kentish denes is not given in individual entries for each place, but included in the account of the 'parent centre'. We find denes without populations or teams recorded (e.g. Orpington, 4b2), sometimes styled 'of the wood' (*silvae* or *de silva*), though their values or swine-renders are often given, and inhabitants and teams are sometimes given for them (e.g. Tinton, 11ai).

The woodland of the country, as many a place-name shows, had been cleared wherever Anglo-Saxon and Anglo-Dane had seen the opportunity of settlement or of colonisation; without the woodman's axe, the thickly forested land could never have accommodated the population which developed during the six hundred years of occupation. It looks as if there had been considerable reduction of the woodland also between the the Conquest and the Inquest, though this can be deduced only from the record for the eastern counties, for here alone are we given the figures of swine 'for which there was wood' in both the relevant years. The decrease is apparent in 33 Norfolk, 38 Suffolk, and 38 Essex villages; it may of course have occurred also in villages for which we have no comparative figures, and may often have been due to the need for timber, not for extension of the arable land, for the number of plough-

---

[1] Darby and Campbell: *Dom. Geog.*, vol. III., p. 527.

[2] *Dom. Geog.*, vol. III., pp. 529, 413: see also *VCH: Sussex*, vol. I, pp. 357–8, 394. In the south-east the number of place-names which contain the 'dene' element is large.

teams often shows no increase where the amount of woodland shows decline. Some of the falls in the number of swine are certainly spectacular; from 60 to 16 at a Maplestead manor (II.84), from 1,000 to 200 at Buxton (II.229), from 300 to 60 at Wissett (II.293).

Of reclamation from the wood we do hear elsewhere. At Marcle in Herefordshire (179b2) 58 acres had been so gained, and interlined is the word 'assart' (*essarz*). This is the only county in which we are specifically told of assarts.[1]

Pasture

Though the instructions stated that the amount of pasture (*pastura, pascua*) was to be recorded, this, if it was returned, was omitted for several counties and only infrequently noted for others. It is absent from Domesday for Yorkshire, Nottinghamshire, Leicestershire, Shropshire, Staffordshire and Worcestershire; it is very rarely given for, e.g., Gloucestershire, Derbyshire, Lincolnshire and Norfolk. The reason might be that since pasture was essential for the beasts of every settlement, it was noted only accidentally or when there was pasture which was not free, but enjoyed only on payment of rent. We hear indeed of free men rendering a customary due 'because they could not do without their pasture' (Fodderstone, II.274). In Cambridgeshire and some other counties, where pasture is recorded for most of the settlements, the extent thereof is not given, but it is merely stated that 'there is pasture for the livestock of the vill', which again suggests its essentiality. Sometimes, as we have seen in the preceding section, swine-pastures are specifically mentioned, sometimes pasture for the sheep.[2] Pasture for horses also appears; Godric the former sheriff of Berkshire had made land into pasture for those he owned, perhaps the 43 acres which had formerly been part of the royal farm of the King's manor of Kintbury (57bi).

[1] We meet them again at Leominster (180ai), Weobley, and Fernhill (184b2); the two last are described as the equivalent of 'land for one team', and their values are given.

[2] Porton (69b2). The Norfolk and Essex entries are almost all said to refer to pasture for sheep, and Round (*VCH: Essex*, vol. I, pp. 368–74), showed how the pastures lay on the marshland and how the large estuary islands were divided between several villages for purposes of pasture.

13

We read in DB, in the majority of instances, not of the several enclosed pasture, but the otherwise unprofitable land which was common to all the inhabitants of the village and their beasts. We are told, for example, that there is a certain pasture common to all the men of the Hundred of Colneis (II.339b). That pasture is common pasture is quite frequently recorded, and sometimes the value of a holding is given and it is then added that this includes 'common of pasture', or that the inhabitants of a certain manor have rights of pasture on the land of a more extensive manor.[1] More than one village might share pasture land, as the Somerset folios show (e.g. Hemington and Hardington, 88b2, 93ai). The burgesses of Oxford are said to hold pasture in common (which may imply common pasture), and which still exists as Port Meadow (154a2).

But for the use of pasture the lord was in not a few instances obtaining a rent, sometimes of money, sometimes in kind. At Kempsford (169ai) he was receiving £9 for pasture, and this did not include the pasture for the oxen. At Guiting (167b2) a rent for wood and pasture was being paid in hens, at Hatfield Broad Oak (II.2), in the form of nine wethers. In a number of instances the rent is of a metallic nature: it takes the form of ploughshares, or of blooms of iron (Abington, 199b2; Whitestaunton, 91b2).

Pasture was indeed of such importance that here and there it got mentioned in DB by name. In the manor of Yatton was a pasture called *Weimorham*, and, though it is not a village, the name Wemberham has survived (89bi). Some entries tell us the type of pasture concerned: we are told of two in Hampshire that one was known as 'the down' and the other as 'the moor'.[2] Indeed, one of the holdings at Exford near Exmoor is said to 'lie in pasture' (95b2), and it is made clear that the whole manor was nothing but a piece of pasture-land. It was thought to be worth recording that there was more than one pasture at Spettisbury, one of which lay 'by the water' (77ai, 82ai). Odstock (73bi) too had two pastures, one said to be 'near the river', presumably marshland pasture of the type frequently

---

[1] Benton and Haxon had common pasture in Braunton (101b2). See also Stockleigh Barton (106a2), Newton Tracy (112bi), Axminster (111ai), etc.

[2] King's Somborne (39bi), Abbot's Worthy (42b).

recorded as being for sheep in Essex, the other being perhaps downland. A Kentish manor (Higham, 9ai) possessed pasture for 200 sheep which was across the Thames in Essex. Pasture, in common with the other leading appurtenances, was sometimes taken into the King's Forest (Bickton, 44b2); it was abstracted from a manor (perhaps because of its usefulness; Mottisfont, 42). At Oakhanger (49b2) the King's reeve claimed half a hide 'for the pasture of the King's oxen', but the shire-jury testified that he could enjoy neither pasture nor pannage of the wood without the sheriff's leave. Twice we hear of pasture which seems to be in process of being converted to arable: there were six acres at Patrixbourne (9a2) which were being ploughed by men from elsewhere, and a part of Swyre (80b2) which had had a chequered history had been pasture but was now cultivable (*prius erat pascualis, modo seminabilis*).

Meadow

The commonest method of indicating the extent of the meadow (*pratum*), which 'implied lands bordering a stream, liable to flood, and producing hay', was by giving the amount in acres.[1] But in a number of east midland counties – Cambridgeshire, Hertfordshire, Middlesex, Buckinghamshire and Bedfordshire – the system adopted was to state the number of teams of eight oxen the meadow was capable of feeding. Comparison of DB with ICC would suggest that each ox required an acre of meadow, for this is the equation the texts give for Westley Waterless and Borough Green (190b2, 202a2, 195b2; ICC 91a), but other entries give variant and unhelpful comparisons. A similar system makes a sporadic appearance in the west midlands. In Haresfield (162b2) and certain other manors no extent is given, but it is said that there is 'meadow for the plough-teams'; at, e.g., Inkberrow (173ai) and Maud Bryan (*Magga*, 185bi) it is 'meadow for the oxen'.

In the east midlands the formula is sometimes enlarged upon; at Cheshunt (137ai) there was meadow for 23 teams and 'for the demesne horses', at *Stiuicesuuorde* (139b2) for

---

[1] The quotation is from *Dom. Geog.*, vol. I, p. 60.

1½ teams and 'for the use of the demesne'. The latter is the implication of 'meadow for 5 teams and hay (*fenum*) for the animals of the *curia*' (Wraysbury, 149bi). Hay – perhaps the sale of hay – is coupled with the pasture dues at Amwell (138a2), and meadow for the teams and pasture for the live-stock of the village are also mentioned. Meadow is, rather strangely, coupled with marsh at Canfield (II.35).

It is doubtful if a manor would require really large quantities of meadow, though the immense manor of South Malling (16b2), had 195 + 38 acres. South Carlton in Lincolnshire (370b2) had 30½ acres; it also had 100 acres said to be 'in Nottingham(shire)', and this may have been a profitable appendage of the manor from which rents were drawn. Meadow was not only essential (though it is not recorded for a large number of manors, and even villages) but could be profitable, if there was sufficient surplus to rent: Shingay (193a2) had meadow for six teams, and 2*s.* from meadow-rent also. Indeed, we very strangely find half a hide of meadow recorded as 'in demesne' in the Ely Abbey manor of Stetch-worth (190bi), while a half-hide manor, whose assessment has been cancelled and which is worth only 5*s.*, contains nothing but ten acres of meadow (Woolfly, 28bi). So it is logical that any interference with the quiet enjoyment of meadow should have been the subject of protest. The meadow at the Abbess of Wilton's manor of Watchingwell (52b2) is 'in the park' – taken, we may think, into the King's Forest of Parkhurst. At Bottle-bridge (203bi) it is noted that the weir of the Abbey of Thorney is doing harm to 300 acres of meadow in this and other manors, presumably by flooding them (or depriving them of the essential moisture). It has already been noted that here and there the lord's power to demand the services of others besides the peasantry to get his hay mown is recorded: at Longden (174bi) the free men had had to mow one day in the year, and there are further references in the next column. The thegns of Derby Hundred (269b2) had to send their reapers one day in August to cut the royal crops; in Newton Hundred those responsible seem to have had to mow for three, but in Salford Hundred not to do this service (269b2, 270ai). At Haddenham (143b2) there was meadow for six teams; this is the number of

demesne teams, while the villeins and bordars have fourteen
– whence did these derive hay? But there is said to be 'pasture
for the livestock', and 'for the Archbishop's farm eight days'
hay'. Does this imply eight days' supply for the demesne
beasts, or eight days' labour in the fields?

Marsh

Marsh is mentioned in the accounts of only a few counties,
and often must have been ignored (as in certain Somerset
entries where we might expect to find it recorded) because of
its worthlessness. When it is noted, quantities are often large;
there were 10 by 3 leagues of it in the Isle of Axholme (369bi),
and 700 acres at South Kyme (337bi). Keckingham (II.205)
had 'marsh for 60 sheep', and in Essex it is plain that the
marshes were all-important as sheep pastures.[1] Though we hear
in the IE of 'the marshland' of west Norfolk and of William
Malet 'going into the marsh' (II.133b)—perhaps in the
Fenland or East Anglian campaigns of 1070–1 or 1075—little
is said about it except that the measurements of the marshland
of Marham (II.212b) are said to be unknown: probably the
witnesses failed to estimate its dimensions. Romney Marsh is
mentioned (12b2).

Rents from property in the marsh are only occasionally
mentioned. Two hundred eels a year from the marsh belonged
to the manor of Croxton (202ai), and renders of eels were
paid to Cottenham (192b2) and other Cambridgeshire manors.
An ore of sixteenpence was due to Wilburton (192ai) for the
privilege of gathering rushes (used for lights and strewing
floors); the manor of Grimsby (347a2) received turbary dues,
for cutting peat from the 'turfland' or for pasture, of four ores
or 5s. 4d. Marshland was not necessarily valueless; when the
royal manor of South Petherton acquired part of the land of
the manor of Seavington St. Mary (91b2), it took in some marsh
as well as meadow.

---

[1] See Round in *VCH: Essex*, vol. I, pp. 368–74.

Moor

As with the marshes, it was not within the scope of the Inquest to consider the moorlands, whether upland or fenland, which were of no use or profit except as rough pastureland. Very occasionally they are mentioned: Wedmore (*160*), below the Mendips but close to the Somerset marshland, is said to include 'moors which render nothing'. The Devonshire manor of Molland (101ai) received one-third of the moorland pasturage dues, 'the third animal of the moors'. Sherford in Devon (109b2) is said to have 50 acres of moor whence, perhaps, peat for fuel was cut. But of the heathland of Surrey, or the Yorkshire moors, we hear little or nothing; one of the few references to the Pennine moorlands is one which says that the manor of Otley (303bi) had moors two leagues long by one broad, and the map naturally shows their upper levels to be empty of settlements. We are however told that at Eaton on Ot Moor (158b2) there were 26 acres of moor, and this is the 'wet moor' of Oxfordshire where fishing and bird-catching helped provide a living. The Welsh land at Rhos and Rhufoniog (269a2) is said to be woodland and moorland which cannot be ploughed.

Fisheries

Fishing was indeed a profitable as well as an essential occupation, and there must have existed far more fisheries than those of which DB tells us. The profit from them, however, was as a rule the lord's, and it is possible that most of the unrecorded fisheries were ignored because he derived no particular profit from them. A few, however, are said to be paying no rent (Marden, Cleeve; 179bi,2); the contrast to these is pointed where a fishery is said to be 'serving the hall' (Holdenhurst, 39ai). But a manor might, apparently, include fisheries some of which were the lord's and some his tenantry's; there were both at Tidenham (164ai), where nearly seventy are recorded, some on the Severn, others on the Wye; and perhaps at Swancombe (6ai) and Kingston (30bi); at Ruyton (257b2) the villeins were renting five fisheries. Tudworth (321ai) had twenty fisheries, furnishing 20,000 eels.

On the whole, though, the profits of the fisheries were the lord's, and the enormous rents in kind recorded for many manors must make us wonder if the totals given had to be furnished altogether by its inhabitants. Wisbech (192ai) was the property of the Abbey of Ely, but six landowners in all seem to have had an interest in the produce of the local waters, and it seems doubtful if all the 33,000 eels and more which had to be rendered to them would be caught within the manor by the local inhabitants.[1] 68,000 herrings seems an enormous quantity for the fishermen of Dunwich (II.312) to have to find; it was not every day in the year that the six fishermen at Eaton (263b2) could make a catch towards the thousand salmon they had to render. Monasteries and baronial households no doubt required great store of salted fish, but it must not be overlooked that fisheries might well produce a surplus and that herring might travel westwards and salmon eastwards to vary dietetic monotony. It is possible, too, that provided the lord received the stated render, the surplus furnished food for his villagers and what they did not need was marketed.

With such requirements, fishing could not be carried on haphazardly. Originally, the lord's capital – if only in the form of the labour of the peasantry and the resources of his estate – must have provided the apparatus and equipment. Weirs and eel-traps, nets and boats, have to be constructed and kept in repair, and to this existence DB bears frequent witness. The number of mills which have to provide an eel-render is very large, and the existence of traps and weirs at their sites must be supposed. Weirs (*gurgites*, *guorts*) appear, for example, at Hoddesdon (137bi) and Shepperton (128bi), a fish-trap (*sagena*) at Soham (192a2), a boat for fishing at Lakenheath (II.392), a sea-weir at Southwold (II.371b), boats on the mere and fishing with nets among the Cambridgeshire fens (Soham, 190b2; Wickham, 195b2), and on the Dee (Cheveley, Huntingdon, 263ai, *bis*; Eccleston, 267ai), seines and dragnets in the Thames (Hampton, 130a2), fish-stews at St. Albans (135bi), Caversfield (148a2), and Sharnbrook (216bi).

---

[1] Fols. 192a2b2, 193ai, 196bi. Mr. Lennard, however, thinks that 'only in a few districts was the fishing on a scale to make much call upon the labour-force of the community' (*Rural Eng.*, p. 249).

It is however of the fish-rents to be furnished that we hear most. Beccles (II.370) was not far behind Southwold in having to provide 60,000 herrings, while at Southease in Sussex (17bi) the villeins had to furnish 38,500 to Hyde Abbey at Winchester, and pay £4 for the porpoises also: this was presumably the fee for catching and selling them. Eel-renders, which run into the 20,000's, are frequently reckoned by the 'stick' (*stich*, 177a2, 257b2) or load of fish (*summa*), and at Staple Fitzpaine (92a2) fifty eels were paid as rent for a garden-close in the borough of Langport. At Iver (149a2) 1,500 eels and fishes were provided for the reeve's use on Fridays, and we can only think that the bulk of these were sold, to the profit of the lord of the manor.

Numerous entries indicate the importance of fisheries in the manorial economy. The existence of a 'new fishery' at Monkton (4b2) is mentioned; this would add to the value of the manor, and so the fact of its newness needed to be mentioned. In contrast, it is recorded that on the land of Milton Abbey (43bi) there had been a fishery, but that in 1086 it was no longer operating. If a fishery had ceased to exist, the fact is noted, for if restored, it would be of profit. Thus 'sites' are recorded (Radcliffe-on-Trent, 288ai). Disputes about rights in fisheries were brought to the notice of the Inquest authorities (Coningsby, 375bi), and a toll in respect of fish is mentioned. It was noted that Earl Harold had 'set up a fishery by force' at Mortlake (30b2) on the land of the manor of Kingston and of St. Paul's; seeing, no doubt, good profit in establishing it, though how his officials could in fact organise its construction on other men's land remains a mystery. The profits of fisheries could be shared between local landowners; many people are said to possess a fraction of a fishery, but it is everywhere impossible always to combine the shares into integral fisheries.

Saltworks

Salt was of enormous importance in medieval economy, for it was upon salted meat that the community largely depended for its winter diet, and much of the products of the fisheries would have gone to waste unless pickled and preserved. Throughout the coastal counties DB includes frequent references to salt-pans, and here the method of production must have been by the evaporation of sea-water. The number of salt-pans in some villages is very large, and it is clear that in certain places the manufacture of salt was the principal local industry. Caistor (II.134, 221) had 45 salt-pans, Chislet (12a2) 47, while the manor of *Rameslie* (17a2) had one hundred pans within it. Many of these must have manufactured salt in quantities far in excess of local requirements, and marketed the surplus over a wide area. In some villages saltworkers seem to form the sole element in the population; in others they exceed the agricultural workers in quantity. The entire population of Ower (78a2) seems to have been engaged in salt-working, for none but fourteen saltworkers is mentioned, and 75% of that of Charmouth (80ai). Some inland manors, instead of buying their salt, seem somehow to have obtained the means of making their salt by the seashore. Wallop (38bi), Honiton (104b2), and Ottery St. Mary (104a2) were three of these, and we know that the Honiton salterns were at Beer and those of Ottery 'in the land of St. Mary of Sidmouth'.

It seems to have been customary to lease the operation of the salt-pans to the saltworkers themselves; it is rare to find salt-pans said to be *sine censu*. Sometimes it is stated that the rent is paid by the *salinarii*, and when it is stated that there are one or more salt-pans 'of' (*de*) a certain value, it is virtually certain that this is the rent which is being paid. There is no consistency about rents; the salt-pan at Gosberton (344bi) rendered only fourpence, while the two at Bedhampton (43ai) were producing 37s. 8d. In Devon an average of 1s. per pan seems to be suggested by the figures; in Lincolnshire the *ora*-unit of 16d. enters largely into the sums. At Washington (28ai) there were five saltworks 'of 110 ambers' (the 'amber' was the equivalent of four bushels) 'or 110 pence', giving a price of one farthing the bushel. At Saundby (281bi), a villein supplied 'salt for the King's fish (caught?) in Bycarrs Dyke'.

The other method of obtaining salt was from inland brine-springs, which occur mainly in two districts, mid-Cheshire and Droitwich in Worcestershire. The Cheshire industry seems to have been concentrated in three 'wiches', Nantwich, Middlewich and Northwich (268ai,2), which DB treats in a way quite unlike that applied to other places. Nothing is said about population, or about anything else except the salt-works and their laws and customs. The profits had in 1066 been two-thirds the King's and one-third the Earl's. Quite understandably, little is said about the actual process of manufacture, though we do hear of a brine-pit and 'boilings'.

Just as town-houses were attached to rural manors (p. 152), so Cheshire 'salt-houses' are found in association with a few holdings. These are so few that we might see here a great contrast to Droitwich, where the number of holdings so associated is high, and perhaps deduce a virtual monoply of supply, but we are told that 'many men of the county' had *salinae*.[1] One of the seven salt-houses belonging to Weaverham (263bi) provided the 'hall' with salt; the others were waste.

The industry seems to have suffered severely as a result of the local rebellion in 1070. The total of the renders from the three places was in 1086 less than one-third what it had been in 1066, and for 1070 the record says 'waste', except for one Nantwich salt-pit. Perhaps we must not see in this statement a totally ruined industry. But we may take it that in 1086 conditions in the wiches were still abnormal. The system of tolls was an elaborate one; toll varied, for instance, for carts drawn by two or by four oxen, for horse-loads, or for loads carried by men on their backs, and they were increased where purchasers came from another Hundred or shire. Even the fine for overloading a horse so that its back was broken is mentioned.

We have a rather different picture of Droitwich (172a2), for the entries concerning it are not confined to a single county, but are to be found in the accounts of half-a-dozen neighbouring shires, and it seems that a considerable number of manors had salt-pans, or rights in salt-pans, within the borough. Sometimes it seems as if the salt-pan was rented to an operator, and the manor drew the revenue; probably in every instance the manor acquired the salt demanded by its own needs, and perhaps a surplus also.[2]

---

[1] William de Malbank's manor of Acton (268a2, 265bi) included a *salina* at Nantwich, which in his predecessor's day had each year produced sufficient salt for his own household. But it seems that there might have been a surplus, for the division of the tolls 'if any were sold thence' is given.

[2] e.g. Alvechurch with its four berewicks (174a2) had eight salt-pans, and it would hardly need all these produced.

The evaporation of salt from brine required huge quantities of wood, and DB notes this for us: Bromsgrove (172a2) provided 300 cartloads of wood in exchange for 300 *mittae* of salt from the thirteen salt-pans the manor possessed in Droitwich.[1] The measures in which renders of salt are given are never defined, but the *mitta* may have been eight bushels, roughly the equivalent of the horse-load or *summa*, a measure which also appears in connection with salt. There are references also to brine-pits (*putei*), lead vats (*plumbi*), furnaces (*furni*), and to a further measure known as the *hoccus*.[2]

As in Cheshire, the fortunes of the industry seem to have been declining (we hear of waste here also). Before the Conquest King and Earl had shared the rents roughly in the usual proportion of 2:1, and the proceeds had amounted to £76, but in 1086 the whole was being farmed by the sheriff for £65. Of no industry are we told more in DB, but the information is still very fragmentary.

Mills

The number of mills mentioned in DB is very large, probably in the neighbourhood of 6,000, and the reason for their inclusion among the statistics is that they brought their owners considerable profits in rents. Some – but not a high proportion of the total – are said to be unrented, *sine censu*, which in the Exeter Domesday reads *molit annonam suam*, grinds its own (that is the lord's) corn. A manor might contain both a mill which was rented and one which was not.

One striking feature of the mill entries is the very large number ascribed to what are often complex or dispersed manors. Wells (89a2) had nine, and they seem to be on five of the numerous constituents of the manor. This is only to be expected, for a single mill could not cope with all the corn of the manor, and the existence of mills in some or all of the

---

[1] Mr. Lennard quotes an interesting entry which shows the deceptiveness of the plain Domesday text. The villeins of Martin Hussingtree (174b2) had to render 100 cartloads of wood to the Droitwich salt-pans. But no woodland is recorded for the manor, and presumably the wood came from a different Westminster Abbey manor (*Rural Eng.*, p. 247, n.2).

[2] In Gloucestershire the sextary and *mensura* are also used as measures.

component villages would obviate transport.[1] But in some manors the number of mills seems unreasonably large. Why Nettleton, with a recorded population of only 52, should need nine, whose values totalled only £1, is not easy to deduce.[2]

The distribution of mills does indeed produce some curious puzzles. Only half-a-dozen are recorded for the whole of Cornwall, and we have no means of determining whether we are to deduce that only these were profitable, the remainder being local handmills, or not. We do not know if the absence, or almost total absence, of mills from some Hundreds reflects a similar state of affairs, or whether the local crops went elsewhere for grinding. We have no means of knowing if, where a river divided manors, each manor had its own mill, or the rent of a single mill was shared, perhaps unequally, between them. Certainly villages did share mills, as Round proved in the instance of Rivenhall and Great Braxted.[3] A mill seems to have been shared in the proportion 2 : 1 between Manhall and Saffron Walden (II.31b, 62b). Ashton Giffard and the two Codfords (70b2, 71b2, 72b2) shared a mill in the proportion 2 : 1 : 1. We can see why evidence was forthcoming at the Inquest that a mill at Hendred which Cola claimed 'had always lain in Ardington', Robert d'Oyly's manor (62a2).

Mills are usually said to be worth, or to be of (*de*) a certain sum. They varied enormously in value, and therefore, presumably, in capacity, and many must have ground corn not produced in their immediate locality and for areas not their own. The average value varies sharply with the county, but this may obviously be the wrong unit for consideration of averages.[4] Still, it is strange to find a high average value in Huntingdonshire (23*s*. 3*d*), and one of only about one-third of this in its neighbour Northamptonshire. But Wiltshire (12*s*. 6*d*.) compares favourably, as we might expect, with its neighbours to west and south. Devon's mills, which are very few, average only about 6*s*.

---

[1] Dr. W. G. Hoskins is reasonably sure that the three mills attributed to the manor of Silverton were actually at Thorverton, Traymill, and Old Heazille Farm (*Devonshire Studies*, pp. 124–5).

[2] Fols. 342a2, 352bi, 362a2, 365ai, 371bi.

[3] *VCH: Essex*, vol. I, p. 379; DB fols. II.27, 49.

[4] Mr. Lennard has considered the relation of the number of mills to that of plough-teams as a means of making comparisons. (*Rural Eng.* pp. 278–9).

We find mills which are valued at a few pence only (e.g. Clatworthy, 95b2 – sixpence), while the two mills at Hemingford Abbots (207ai) were together worth £6. What again is surprising – unless the mill values are not included in the total values of the manors – is the often high proportion of the mill value to the whole. Battersea (32a2) had a total value of just over £75, and its seven mills contributed over £42 to that sum, or corn to the same value. Mill-rents do not readily lend themselves to comparison. In the eastern counties we are hardly ever given their values, and there is an artificiality about some of the figures elsewhere, many of which are obviously derived in terms of the *ora*, whether of sixteen or twenty pence, the latter of which is markedly apparent outside the counties with strong Danish backgrounds – e.g. in the south-west.[1] Rents may of course often have been paid in kind, to the value of the amounts stated, and both money and goods seem here and there to be required. Eel-renders are the most common, for the mill with its weir was the natural site for an eel-trap.[2] The owner of Swaffham (196a2) got 300 eels as well as 29*s*. 8*d*. for the mill. We hear of rents paid in kind, other than by means of eels, in a few counties only. They include loads of salt (Wasperton, 239ai), a pig (Lydham, 253bi), and honey (Cleeve Prior, 174ai).[3] But the majority are by means of different kinds of grain, though it is not always easy to determine just what variety is meant. But there can be no doubt that the medium was malt at Bledlow and Yockleton (146ai, 255bi) and rye at Ryton (257b2), but most entries indicate 'grain' only, though at Arundel (23ai) both *annona* and *frumentum* were required. The mill at Marcle (179b2) which provided 'nothing but the living of him who keeps it' seems to be quite exceptional.

Some mills, on streams where the summer flow was insufficient to turn the wheel, are recorded as *hiemale*, or *hiemale non aestivum* (Cockfield, II.359, Welbatch, 255bi); a point stressed, we may think, to indicate that they were not adding greatly to

---

[1] For the *ora*, see p. 226.

[2] At Barking (II.382b) we hear of 'one mill and the weir of another mill'. The mill-dam and the sluice are mentioned at Creeting (II.304b).

[3] At Shelford (ICC 99a) two pigs were 'fattened from the mill' – this may imply a two-pig rent.

the manors' revenues. Care seems to have been taken to note that
mills which had been operating in 1066 were not doing so twenty
years later, that a mill had not been at work in King Edward's
time (Farnham, 151bi), or anything else which affected the
value of the manor. Thus the effect on a garden of a mill constructed since the Conquest (Croxby, 376ai), and the facts that a
mill was damaged (Shillington, 210b2), or was broken but could
be restored (Duxford, 196ai), were all found worthy of mention.
So was the fact that the King's pool at York (298a2) was
damaging two new mills – it probably cut off their head of water.

The profits from mills are not infrequently divided between
several owners. The details suggest that a number of individuals
– often, perhaps, minor landholders only – had combined to
erect the mill, drawing rent in proportion to their outlay.
At *Langhedana* (II.404b) a man was receiving one-twelfth of the
rent, described as 'one-quarter in every third year'. A classic
example is that of Rode (88b2), said merely to have 'mills'
worth 27*s*., but the Exeter Domesday (*148*) enables us to
determine that there were two mills of unequal value divided
into a half-share worth 6*s*., a quarter share worth 3*s*., a sixth
part worth thirty pence, two 'parts' of the pair worth 8*s*, and a
half-share worth 7*s*. 6*d*. – the two mills being worth 12*s*. and
15*s*. respectively. 'Half', 'part', etc., seem to have been loosely
used: at Hampole (316ai, 319b2) one man had 'half of a mill'
paying 3*s*., and another 'half a mill' worth 40*d*.

Millers, as such, figure hardly at all in DB. We do indeed
hear of the 'keeper of the mill' (*custos molini*) at Moreton
(276bi) or Tilston (264ai), but sometimes it is the owner or
lessee who seems to be indicated; e.g. we hear of a Frenchman,
a reeve of the vill, and a named sokeman having mills (fols.
260b2, 182ai, 139b2). Often enough, maybe, the miller's
occupation was not a full-time one.

Churches

It was not piety, but the fact that churches were of profit to
their possessors, which governed the inclusion of information
about churches in DB. But the shires seem to have treated the
churches within them in altogether different ways, and the
information we receive is obviously incomplete and most un-

satisfying. In the accounts of some shires, e.g. Oxfordshire and
Cambridgeshire, churches are only rarely mentioned, and
when we find fairly frequent mention of priests, without a
corresponding mention of churches, we cannot be certain that
the existence of churches is implied, for the priests may be
landholders, and unconnected with village churches; some said
to be priests may have been monks of monasteries such as Ely.
In Cornwall less than a dozen churches are recorded, and it
may be that here a system of village churches and 'parish'
priests had not yet fully developed, but that an older system
whereby the rural districts were served by a community of
clergy attached to a central 'minster', still obtained. Against
this view it may be said that so many places in Cornwall are
named from saints (implying the existence of a church dedi-
cated to the saint whose name the settlement bears), or include
elements meaning 'church', that it may be that the Inquest
officials here often ignored the existence of churches.[1]

For some counties, however, e.g. Suffolk and Huntingdonshire, the record appears to be reasonably complete. It is
true that a map of places with Domesday churches shows
almost empty areas, but that might be the result of clerical
omissions rather than an absence of churches. We cannot
indeed adequately map the churches of 1086, for entries
commonly tell us of more than one church, but not where
each lay. On an enormous manor such as Chilcombe (41ai)
there were nine churches, but we do not know at which of the
numerous villages making up the manor of Chilcombe they
were situated. Often, when we find more than one church
mentioned in an entry, there are today as many parishes with
a common name as there are churches in DB, and presumably
in 1086 there were as many distinct settlements. Tivetshall, for
example, is said to have two churches (II.210b), and to-day
there are two parishes. Fornham is now three parishes, and DB
tells us of two churches in different Hundreds and also of a
third, *Genonefae Forham*, the modern Fornham St. Genevieve

---

[1] Names including *eglos, cirice, lan,* are common; but *lan* may often mean no
more than 'enclosure'. Even if DB does not record one, there were surely churches
at places whose names contained the element *minster*, or at those with names such
as *Jacobescherche* (118bi) – St. James's, Heavitree – or *Sanctae Mariae Cerce* (the
village of St. Mary Church, 105ai).

(II.357b, 361b, 362). To the royal manor of Corsham (65ai) belonged the church of Poulshot, but the church of Corsham itself belonged to the Abbey of St. Stephen of Caen; this possessed land assessed at as much as three hides and which included five ploughlands.

That hardly anywhere does DB give us the full tale of churches existing in 1086 we can be certain. Two Lincolnshire churches, Winghale and Long Sutton, are mentioned only in the *Clamores* section (377b2) and are ignored in the text of DB. The number of Kentish churches DB records is appreciably under 200. But three documents which we know deal with conditions as they were little, if at all, later than 1086, bring the number to more than double the Domesday figure.[1] On the other hand, the lists for the principal towns are probably fairly comprehensive, and frequently they even tell us the dedications of the churches. Of the 12½ churches at Thetford, five are named, as are six of the 15 at Norwich, in which town there were 43 chapels also.[2] Seven of eight churches mentioned at York are named.

DB shows us something of ancient ecclesiastical organisation. It does not, indeed, tell us very much of the cathedrals and abbeys except in their capacities as landowners; it shows us, however, that the ultimate universal system of division of the dioceses into parishes, each with its church and priest, was still distant. Some of the churches it mentions are not parish churches, but collegiate churches, minsters whose canons served a wide area, from which they drew material benefits. At Ramsbury (66ai), the seat of a former bishopric, we hear of 'the priests', who have four hides of the land of the manor; they may have been parish priests serving the villages making up the vast 90-hide manor of Ramsbury, but equally a collegiate church may have persisted. The *presbiteri parrochiani* mentioned in the geld account for the lands of the bishopric of Wells (*78b*) may well have been members of a 'minster' who served the various churches of this scattered territorial agglo-

---

[1] The *Domesday Monachorum*, the *Textus Roffensis*, and the White Book of St. Augustine's.

[2] There was not, of course, a portion of a church at Thetford: it happens that we are only told who had a half-share in it.

meration of estates. The Canons of Plympton, who with 'St. Peter of Plympton' appear in DB and the geld accounts (*70, 86,* 113bi), sound like members of a collegiate church. So do the *sacerdotes de Nieuuetona* (*65b*) – Newton St. Petrock, connected with St. Petrock's collegiate church at Bodmin.

The existence of chapels (*capellae*) and minor churches (*aecclesiolae*) is noted in DB. At Mottisfont (42a) there was a church, and also six chapels at named places in the neighbourhood; the owner, the Archbishop of York, had from these 'the dues of the living and the dead'. They were dependencies of a mother-church, whose owner's rights needed to be recorded, for he received revenues from them. At Thorney (II.281b) the local free men had built a church on their own land near the cemetery of the mother-church, because this could not serve the needs of the whole 'parish', and a dispute arose as to who was to have the burial-fees.[1] At Wisset (II.293) there was a chapel 'under' – subordinate to – the church.

DB mentions only occasionally and incidentally the revenues which the existence of a church implied – the fees charged for specific religious offices, church-scot, tithes, etc. But these, and former endowments, made certain churches worthy of special mention, and of considerable profit to their owners. We find churches possessed of estates assessed at figures which compare very favourably with those of all but the larger manors. Some may indeed derive from older minsters, but this does not alter the fact that in 1086 the ownership of such churches was well worth having. Calne (64b2) is perhaps an extreme example: there are six hides, a recorded population of 26, and it is worth £18. Moreover, Nigel claims five hides at Yatesbury as belonging to the church lands. Netheravon church (65a2), which was also Nigel's, was worth, with its appendages, £32, and these 'appendages' were the wealthy manors of Stratton St. Margaret and Chisenbury, which with the hide of church land taken out of the royal manor of Netheravon were assessed at 39 hides, had land for 19 teams, and a recorded population

---

[1] When the lords of certain lands associated with the manor of Taunton died, they were buried at Taunton (87bi). This was perhaps recorded because the Bishop of Winchester was anxious that no one else should secure profitable burial-fees. See also Bishamton (173ai).

I.D.B.

of 66, two mills, meadow, and pasture. These look like the components of a former 'minster', but we hear of no priests, nor of churches at Stratton or Chisenbury, while the church at Netheravon is 'ruinous, and the roof so out of repair, that it is almost falling down'. (The church at Collingbourne Ducis, in the next entry, whose tithe was valued at 10s., is also said to be 'ruinous and decayed'.) To Alderbury church two estates are credited, one of five, the other of two hides (68bi). Wiltshire is not the only county which includes a special list of churches (65bi), with various owners, and assessed at anything up to three hides. The endowment of SS. Simon and Jude, Norwich, included the revenues from 'three parts' of a mill, half an acre of meadow, and a house in the city (II.117b). The glebe land attached to churches is most regularly given for Norfolk and Suffolk.[1] The amount varies from a single acre to a couple of carucates, and while it is common to find proper fractions of the 120-acre carucate – 10, 12, 15, 30 acres, and the like – many extents are irregular and look as if they might be the product of a number of small endowments. The glebe of Slinford (II.24b) was 30 acres, which 'had been given by the neighbours in alms'; this suggests that local small proprietors wanted their own church and were willing to abandon a share of their own lands to meet its needs. Leave to found a church would be required, for endowment of it could normally only be made at someone else's expense. We hear of a priest called Colebern who built a church (whose revenues would presumably be his), with the King's leave, 'and if the King permits he will endow it with 20 acres' and 'will sing for the King a Mass and the Psalter every week'. (II.263b).

These co-operative foundations are perhaps reflected in the numerous instances in which several people are said to have varying shares of a church. While churches had been founded by great men and also by lesser thegns, some, like the mills, look as if they result from the combined action of a number of small proprietors, especially in the eastern counties.[2] The

---

[1] When a church here is said to have no land, the statement is made as though this is an exceptional circumstance. (e.g. Cornard, II.286b).

[2] It is suggestive that quite often in a holding the varying shares in church and mill are identical – see R. Lennard, *Rural Eng.*, p. 320.

shares will not always combine into integers, and from the fact
that they are found as small as one-twelfth, they must have
been those of very minor thegns, or of sokemen and free men.
These are indeed true village churches, and their priests were
probably of humble origins.

Some entries record a church without mentioning a priest,
and priests are recorded where no mention is made of a church,
but many of these must be among DB's numerous lapses: a
church without a priest is noted at Houghton (204bi) as though
this is not the usual state of affairs. Both church and priest
are often described as 'of the vill' or 'of the manor', as though
the implication is that the revenue-producing functions of
both are items in the manorial or in a landowner's economy.[1]
At Morley (373b2) the priest is said to 'serve the church'. We
find priests with more than one church and churches with more
than one priest; in the latter instances one may not be a
'parish' priest, though at Market Bosworth (233ai) there were
both a priest and a deacon.

The instructions do not ordain that priests shall be enumer-
ated in the way that sokemen or villeins were to be counted,
but only that they should with the reeve and six villeins assist
with the Inquest. From the wording of many entries, the
village priest seems often to be associated with the villeins.
Commonly we find phrases saying that so many villeins and so
many bordars with the priest have *n* teams, or that there are
so many various categories, among whom the priest is mentioned, and that 'between them all they have *n* teams'. It looks
as if the priest as a rule had a share of the village oxen and thus
of the land which these ploughed. Whether he had to pay rent
for his glebe land, and whether he had to labour on the land in
company with the villeins and bordars, cannot be discussed
here. Quite obviously he was performing a parish priest's duties,
for some unknown stipend, while the owner of the church, lay
or ecclesiastical, drew the revenues.

For DB frequently shows us the church of the manor or of
the vill treated much as any profitable manor might be treated.
The Nigel who held Calne was a physician, and successor in

---

[1] St. Peter's, Shrewsbury, is said to 'hold' the church and the priest of Berrington
(254bi). The priest at Beeford (324a2) is spoken of as 'Drogo's priest'.

his estates to a priest named Spirites who had held numerous churches and had been exiled. Regenbald 'the King's priest' is found holding seven wealthy churches, and he may have held several more.[1] The Bishops of Exeter, of London, and of Salisbury, are not the only ecclesiastics to be holding churches whose duties they did not discharge. Churches were bestowed on continental religious houses; Robert of Mortain had obtained a church which must be St. Lawrence, Exeter (104bi). Hugh fitzBaldric would not have bought St. Andrew's, York, if he had not expected financial or spiritual profit from the transaction; laymen are holding churches of ecclesiastics, and priests are holding churches of laymen. A certain Ulwi of Hatfield sold two Hertford churches to the sheriff, Peter of Valognes (132ai). A Domesday passage tells us how within a short space St. Mary's, Huntingdon, changed hands five times (208ai). When we read that 'all the churches' on the land of William of Warenne in Norfolk 'are valued with the manors' (II.172) it reminds us that a church was an asset – a financial asset – to a manor, and treated as part of it unless it had been alienated by bestowal on some ecclesiastic or religious foundation. A statement that twelve sokemen used to be *parrochiani* – though this implies that they were liable for church-dues rather than 'inhabitants of the parish' – in Stow church, but are now in that of Combs, argues that the recipient of the revenues from Stow had protested against their loss.

The rents paid for churches were often considerable ones; Bishop Maurice of London was getting 60s. for that of North Curry (86b2). Three churches were attached to the Bishop of Winchester's manor of Alresford (40ai) and had been paying £6 a year, but could not afford to do so, for they were worth only £4. Upon occasion, at least, it was the parish priest who was renting his benefice and land (West Wickham, 9a2).

The glebe is at times said to be 'free land', *libera terra*, especially in the eastern counties. Churches are said to be held 'in alms', *in elemosina*, but this does not necessarily imply that they were free of all burdens. Often enough, when we are given the hidage of an estate credited to a church (which is

---

[1] Among them was St. John's, Frome, (86bi, 91a2), which was worth £6, and had eight carucates of land.

often distinct from that of the manor of the same name), some is said to be in demesne. The three hides of Highworth church (65bi) were geld-free, and the Calne Hundred geld account shows that one of Nigel's five hides was exempt. But many a church's land must have been liable for geld; where a rich church estate had been bestowed on an ecclesiastic, there was no reason why he should not pay geld just as the holders of other manors did.

But of the church's revenues from their parishioners we are told comparatively little. From the eight Hundreds around Aylesbury each sokeman who had had one hide or more gave one load of wheat to Aylesbury church, also one acre of grain or fourpence (143b), but the latter due had not been paid since the Conquest. The first is certainly a reference to the due known as church-scot (or 'shot'), for it corresponds to the *circset* payable to Pershore Abbey on St. Martin's Day (175bi).[1] The bishopric of Worcester had a 'seam' (horse-load) of corn from every hide it owned whether the hide was 'free' (that is, probably, immune from geld) or not. Tithes are noted as a rule when these had been alienated: those of the manor of Basingstoke (43ai) had been granted to the Norman abbey of St. Michael's Mount; Richer the clerk had those of the vill of Stoneham (41b2) and of the King's land, Twynham Abbey had all the Twynham tithes and one-third of those of Holdenhurst (44a2). The church at one of the Wallops (38bi) had half the tithe of the manor and all the church-scot, and 46*d*. 'from the tithe of the villeins', while the chapel at a neighbouring Wallop (Over or Nether?) had 'eight acres of tithe'. The Abbey of St. Mary of Lyre had half-a-dozen churches in the Isle of Wight, and 'tithes of all the King's renders' (52bi). Even if they were only those from the demesne land, they made the priest so much the poorer. That the owner had a right to bestow tithes is shown by a passage which tells us that a Derbyshire thegn 'could build for himself a church on his own land and in his own soke and could send his tithes where he would' (280a2).

---

[1] Church-scot is not often mentioned in DB, but is noted at, e.g. Alveston (238bi), Benson and Headington (154bi), Hurstbourne Tarrant (39a2). If that due to Pershore was not paid at the proper time, the penalty was to pay twelve times the sum due.

Of the obligations of priests in return for their benefices we hear a little; usually they are those of singing a certain number of Masses a week for their benefactors' souls; e.g. at Heveningham (II.133). The priests of three royal churches in the district of Archenfield had to bear the King's embassies into Wales (179a2).

Farm animals

In volume II of Domesday Book, in the Exeter Domesday, and in the ICC and IE, we are given the number of livestock on the demesnes of manors. It is made quite clear that only the demesne livestock is recorded: the ICC entry for Kennett (76a) speaks of *pecunia in dominio*, and in vol. II the numbers are often given as being *in halla, in aula dominica*.[1] What too is made clear is the frequent comparative smallness of the demesne flocks and herds. East Bergholt (II.287) had woodland for a thousand pigs, but there were only 29 on the demesne. The figures available are thus virtually useless for statistical purposes; the more so because often we find a manor with demesne but with no livestock recorded, and livestock where the amount of demesne was apparently omitted.

In the eastern counties, where we should be given the information for three dates as stated in the I.E., we are quite often given none for 1086; merely that 'when he received it' or 'then' there were so many of different kinds. Thus we have no means of knowing how many, if any, livestock there were in 1086. There may well have been a number of places on a par with Yalding in Kent (14a2), where 'the land was wasted by the destruction of the stock'; this was certainly so at, e.g., Eaton (II.444b), where there had been 86 various beasts – 'now, nothing'.

We can be reasonably sure that the demesne livestock were returned for all England, since the figures appear in ICC and IE for Cambridgeshire and the Ely manors in Huntingdonshire also. It seems, too, as if a few times the Exchequer clerks failed to omit them when condensing texts which included them. In an unnamed manor of Eudes fitzHerbert (139a2) it is noted that when Humphrey took it over he received

[1] e.g. on fols. II.41b, 131, 186, 257b.

'68 animals, 350 sheep, 150 swine, 50 goats, and one mare'. Nine *afri*, or pack-horses, are mentioned at *Clive* (165ai). *Animalia*, normally non-working beasts, also appear intermittently in the Exchequer text, but we cannot be sure that here they do not stand for beasts of the plough.[1] Eynesbury (206b2) had a sheepfold for 662 sheep, and at *Sudtone* (354bi) the owner of the manor is said to have a flock of sheep. Occasionally, too, we are reminded of the existence of the livestock by mention of rents in kind; e.g. of wool and cheese at Bloxham and Adderbury (154b2).

Sheep

Sheep are everywhere by far the most numerous of the categories of animals recorded. In the eastern counties the flocks seem largely to have been kept on the marshland, and the expression 'pasture for sheep' is a regular feature of the Essex Domesday.[2] Flocks were often very large – Southminster (II.10) had pasture for 1,300, and a demesne flock of 696 – and in contrast to some other figures those for the demesnes are often high; in Devon there are nearly 50,000 in all. Large flocks, too, are found in the Norfolk and Suffolk marshlands and in the fenland. But, if the situation of manors with many sheep is any guide, the upland regions and the south-western downland supported large flocks also. Cranborne (*29*) had over a thousand, but there must always remain a suspicion that some of the south-western sheep may have been pastured on the coastal marshes.

In the eastern counties we find frequent reference to foldsoke, the right of the lord to make his peasantry shut up their beasts in his fold so that he might have the benefit of their all-important manure, (e.g. at Hesset or Hillington, II.362b, 203b). We shall presently see how sheep and their lambs are among the renders of various manors (p. 238). A few other incidental references have crept into the Domesday folios: wethers or *berbices* are twice mentioned in Devonshire, and the theft of 380 sheep is recorded in connection with Abington (190ai,

---

[1] At Lower Sapey (176b2) there was 'nothing but nine *animalia*' in demesne; at Weston Favell (227b2) was 'a villein with three *animalia*'.

[2] At Heckingham in Norfolk (II.205) there is said to be 'marsh for 60 sheep'.

199b2). A share in a shearing-house is mentioned in the account of Stallingborough (340ai), and in that of Cirencester Hundred (162b2) the 'wool of the sheep' being one of the Queen's perquisites is mentioned.[1]

Cows

Cows (*vaccae*) are mentioned in small numbers only, and are rarely recorded in an entry which includes *animalia* (which are frequently described as *animalia ociosa* or *otiosa* – non-working beasts). Round thought that the few which are mentioned were kept to provide milk for the lord's family.[2] Whether this theory is right or not, both *vaccae* and *animalia* occupy a very minor position among the beasts of DB. Accordingly, milk and cheese may have been provided by goats and sheep rather than cows. Certainly there are very few references in DB to cheese-making, or to renders in the form of cheese. The Pershore Abbey *vaccaria* or dairy-farm seems to have been at Wadborough (175a2), and at Bisley (180b2) there were both dairy-farm and dairy (*daia*). A render of 56½ weys of cheese from Milton Regis to the manor of Newington (14bi), and one of 10 weys or 22*s*. 4*d*. at Buckland (58bi), are mentioned, but on the whole, DB remains silent about milk-production. The primary function of the cattle seems to have been the breeding of the plough-oxen. Calves (*vituli*) are very rarely mentioned; a bull only once (Bodardle, *249b*). Once the pasture is said to be for the use of the *animalia* (Birling, 7bi).

Goats

The majority of the entries which mention livestock include some goats, but none is of special interest, and the numbers on the demesnes are never really large. It is always she-goats (*capreae*) which are mentioned.

Horses

Horses are variously classified; the *runcini*, *roncini*, or rounceys were probably pack-animals, and no manor had any appreci-

---

[1] At Kingston (30bi), Humphrey, the Queen's chamberlain, had a villein whose duty it had been to collect the wool owed to her.

[2] *VCH: Somerset*, vol. I, p. 424. *Animalia* may often represent cows.

able number of them. Once (Clopton, ICC 101b) a *hercerarius*
or animal used for harrowing is mentioned. Studs of horses
variously described as 'unbroken' (*indomitae*) or 'forest' (*silvestres*
or *silvaticae*) are noted both in the eastern counties and the
south-west, and the latter were probably Exmoor ponies.
Numbers were often quite large; Brendon (*337*) had 104 and
Lynton (*402*) 72, but it is not always clear whether horses or
mares are indicated. There is also a stray Surrey reference to
'the King's forest-mares' (36ai). Foals are very rarely mentioned;
the reference to a 'lame mare' at Wilburton (IE 46bi) is
altogether exotic.

Donkeys, asses, and mules make occasional appearances.

Swine

Some reference to these has already been made in considering
the woodland and the *porcarii* as an element in the population
(pp. 173, 132). Herds were probably very large indeed, even
if the figures for demesne swine are not as great as might be
expected. When, as not infrequently happens, we find DB
attributing wood for a thousand, sometimes over two thousand,
swine, to a manor, we are entitled to think that capacities
and herds were sometimes not appreciably less than the figures
implied. Swine-keeping seems to have been a matter for the
peasantry rather than the maintenance of a large herd by the
lord; those *porcarii* who are numerous in the Exeter Domesday
and appear occasionally in the Exchequer Domesday, and who
pay considerable swine-rents, seem to be, not village swineherds, but small farmers engaged principally in breeding and
rearing. Money as well as swine-rents were paid by them for
the privilege: twenty at North Petherton (*88b*) paid one
hundred shillings a year; and at Hanley Castle (180b2) the
rents average ten pigs a man.

Perhaps when the Domesday Geography of England is
complete we shall have a better idea of the place of the livestock in eleventh-century England than we have to-day. But
there will always remain difficulties; for example, so far as the
Domesday text goes, there were no *porcarii* in Dorset or Cornwall, though swine are recorded. It seems most improbable

that there were none; and we find ourselves faced also with suspicion that in some Hundreds a particular category of livestock was completely omitted from the record.

For the three eastern counties over 180,000 livestock are mentioned. Very roughly, sheep contribute 70% of their number, swine 17%, goats 6%, *animalia* and cows 5%, and the various categories of horses under $1\frac{1}{2}$%.

Miscellaneous information

The preceding chapters will already have shown how, presumably as a result of information volunteered by the witnesses, extraneous information crept into the Domesday folios. There are in addition a number of passages which are concerned with items many of which, if not covered by the terms of reference, had to do with the economy of the manor, and so are relevant.

Nearly forty vineyards are mentioned, and since a number are said to be 'new', it may be that the foreigners were trying to introduce or widen viticulture in England.[1] For the most part they are measured by the arpent, a French unit of mensuration. They are recorded as far north as Ely.

Beehives, of great importance because sugar was an expensive commodity and wax in demand, must have existed wherever possible, but are only spasmodically mentioned. About 600 are mentioned on the Essex demesnes alone. Renders in terms of honey are common, and the beekeepers themselves are occasionally mentioned (e.g. at *Sutreworde*, 111b2; Suckley, 180b2).

Whether orchards are specifically mentioned or not is somewhat doubtful. *Ortus* or *hortus* seems usually to imply a garden-close within a town, but *virgultum* may imply fruit-growing, especially as the term is found at the place now known as Orchard (84ai).

A warren of hares (which again must have been common) is recorded only at Gelston (347b2). 'Provision for horses' (implying perhaps pasture or a render in kind) occurs in four Lincolnshire entries (347b2, 348ai): we hear also of the pasture a former sheriff of Berkshire made for his horses (Kintbury,

---

[1] Of other vineyards it is said that portions of them are 'not in bearing'. A pre-Conquest wine-render is mentioned at Lomer (43ai), but the wine may not have been local.

57bi), and of 'pasture for the King's mares' (Kingston, 36ai). The fact that Earl William fitzOsbern had had a bakehouse and a baker in the Isle of Wight (Cheverton, 52b2) is also mentioned.

Ferries make occasional appearances (e.g. at Weston-upon-Trent, 273ai), since their rents or the tolls for using them were of profit. Other tolls, and the 'custom of ships', some of which are innovations, are also mentioned: one at Barton and South Ferriby (375b2) is concerned with 'bread, fish, hides, and very many other things', while at Southwark (32ai) a toll was exacted along the strand or the water where ships used to berth. Such landing-stages (hithes) are mentioned at, e.g., Dartford (2bi).

Much less is said about extractive industry than the demand for metal and stone would warrant. Mention of iron-working is of surprisingly infrequent occurrence, though iron mines are mentioned under Rhuddlan (269ai). Forges and ironworkers' premises do occasionally appear (e.g. *fabricae ferri* at Castle and Little Bytham in Lincolnshire, 360b2; a *ferraria* at Stratfield, 45b2); but the smiths themselves, who must have been numerous, are not prominent. A forge could be 'for the use of the hall', as at Chertsey (32b2). The ironworks at Corby and Gretton (219bi) seem to have suffered in the troubles following the Conquest. Renders in terms of ploughshares and horseshoes are sometimes mentioned; so is one of rods (or iron) for making nails for the ships (Gloucester, 162ai).

Quarries (*quadrariae*) must have existed in many more places than are mentioned. Sometimes, e.g. at Bignor (25ai) or Whatton (290bi) they are said to be for producing millstones (*molariae*). Lead-mines appear in the Derbyshire folios. Among the entries is one stating how three royal manors rendered five cartloads of lead of 50 slabs (273ai), and the fact that five other royal manors rendered £40 of 'pure silver' (272bi) may suggest a connection between lead- and silver-mining.

Pottery-making is recorded at Bladon (156ai), and there were an unspecified number of potters in the manor of Westbury (65a2).

Perhaps the oddest introductions into the formulistic text are a reference to a road separating Staffordshire royal property from that of Robert of Stafford; and a man's liability at Poston (252b2) to furnish a bundle of box for rods on Palm Sunday.

CHAPTER XI

The Forest and the Waste

The Forest

Only about a dozen of the numerous Forests in England are mentioned by name in DB. But there can be little doubt that most of those made famous in later days – Epping, Sherwood, Savernake, Selwood, Clarendon, Galtres, Charnwood, for example – though not named, were then in existence. Few counties are without fairly frequent reference to the royal Forests, and there is every reason to believe that there would have been many more passages dealing with them if they had not been in some sense outside the scope of the Inquest.

For the 'forest' is not necessarily woodland, but something *foras*, outside, the normal systems of administration and of agricultural and pastoral life. It may be that it was in 1086 an agreed principle that land wholly 'in the Forest', as being outside such systems, on which otherwise the Inquest depended for its structure, would not be considered. If so, it was once departed from, and then only in order to record the details of the New Forest.[1] We have no special accounts of other named Forests, such as those of Dean, Wychwood, Malvern, or Windsor. All we receive is frequent mention of the fact that some of the land of a vill is 'in the Forest', and often it is added that the Forest is the King's. We hear very little of the Forests of other lords, but this may be because it was not part of the Inquest's scheme to include them, because land 'in the Forest' seems on the whole to have been quit of liability for geld and service (except for duties specifically connected with the Forest), and because DB is primarily a record compiled in

[1] It does not seem probable that similar records of other Forests were drawn up, but omitted from the Exchequer Domesday. Probably appreciable portions of Wiltshire were Forest land, in what later were Groveley, Clarendon, Melchet, Chute, Savernake, Melksham and Selwood Forests, but there is no textual suggestion of there having been a separate account of any or all of them.

the King's interests. But we do hear that, in the palatine county of Cheshire, Earl Hugh had placed Kingsley (267a2) 'in his Forest', that he has put all the woodland of twenty hides of Atiscros Hundred in his Forest, thus greatly depreciating the prosperity of the manors concerned (268b2), and that he has half of the woodland which did not belong to any vill of the manor of Rhuddlan (269ai). Ripple (173a2) was in the King's Forest of Malvern, but the Bishop of Worcester could hunt there, and also derived profit therefrom. Gloucester Abbey enjoyed hunting rights in three enclosures at Churcham and Morton (165bi); Osbern fitzRichard hunted in the waste lands on the Radnor-Hereford border (186b2); William fitzNorman held what was later the Forest of Treville (129bi), and got enough out of it to pay the King £15 for it. Several lords, and the King also, had made themselves 'parks for wild beasts'. The Bishop of Winchester had one at Bishop's Waltham (40a2); there are few counties which show no record of them.

Frequently we are told of some holding that 'the King has it in his Forest' (e.g. Enville, 249b2). It was important to mention its inclusion; first because this placed it 'outside' the manor in which it had lain, secondly because it militated against local agricultural and pastoral activity, which was forbidden to disturb the game, reducing the availability of swine-pasture or preventing timber-gathering. It is clear, though the form of the expression varies, that the King and his lieutenants had been greatly enlarging the area under Forest Law. Bullingham (186a2) has been 'placed in the King's wood', parts of Laverstock and Milford have been included in what must have been the King's Forest of Clarendon (68a2, 71a2, 74a2). At Harewood (187ai) 'the land had all been converted into woodland'. Hewelsfield (167ai) is in the Forest 'by the King's order'. Often enough it is said that land is 'waste' (which often implies barred from use rather than unusable) '*because* of the King's Forest'; e.g. *Haswic* in Cannock (247b2). One hide at Ellington (204b2) is waste 'because of the King's wood'. Many phrases which do not specifically mention inclusion in the Forest imply it: Didley (181bi) and other places are 'in the King's enclosure', *in defensione regis*. The woodland at Littleton and *Clatinges* (45b2, 46ai), in Forest areas, is said to be *inutilis*, which may well mean 'not to be used' rather than useless. At Botley (46b2), the woodland is wanting (*deest*), which probably implies the same; at Chilworth (47b2) the owner 'has no power in his wood'. There had been woodland at Durley (50b2), the pannage of which had been six pigs, but this has gone – *sed non est*; gone 'into the Forest' most likely. The men of Oakhanger (49b2) can have neither pasture nor pannage in the King's wood except by authority of the sheriff.

Of the appurtenances of the chase itself we learn little, but to record these was not the business of the Inquest. The customs of the borough of Hereford (179ai) note that when the King hunted locally, one man went from each house to his station in the wood, to assist in driving the deer. 'Hays' or hedges for controlling the course the quarry must take are frequently recorded; they are mentioned in connection with thirty-six Shropshire places, and at *Lege* (254bi) are said to be of permanent character (*haie firmae*). The Crofton entry (256bi) and others add that they are to aid the capture of roedeer. Renders of hawks, or sums paid in lieu of such renders, we encounter also (e.g. at Malmesbury, 64bi). Hawks' nests are also mentioned; e.g. at Forthampton (180b2) and Bromsgrove (172a2), for it was of importance to know where to obtain replacements for training. Ailey (187ai) is said to include 'a great wood for hunting', and the value of Fotheringay (228a2) is given as for occasions when the King did not hunt in it.[1] Gloucestershire manors had had to find 3,000 loaves for feeding the hounds (162b2), and the obligation occurs in other counties also.

Huntsmen and foresters we meet with everywhere in DB. William's predecessors had been as devoted to the chase as he was, and the number of persons with the epithet *venator* after their names is large. Several of these, or their sons, are to be found still holding at least a portion of their estates in 1086.[2] The fief of Waleran, the King's foreign huntsman, is of considerable extent, and almost entirely in the neighbourhood of

---

[1] The value would be lessened when it was preserved, for entry into it for pasture or wood-collecting would be forbidden. It must be remembered that deer do much damage to crops.

[2] Even in a score of years, the newcomers could not have assimilated the forest lore or topographical knowledge accumulated by generations of natives.

the chief southern Forests. The 'King's foresters' have a small estate 'in the Forest of Groveley' (74a2). Even in counties where the Forest is not specifically mentioned, we encounter occasional suggestions of it. An Ædelraed the forester ('Aderet') appears in the geld account of the Devonshire Hundred of Exminster (*69*), and in Essex Robert Gernons is said to have made a swineherd 'forester of the King's wood' (Writtle, II.5b).[1] But a very large proportion of the entries which refer to the Forests come from those parts easy to reach from the cities to which the Kings of England and their households paid frequent visits – Winchester, Salisbury, Gloucester, Hereford – though medieval economy as well as the desire for sport must have necessitated the scientific care of Forests everywhere. We hardly think of Cambridgeshire as a hunting county (and perhaps much of the practice was concerned with the hawking of wild fowl); none the less, we hear under Snailwell (199a2) of the 'King's wood' of Cheveley and of parks at Borough Green (195b2) and Kirtling (202a2).

The New Forest

The New Forest does not altogether owe its origins to the Conqueror, though DB bears ample testimony to his enlargement of it. The geld account for the Hundred of Downton (*2b*), which was co-extensive with the manor of that name (65bi), tells us that some of the inhabitants have fled 'because of the Forest', and DB that two of its 97 hides are not the Bishop of Winchester's, but were taken away, with three others, 'in the time of Cnut'.[2] Obviously there was a royal Forest on the Wiltshire-Hampshire border long before 1066, and the situation suggests that this was what was later reckoned as in the New Forest.

Apparently this Forest was considered to be of special importance – or it was reckoned to be of such character as to be inappropriate for inclusion in the body of the Hampshire

---

[1] A swineherd, from driving his charges to woodland feedings, would inevitably pick up much knowledge of wild beasts. This is the sole reference to Forest in a county which included Epping and Hainault.

[2] Probably the 'New Forest' is meant; if this extended over the Hampshire border. There was Forest land all along the south-western and -eastern boundaries of Wiltshire.

Domesday – and worthy of a special section of DB, headed 'In the New Forest and round about it', placed between the mainland manors and the Southampton and Isle of Wight sections (51a,b).[1] The use here of 'New' suggests recent enlargement of the former extent, and its isolation from the general record its importance and size. King William has long been accorded bitter criticism for his part in making this Forest, and responsibility for eviction of its inhabitants. But while inclusion 'in the Forest' was surely damaging to these, the extent of eviction seems greatly to have been exaggerated. In the first place, the area can never, by reason of the character of its soils, have been of even average prosperity. Secondly, the record of DB is altogether against wholesale eviction. Thirdly, there is no proof that the harm done to local economy was anything like so great as the chroniclers would have us believe.

The entries fall into three classes: those which deal with holdings which are altogether 'in the Forest', those where some part of a village or hamlet has been taken into it, and those holdings which, so far as we know, were unaffected. The first category, from the statistics, seem to have been mostly small and unprosperous estates, for the most part in the heart of the area, remotest from civilization.[2] On cursory inspection, we should deduce that in 1086 they were deserted. As a rule no population is recorded, and often it is said that there *were*, not are, so many ploughlands, no teams are recorded, and any small assessment to the geld for which they were formerly liable has been reduced to nothing. Usually it is said of these holdings that somebody had (*habuit*), not 'has' them (e.g. *Achelie*, 51ai); it is added that 'the King put it there' (i.e. in his Forest). *Truham* (51a2) now gelds or defends itself 'for nothing', because 'the whole is in the Forest'; Canterton (50b2), which had gelded for half a virgate, now did so for one ferding, 'because the other ferding lies in the King's forest'. Also, it is

---

[1] Some relevant entries, however, are in the body of the Hampshire text; e.g. Avon (44bi), Fordingbridge (this seems to be postscriptal – 47a2), *Slacham* (39ai). The Forest section is arranged by fiefs just like any other part of the record, and the Hundred in which each holding was is given. Round thought it was postscriptal; certainly some entries had to be added in a blank space on fol. 50b2.

[2] The Domesday names of many of these have not survived in modern form; clear evidence of their lack of prosperity.

stated that though they 'were worth' sums which rarely exceed £3, though amounts of £8 and £10 are recorded, no 1086 value is given. But we find some nineteen out of forty-seven entries where 'it is now in the Forest, except for *n* acres of meadow'. The hay, perhaps, was used for the horses of the hunt. Someone must fence and mow that meadow, and make use of its hay: perhaps the holdings were not so empty as at first sight they would seem to be. Quite often we are told that someone is holding this meadow; at *Oxelei* (51ai) it is Nigel, the sub-tenant; at *Sclive* (51ai) it is 'he who held the manor and still holds it'. This does not look like total emptiness and complete desertion; nor does the account of *Bile* (51a2), which is all in the Forest, and yet is called *villa*. Would a deserted settlement be so styled? Who, too, if there were no surviving inhabitants, gave the Inquest officials the information preserved for us?

The record of the second group makes use of varying formulae: a proportion of the hides are 'now in the Forest', or what has been taken into the Forest is specified. Always it seems to be known what proportion of the assessment is now 'in the Forest'. Perhaps this was estimated (and it had to be reckoned in order to arrive at a judgment of how much liability for geld had been withdrawn); perhaps only some outlying components of the manor had been afforested, and their individual liabilities were known. This may have been the case at, e.g., Ringwood (39ai), some of the land of which was in the Isle of Wight, and four of whose ten hides had been taken into the Forest. In all but a very few instances, the value has dropped appreciably from that of 1066; e.g. from twenty to four shillings at Canterton (50b2), from forty to three at Testwood (51ai). Often we are given also the value of what 'the King has in his Forest', but rarely does this, together with the value of the undisturbed portion, equal that of 1066. At Barton (*Burmintone*, 51a2), the value had fallen from 40*s.* to 20*s.*, but what the King has is worth only 6*s.* Often it is said, as we might expect, that the King has the woodland of the manor in his Forest, and what swine-rent this paid, but meadow, pasture, and honey-renders are also mentioned as having been 'taken into the Forest'. Often we are told how much pannage, expressed in terms of pigs, in the woods had become Forest

15   I.D.B.

land. We are not told that this still left some wood for the inhabitants' use, so we cannot say that this figure is an estimate of the proportion of woodland lost to them. But either some was left for the feeding of their beasts, or swine- and goat-keeping must have ceased locally. It is a great pity that we do not possess the earlier drafts which would have shown us the number of livestock on the demesnes.

Values had mostly declined, in varying proportions, from 1066 to that date described as *post*, and from then to what is said to be *modo*. But an appreciable number show no fall between *tunc* and *modo* – this suggests that inclusion in the Forest might be comparatively recent – and several a fall between *tunc* and *post*, but none between *post* and *modo* – which with the above may suggest that the Forest was not extended as the result of a single action. A few show no reduction at either period.

The third group is one of a few holdings in the account of which nothing is said about any of their land being in the Forest. It is just possible, from occasional improvements in their values, and a superabundance of teams over recorded ploughlands, that they might have absorbed some of the inhabitants from those holdings from which they are supposed to have been driven.[1]

We are never specifically told that these have been evicted. There are indeed only six entries in which the past tense is used of inhabitants; at Eling (38b2) there were taken into (*occupatae*) the Forest sixteen dwellings or plots (*mansurae*) for villeins and three for bordars; at Holdenhurst (39b1) thirteen villeins and three bordars with eight teams dwelt (*manebant*) on the portion taken into the Forest; at Hordle (51a2) the King has the wood in his Forest, where six men used to dwell. The total for the six amounts only to 51 villeins, these 6 'men', and 12 bordars, with 19 teams. The expressions may indeed merely mean that some or all are still there, but under Forest law and custom rather than that of the country and manor.

---

[1] e.g. Brockenhurst (51b2). Its assessment has been halved, but there are three and a half teams for a single ploughland, and its value has doubled from what it was T.R.E. and *post*. It may have received an influx from neighbouring holdings; the Alfric who holds it might be the Aluric, *venator*, of other entries. The Hampshire chapter in vol. III of the *Domesday Geography of England* includes elaborate tables drawn up by Professor Darby to illustrate all the points discussed in this section.

The New Forest may seem to have been dealt with in disproportionate detail. But the entries are unique, and an appreciable part of the country was also 'in the Forest'. These entries throw much light on what the phrase implies.

Waste

But not all the land recorded in DB as waste – and the number of such entries is considerable – was so described because the requirements of the Forests prevented its full exploitation. Some of it was the result of the hazards of farming, especially where marginal land implied an ever-precarious balance between partial cultivation and a return to the wild. Much of it was due to deliberate harrying in punishment for rebellion, as in Yorkshire; some to the inevitable concomitants of military campaigns. Harbury (239ai) is said to be waste 'by reason of the King's army'. In the marchlands, Welsh raids and countermeasures had produced many wasted vills and holdings, both in King Edward's day and those of the Conqueror's border barons. Wrangle in Lincolnshire (367b2) was waste 'through the action of the sea'.[1]

Much of this waste we should expect to be the result of a decline or absence of men and beasts to exploit it, and probably not so far distant from settlements and land in cultivation that it could not indeed be used at all. Mullacot (*469*) 'lay waste as pasture', and we can only think that it had once been inhabited and that in 1086 the beasts of the men of a neighbouring holding grazed it. Of the two holdings at Hilderstone (246b2, 249ai), the King's was waste, but Robert of Stafford's well stocked, and this suggests neighbouring settlements of unequal potential prosperity, of which the less favoured had gone back to its unreclaimed state.

But what are we to make of holdings which, though said to be waste, are being cultivated? Of the two holdings at Butley (264b2, 267a2), both are waste, except for twelve and seven acres which are sown. The only inhabitant mentioned at either (though they may be duplicate entries, with vii misread as xii, or *vice versa*) is Wlfric (Uluric) and any unrecorded family he

---

[1] Of two carucates of land at Dunwich (II.311b), there was in 1086 one only; the sea had 'carried away' the other.

may have had, but if the land is growing a crop, how can it be 'waste'? Again, Keisby (371ai) is 'waste', but there are three villeins with six oxen there; so is Stubton (361b2), with its solitary bordar and 37 acres of meadow. We cannot help noticing, too, how often in DB places said to be 'waste' are yet of some small value. Besford (174bi) is waste, but none the less 'it was and is worth sixteenpence'; Foxley and Challons Weston (223bi) are both waste; however (*tamen*) each is worth 5s. Do such phrases imply that, though partially 'waste', like those holdings of which some portion has been taken into the New Forest, enough has been left outside the Forest to enable some manner of agricultural or pastoral life to continue, or that, after recent devastation, recovery has begun, but is insufficiently advanced for the struggling settlers to be considered as having anything but 'waste'? The 'waste' – the uncultivable land – woodland and pasture and marsh – may still produce enough and support enough beasts to make it possible for the inhabitants to pay the modest rents of which we read. Men were herdsmen as well as workers in the fields.

Another explanation of some of the entries is possible. There were two bovates for geld at Elstorpe and Bulby (368ai), and they 'are empty' (*vacuae*); however, they are cultivated (*coluntur*). Since no population is recorded, men from another holding must have tilled the fields. But they might well have been noted as 'waste'.

Of the waste which is of man's rather than nature's doing we hear a good deal. One-third of the hides recorded in the Northamptonshire geld account are 'waste', because of the treatment of which the *Anglo-Saxon Chronicle* tells us meted out to the shire during the Northumbrian revolt of 1065. Entry after entry in the Yorkshire Domesday speaks to us of King William's harrying of the north in 1069–70 after the Anglo-Danish revolts. Earl Alan of Richmond had 199 manors in his castellate (381a2): 101 of them were still waste in 1086. There were 61 vills around Preston-on-Ribble, then surveyed with Yorkshire (301b2): 'of these sixteen are inhabited by a few, but it is not known how many the inhabitants are – the rest are waste'. The frequent mention of waste and the falls in value amply demonstrate Norman reprisals for the revolts in the midlands early in the reign. One-fifth of the Staffordshire vills were still waste in 1086, and in such a county, with much marginal land, recovery would naturally be long delayed. Leicestershire is another county which had suffered severely; there is much which is waste in 1086, much which was 'found' waste (i.e. when the new owner acquired it, *c.* 1067–71). But some land which had been waste now has a value; though there were not a few places, such as Donington-le-Heath (236ai), worth 20*s*. T.R.E., which had later been waste, and by 1086 have recovered no more than 10% of their former value. Similar figures, and similar formulae, mark the Welsh raids which were most vicious in 1055, 1069, and 1074, and the ruin inevitably caused by reprisals and Norman penetration into Wales. Land for 31 teams which is waste (Cause or *Alretune*, 253bi), is a comparatively large area for waste and a suggestive figure. But it is the number of places waste at one or more of Domesday's three dates which is the most striking feature.[1]

'Waste' is most fully dealt with in the volumes of the *Domesday Geography of England*, whose maps are illuminating. They bear ample testimony to the number of stricken vills and the suffering the Conquest and its consequences had induced, and especially to the harrying of the north. But an explanation alternative to punitive military operations has been given of the condition of Yorkshire.[2] It has been suggested that the upland vills are deserted not solely because of deliberate destruction but because their inhabitants were in some instances transferred to more fertile lowland settlements to supply the deficiencies caused by the campaigns and the reprisals of 1069–70. This would explain occasional surpluses of teams in the lowland manors, and while the uplands would be the natural refuge of the discontented, it may not seem altogether probable that their isolated and impoverished hamlets should be the target of systematic destruction.

[1] But, in considering the extent and distribution of 'waste', we must always pause to ask ourselves whether it is 'waste' because it is 'in the Forest'.

[2] T.A.M. Bishop: 'The Norman Settlement of Yorkshire', in *Studies in Medieval History presented to Frederick Maurice Powicke* (ed. R. W. Hunt, W. A. Pantin, and R. W. Southern; Oxford, 1948).

Though we read of places which are 'altogether waste', *penitus vastata*, and which are 'empty', *vacua*, (Furzehill, *366* – the Exchequer version, fol. 111ai, says *vastata*; *Celvertesberia, 133b*), it is more common to find that of the land of a manor some portion, often perhaps far removed from the *caput*, and somewhat unsuitable for settlement, is waste. Of the twenty-three hides of Tredington and Tidmington (173a2), one only is said to be waste. Of 'land for nine oxen' at Addlethorpe (360ai), four bovates were waste. Occasionally we are told what, since the holding is waste, makes its mention necessary; Bicker (367ai) is waste 'except for one salt-pan'. Very rarely are we told just what it is which is waste, but we do occasionally meet passages such as that which tells us that a church, and a virgate in Guilsborough, and the site of a mill, and one-third of a virgate in Hollwell, are all waste (Nortoft Grange, 224ai). Sometimes an entry is precise and presents a vivid picture of an empty countryside: of a moorland Derbyshire valley it is said that 'the whole of Longdendale is waste; there is woodland there, but it is suitable for the needs of the chase, not for pasture of swine' (273ai). Sometimes, though waste is not specifically mentioned, we can visualise an impoverished and stricken community: 'many things belonged T.R.E. to this manor in wood and ironworks and other things which are now wanting' (Corby, Gretton, 219bi).[1]

But in addition to the recovery from former misfortunes, if often only partial recovery, implied by increases in value after sharp declines, we do also hear of the reclamation of land once deserted and idle. 'It was waste; now a certain man ploughs there', and he is in a position to render 2s. (Hadlow, 263b2). Little Grimsby (340b2) had been waste, but in 1086 it is being cultivated (*colitur*). Moreover, though these were not necess-arily instances of a former return to the waste after earlier settlement, those mentions of *hospites* (p. 134) tell us of use of a formerly idle soil. The Norman, avid for profit, may have planted numerous new outposts about which DB is silent, and in some measure adjusted the balance his ravages had disturbed.

---

[1] A suspicion that some of the land of these manors had been taken into the Forest (that which later was Rockingham?) is inevitable.

Part Three

THE
MAGNATES AND THEIR REVENUES

CHAPTER XII

The Magnates

DOMESDAY Book lists, besides the King, a couple of hundred tenants-in-chief, and an indeterminable number of sub-tenants who for the most part rank rather higher than those persons dealt with in previous chapters. In practically every shire the pattern is the same; except in the palatinates, the King has a large number of manors, usually large and prosperous ones, and which are often complexities of holdings. Bishops and their episcopates, abbots and abbesses and their houses, are credited, in the case of the more influential ones, with broad lands the majority of which have long been the property of see or abbey. Generally speaking, each ecclesiastical fief is confined to a comparatively small number of shires around its headquarters. The magnates range from the half-brothers of the King, with estates scattered throughout England, to men who in no sense rank with the palatinate Earls, but whose property, often extensive, is to be found within the confines of from two to half a dozen shires, which are not necessarily adjacent ones. At the foot of the scale come men, minor royal officers or servants, with half a dozen or so small estates, and those Englishmen, often also royal officials, who had retained at least a portion of their former property.

By the eleventh century the kings of England were no longer holding vast amounts of land, owing to bequests and sales, especially to the Church, though their manors were usually among the largest and most profitable. Many a Saxon Earl's possessions compared favourably with those of the monarch. But the Conqueror's coming had changed the picture. He had taken to himself the bulk of the possessions of the House of Godwine, and many of the estates at his disposal on the forfeitures of rebellious Earls or on the death of a former holder. In 1086 more than 15% of England is ascribed to *Terra Regis*;

in Wiltshire, for example, when allowance is made for the unhidated ancient demesne of the Crown, it is fair to say that no other single landowner possessed half as much as King William did.

It must be remembered that DB gives us a picture of the ownership of English land as it was in 1086, and not at the time of the original redistribution thereof. King William had allowed the Confessor's widow to retain her lands (some of which were transferred before her death and the royal inheritance of the remainder); he had made provision for his wife, and only came into possession of her estates in 1083; he had acquired a good few manors on the forfeiture or death of their earlier holders, e.g. Edric of Laxfield's. If we add to the *Terrae Regis* forfeitures such as those of Earl Aubrey, and conceive the King to be enjoying the revenues of Odo of Bayeux's vast fief after the Bishop's disgrace in 1082, the royal possessions look even more impressive. We have to take into the reckoning, too, the extensive private estates of Archbishop Stigand, some of which became the King's, and, for some tenants-in-chief, the fiefs of Earl Waltheof, not all of which passed to his widow the Countess Judith, and of Brian of Penthièvre, and the baronies of men such as Frederic, the brother-in-law of William of Warenne, which by 1086 had not necessarily been preserved as solid inheritances. Many men must have held in 1086 a good deal more than they had held in 1067/71.

The Church lands occupy a large proportion of the folios of DB, and amount to over 25% of English land. It is noticeable that Holy Church is much richer in the stable south and west of England than she is elsewhere. Foundations were here rather more numerous, and royal and lay generosity seems to have been more marked. Canterbury's Archbishop's property is almost four times as great as that of York's.[1] The Bishop of Winchester's lands were finding work for over a thousand plough-teams in 1086, and other wealthy bishoprics, such as Exeter and Worcester, give figures little lower than this. The richest abbeys, such as Glastonbury or Westminster or Abing-

---

[1] The proportion would be less if so much of Yorkshire had not been waste and we had an account of the Archbishop of York's estates in Durham.

don, had over 500 hides of assessment (Glastonbury owned nearly 900); Ely and Peterborough had each round about 500 plough-teams on their estates. A few foreign religious establishments were granted English lands after the Conquest, but the gifts were neither spectacular nor especially rich ones.

The King's half-brothers had done particularly well for themselves. Each had estates in about a score of shires, and between them they possessed almost half as much as did their royal relative. In Cornwall, of which he was Earl, Robert of Mortain's possessions fill $7\frac{1}{2}$ out of the 11 folios the county occupies in DB. In both Devon and Somerset the accounts of his lands fill five columns. Odo of Bayeux, profiting perhaps by his intermittent regencies, spent the years before his rebellion accumulating estates in every part of the country. The legality of some of his acquisitions is more than doubtful, and seems frequently to have been challenged at the Inquest. Geoffrey, Bishop of Coutances, in his capacity as royal adviser and official, is another who had become possessed of vast holdings. His Devon and Somerset lands alone fill eleven columns of DB.

In almost every county we find a few barons with a large number of estates, and twenty or thirty more whose local fiefs are small. The great lord of one shire usually has a smaller number in several others, and the aggregate of those who, viewed from the aspect of a single shire, are not especially well-endowed, is in the sum far from negligible. Roger of Courseulles's Somerset lands occupy more than five columns of its record, but he has only one manor in each of Wiltshire and Dorset, none in Devon or Gloucestershire. Eudes the Steward, Eudo *dapifer*, held land in eleven counties (including houses in boroughs), with the bulk of his fief in the eastern and east midland shires. The total value of his fief was in the neighbourhood of £400, which is greater than that of Ramsey Abbey, which may be reckoned as among the richer abbeys. The sheriff of every county appears as a substantial landowner within it, and his suitability to be the royal representative is marked by his possession of estates in neighbouring shires also. Baldwin of Exeter's Devonshire lands occupy eleven columns of DB, and he has property in several other counties also.

To estimate the relative wealth of the King and his barons

and of the religious houses is a difficult matter. The number of manors held is no guide, for manors varied enormously in extent and value. Most of the relevant chapters of the *VCH* give figures for the individual local fief, but these can be misleading. Little has been done since the estimates of Mr. Corbett were published to arrive at more satisfactory figures.[1] His calculations, however, do enable us to form some kind of comparative picture.[2] He reckons the yearly revenue from the royal manors at over £12,500, of the King's half-brothers at over £5,000 between them, of the Archbishop of Canterbury at £1,750 and of Glastonbury Abbey at almost £900: such figures, of course, in no sense represent total wealth. Only eight magnates' lands exceed the figure of £750, and of the major baronies, in number about 170, less than half exceed £100. They do, too, enable us to visualise how military reprisals and soil characteristics affect the issue. Though Earl Hugh was in possession of the bulk of Cheshire, his land-revenues were less than those derived from his Lincolnshire possessions which fill four columns of DB only. But King, Church, and magnates, as will be seen (pp. 237, 266), had many sources of revenue besides their estates.

A characteristic of almost every county is the number of minor barons who have in it only a manor or two, though we may find them with similar estates in five or six other shires also. The apparent smallness of a man's local fief may be somewhat deceptive, for he may appear under the heading of the King's *ministri* or *servientes* also.

The land as noted in DB by individual fiefs is however somewhat misleading as a guide to the resources of the individual baron. Much land had been granted out by the tenants-in-chief to sub-tenants, and major barons were themselves the tenants of other lords. It is clear that many magnates were renting and farming royal manors, and that the Church had let much of her land to lay sub-tenants. Such complexity makes

---

[1] W. J. Corbett in *Cambridge Medieval History*, vol. V, pp. 481–520 (Cambridge, 1926).

[2] Readers may make their own estimate of the value of the pound in terms of modern money – especially in view of recent falls in value of the twentieth-century pound.

it impossible to arrive at satisfactory comparative figures for the individual fiefs, or to estimate their true values.

For example, in Wiltshire the Bishop of Winchester held 257⅝ hides, valued at £269 10s. Of his dozen manors, nine were 'for the maintenance of the monks' of the cathedral monastery. On eight of the manors there exist seventeen sub-tenancies, rated at 63⅜ hides, and while the Bishop was getting rents for these, presumably the lessees were making a profit from them, so that their value to him was not all it might have been. We are not given values for all the sub-tenancies, but on the seven manors where we are they amount to £58, and this is most likely the figure for the rents paid.[1]

Many of the holders of sub-tenancies were probably minor men (only two in the above example – William de Braiose and William Scudet – are certainly identifiable). But William de Braiose was a baron of at least the second rank. He held a Sussex fief which occupies six columns of DB, a couple of manors in Surrey, thirteen small properties in Dorset, and one in Hampshire. One wonders if he rented his extensive Wiltshire property so as to have an establishment conveniently close to Salisbury and Winchester when the King required his services there.

We do indeed find some of the greatest men in the land holding sub-tenancies. Quite often the text of DB may be deceptive: they may indeed be holding thegnland and occupying it on the grounds that it had been leased to their *antecessor*. The sub-tenants of Glastonbury Abbey in Somerset include such powerful west-country barons as Roger of Courseulles, Serlo de Burcy, and Alfred d'Epaignes, while part of Monkton (90b2) is held by the Bishop of Winchester. It is plain that a number of such tenancies were not in accordance with the Abbey's wishes. Robert of Mortain is holding four manors (91ai) and is said to hold them of the King. But they had been Glastonbury thegnland, and 'could not be separated from the Church'. Moreover, these and others are recorded in *Terrae Occupatae*, showing that occupation of them was in dispute.

---

[1] Actually not all the holdings are true sub-tenancies; e.g. four hides at Downton (65bi) belong to the church of the manor, and the King has taken four hides into his Forest.

Thus we can visualise the complications which make comparative estimates of wealth and influence so hazardous. Since it was no part of the purpose of DB to set down the feudal services owed by a baron to the King, or a sub-tenant or a holder of thegnland to his superior, or the duties of the peasantry to the lord of the manor, we are for the most part totally ignorant about the forms of tenure or what these implied. The arrangement of DB, too, is somewhat misleading. Where a manor, or part of a manor, had not been sub-let; where the owner, in fact, held it 'in demesne', all is fairly straightforward, and really it is the demesne manors which form the fief. For the sub-tenant possessed what Mr. Lennard calls 'the primary economic rights of a landlord': his lord owned, not the land itself, but a superiority over it. Finally, DB does not often clearly tell us where the King had leased a royal manor, or a group of manors, to a local lord, and this makes estimates of true wealth uncertain. Also, there was a large area of England which was not highly manorialised. Here, more even than in the south and west, it was largely a matter of superiority over the land and its occupants rather than ownership.

Moreover, as succeeding chapters will demonstrate, Domesday Book was a series of documents compiled very largely in the royal interest. In consequence, what we learn from it about profits to be derived from the land and its inhabitants is, save for manorial valuations and the advantages of special franchises, largely what the King himself might expect to get from his new kingdom. The final phrase of the instructions in the IE, 'and if more can be obtained from it how it is to be obtained' contains the suggestion that it was King William's object to discover how his revenues and profits might be improved.

Such figures as DB can furnish make it extremely plain that quotas of knight-service, with which the Inquest was not concerned, seem in no way to depend on the extent or value of a fief. It is however a possibility that the results of the Inquest might well have been used to revise these. References to knight-service as such are infrequent in DB. We are however told that the man who holds Long Ditton from Wadard, who holds it of Bishop Odo, does so by the payment of 50s. and 'the service of one knight' (32ai): there are similar passages in the entries for *Cumbe* (10bi) and Sundridge (3ai).

DB's treatment of sub-tenants (and also of tenants-in-chief) is often unsatisfying. Frequently we are not told the names of the holders of manors T.R.E., but merely that so many thegns or free men held it. We have no means of knowing whether, in a shire or group of shires, the often numerous entries including a single proper name refer to an individual, or to an unknown number of men with a common name. The Exchequer clerks, as we can see by collating their text with the Exeter Domesday, omitted the sobriquets of Englishmen and Anglo-Danes and newcomers alike. Such by-names, especially where these relate to pre-Conquest tenants, are often hard to translate.[1] The distortions of name-forms contributed by the Inquest clerks intensify the difficulties. Some are plain enough: a swarthy man is styled *blac*, a blind man *c(o)ecus*, a bald man *calvus*; and we have personages styled Dane (*dacus*), or *forst* (? forester) or 'the steersman'. But few of the epithets – e.g. *mele, tope, biga, pic, uuelp, scoua, musla* – can be interpreted at sight. The newcomers are far more manageable; their names often derive from the places on the continent whence they had come, from their fathers, or from an office they held. Often, though, the orthography is so distorted that recognition is not automatic. William de Faleise or William fitzOsbern present small difficulty, but Auberville can appear as *Otborvilla*, Raimbeaucourt as *Reimbuedcurt*, Sassy as *de Salceid*. In a single county we have landholders described as 'the cook', 'the carpenter', the 'doorkeeper', the 'chamberlain', the 'keeper of the granaries', the 'bowman', etc. We have falconers and goldsmiths, crossbowmen and stonemasons, minstrels and interpreters. Some of these need not be thought of as artisans or of lowly origins. Abroad, it is true, they may have been of humble status, improved on acquiring English estates, but equally they may have been technical experts, the supervisors of the erection of wooden castles and the planners of the ditches which defended them, the commanders of bodies of archers or in charge of royal

[1] See Gosta Tengvik: *Old English Bynames* (Uppsala, 1938) and Olaf von Feilitzen; *The Pre-Conquest Personal Names of Domesday Book* (Uppsala, 1937).

store-houses. The newcomers too had epithets attached to their Christian or family names, and though the origins are lost, 'Poingiant' implies 'biting', 'Escuet' a shield, 'Aculeus' a goad. It is a pity we do not know how 'Roger God-save-the-ladies' got his name.

CHAPTER XIII

Valuations and Renders

Treatment of values

THE Inquisitors were apparently to cause to be set down what the whole of each manor had been worth and was then worth, and, as for the other items, details were to be given for the time of King Edward and when King William gave it. An appreciable proportion of entries do not give any figure for 1066: indeed, once we are told that T.R.E. it was not put out to rent, and therefore it was not known what it had been worth (Lugwardine, 179bi). It may well be, too, that many valuations given for a former date do not refer to King Edward's day. Frequently the wording is merely *valuit* or *valebat*, 'it was worth', and another formula which merely says that the holding was worth so much 'formerly' (*olim*), or the use of 'afterwards' (*post*), equally do not enable us to relate the information to any particular date. Sometimes we are given the 1086 value and that for the time when its owner received it, *quando recepit*, but we do not always know when the holder at the time of the Inquest obtained the manor. It is not impossible, too, that the implication may be 'when the holder took it over at a farm-rent'. Occasionally we are given a definite date: the values are given for Ilminster (91ai) 'when Abbot Leofweard died'; for Longbridge Deverill (68bi) while the late Queen Matilda, who gave it to the Abbey of Bec, was alive; for Long Itchington (244a2) when King William gave it to Christina, sister of Edgar the Atheling. Chewton Mendip (87a2) is said to have been worth £30 when Queen Edith was alive. The figure for a score of years earlier may often have been something the witnesses could not give.

The values are given in terms of pounds, shillings and pence, and often their numbers are round ones. Neither of the first two existed as a coin at the time – they were merely expressions

16   I.D.B.

of account – but the reckoning is in terms of twenty shillings to the pound and twelve pence to the shilling. Halfpennies and farthings appear intermittently; so does the 'pound of pence', which on current value makes the penny one-twentieth of an ounce. Sums are frequently expressed in terms of the number of pence to the ounce or ore: e.g. the render of Tidenham (164ai) is given as £25 *de xx in ora* – of 20*d.* to the ounce. But the Scandinavian reckoning was of 16*d.* to the ounce, and this equation is common both in the shires in which Danish influence is marked and elsewhere. So are sums which include 1*s.* 4*d.* or 2*s.* 8*d.*, and, where 20*d.* to the ounce is reckoned, we often find amounts of or including 1*s.* 8*d.*, 3*s.* 4*d.*, and their multiples. Some figures make use of the mark of silver (13*s.* 4*d.*) or the mark of gold (£6).[1] Many of the Cornish manors of Robert of Mortain include the curious figure of 18*s.* 4*d.* – a figure we shall meet again in Cambridgeshire. The Devonshire manors of the Abbey of Rouen are valued in 'Rouen money'. Payments might be made in two ways; coins were normally counted and accepted at their face value, despite debasement: this was recorded as payment by tale or number (*numero*). But coins were also burnt and assayed and the good metal weighed: consequently we hear too of payments of 'white silver' (*de albo argento*), of coins 'burnt and weighed' (*arsae et pensatae*) – (Berkeley, 163ai,2). The entry for Bosham (16a2) shows us that £65 worth of unassayed coins were reckoned to be worth only £50 when reduced to good metal.

The basis of valuation

What do these 'values' represent? Maitland thought that what guided those responsible was their judgment of 'what will this estate bring in, peopled and stocked as it is?'[2] Such an interpretation would explain the frequent round figures, £5, 50*s.*, 15*s.* and so on. But some values are apparently given with great precision. Water Upton (256bi) is said to be worth 30*s.* 2¼*d.*;

---

[1] The figure for Tintinhull (*266b*) includes one silver mark; Lugwardine (179bi) pays £10 of 'white money' and an ounce of gold; Birstall (232a2) had paid 40/–, but in 1086 five ounces of gold. When the manor of Blakenham (II.353b) was let, those who rented it gave a premium of a mark of gold in order to obtain a lease of it.

[2] *DBB*, p. 413.

Titchwell (II.183) had been worth 13*s*. 4*d*. and was valued at
12*s*.; for the village of Ashley (225a2) the figures are 37*s*. and
48*s*. 8*d*. It may be that strange figures sometimes appear because
we are being given the sum of actual individual rents, or the
previous year's income.[1]

How far the figures cover manorial appurtenances it is
impossible to say. The value of a lord's mill is usually given
separately, and at times we hear of rent paid for pasture, of the
profits from woodland, of what seems to be commutation of
renders in kind.[2] Who, too, was responsible for the valuation?
– the lord's bailiff, or the Hundredmen?

DB gives us occasional hints as to the process. 'No one
answered' for a holding in Langtree Hundred (166bi), but 'the
men of the shire' valued it at £8. It would hardly be a steward
who reported that Aldwinckle (222ai) had been worth 20*s*. and
was worth 30*s*., but that 'if it were well worked it would be
worth £5'. Valuations could apparently be challenged, and
the fact that the lord was requiring impossible rents recorded.
Newton Tony (70a2) had increased in value from £10 to £18,
but the English did not value it at more than £12. This could
often happen: Barking (II.18) was estimated to be worth £80,
but the Frenchmen valued it at £100. Coggeshall (II.27) was
valued at £14, £4 more than its worth in 1066, but it was in
fact rendering £20. Kembrook (II.343) had been and was
valued at £6, but the men of the Hundred gave its worth as
48*s*. only. In consequence of such uneconomic rents we are
several times told that 'it cannot bear it' (Fareham, 40bi); that
is, the lessee or inhabitants cannot pay such a sum without loss
to themselves. Combs (II.291) is 'scarcely able to render' the
sum of £16 – £10 more than in King Edward's day – set on it;
the freemen who have another part of Combs, where the 'value'
has increased from £16 to £31, 'cannot suffer it without ruin';
the men who rented Pettaugh (II.440b) for 75*s*. were thereby
ruined, and a reduction to 45*s*. had to be made. Damerham
(66bi), once worth £36, was rendering £61, but the 'men' (the
Hundredmen?) valued it at £45 'because of the ruin (*confusio*)

---

[1] This seems to be confirmed by entries such as that for Lank Combe (114ai),
where in one place it is said to 'render' 3/–, in another to be 'worth' the same sum.

[2] See p. 236.

of the lands, and the *feorm*, which is too high'. Does 'ruin' imply that there were too few men, following some disaster, to furnish this large sum? Clandon (34ai) was valued at £4, but the villeins who held it from Chertsey Abbey were in fact paying £6. The implications of such figures are, however, not necessarily simple ones: always we must allow for a manor being valued at one sum, but in fact let out at a farm-rent at a higher one.

We must not, indeed, think of many of the valuations as arbitrary estimates, the more so because 'conditions were more various than the phraseology of Domesday suggests'.[1] We have three aspects of the holdings to consider; the demesnes, the feudal sub-tenancies, and the manors or parts of manors which were demesne land but which were 'put out to farm', and for which the tenant paid a fixed rent, hoping to obtain a surplus over and above his payment.

Food-farms and -rents

One of the obligations of many of the royal manors, especially in the south-west, was to furnish provisions for the royal household. Of these DB tells us that 'this vill pays the farm of one day (or night), with all customary dues', or that vills have combined to produce it. The vills are those which are the name-places of the large and wealthy manors which for the most part formed the ancient demesne of the Crown; and it was at them, presumably, that the king's reeve or bailiff received payment, first in kind, and later in money. Vills were sometimes combined, and not necessarily on a basis of geographical propinquity, to furnish such 'farms'. Barton Stacey and Eling in Hampshire each paid, as commutation for their previous *feorm*, £38 8s. 4d. in King Edward's day, Broughton and Neatham double that sum (38ai,bi,2). Round showed that in Somerset the payments, which are never far from £100, were divided between vills in such proportions as 1 : 1, 1 : 1 : 1, 2 : 2 : 1, and that twice £100 10s. 9½d. was split in the pro-

---

[1] Lennard: *Rural Eng.*, p. 109. Chapters V and VI of this book contain a detailed examination of Domesday valuations and rents: my debt to these will be obvious.

portions £79 10s. 7d. and £21 0s. 2½d.[1] In Dorset four groups
of royal vills, with from four to six vills in a group, each found
a night's farm, and one of two and one of four vills each found
that of half a night. There is probably some underlying administrative principle here which it is now impossible to grasp.
That the food-rent system was not entirely obsolete in 1086 is
shown by the fact that Bitton (162b2) had rendered one night's
farm in King Edward's day 'and now does the same'.[2]

Though DB does not tell us so, many of the religious houses
had adopted a system whereby a demesne manor, or group of
manors, had to furnish provisions to supply their needs for a
definite period. Ely, well before the Conquest, had apparently
grouped 33 manors into 56 units, each of which had to furnish
a week's food supply.[3] Bury St. Edmunds, again, had grouped
its manors to supply provisions for thirteen periods each of four
weeks, so we learn from a ms. which dates from the eleventh
century, or only a little later. DB tells us little of this feature of
rural economy, though it is noted that the Canons of St.
Pieran had lost two manors from which they had derived a
farm of four weeks (121a2).

The system persisted (and in some instances may have been
introduced) long after the date of the Inquest, but it is doubtful
if food and drink were the only elements which the demesne
manors incorporated in such schemes had to furnish. In DB
we find many of the Ely demesne manors paying a money-farm
(e.g. Barking, Drinkstone; II.381b, 382b), and this may not
wholly or even partially represent a commutation of an earlier
food-farm. In any case, the fluctuations of the population of a
monastery, and the need for feeding the military quota demanded by the imposition of knight-service (until this had
been furnished with estates of its own), would make too rigid a
scheme of food-rents difficult to operate.

[1] Round: *FE*, p. 111. Such manors are unhidated, and do not geld.

[2] The commutation is not always in the region of £100, nor the period a single
day or night: see, e.g., Laleford (II.6), Writtle (II.5), Linton (179bi).

[3] The figure of 56 suggests that insurance was made against failure to fulfil
quotas. So does the reservation of the manors in the Isle of Ely to furnish supplies
if the crops and stock of the manors within the system failed.

The farming-out and renting of manors

It is quite common to find *reddit*, 'it renders', not *valet*, 'it is worth', in DB, and in the past tense also. The use of the phrase rather suggests that it is indicating the actual rent paid, and it is suggestive that in the Exeter Domesday, especially for royal manors, *valet* has often been struck through and *reddit* substituted.[1] For the royal manors in particular lent themselves to a farm system; singly or in groups they could be let to the local sheriff, the natural guardian of royal property, or to other persons who anticipated a virtual certainty of profit. The farm system meets us everywhere in DB; the owner is prepared to be assured of a fixed sum, and the lessee expects a satisfactory return on his outlay: we shall encounter it again when considering the boroughs (p. 271).

Possibly it is this system, which obviously lends itself to exploitation, to which the *Anglo-Saxon Chronicle* refers when it tells us that 'the King gave his land as dearly for rent as he possibly could; then came some other and bid more than the other had before given; and the King let it to the man who had bidden him more, and the King gave it up to the man who had bidden most of all. And he recked not how very sinfully the reeves got it from poor men, nor how many illegalities they did.' DB, we are going to see, is full of passages showing that the rents received were often in excess of what was fair. It shows, too, that it was not uncommon for a premium – *gersuma* – to be obtained in consideration of a lease being granted. In Lincolnshire there is frequent mention of a *tailla*, and this seems to represent a sum paid by free and unfree alike in addition to the lessees' rents.

It is not uncommon, indeed, for DB to tell us that a manor is 'worth' so much, but that it 'renders' a higher sum. Harbilton (8a2), for example, is worth 60*s*., but 'is at farm' (*est ad firmam*) for £4. Here is one clear case among others of a sub-tenant (of Bishop Odo), renting a manor: we are not always told the estate is held *ad firmam*, but the expression used is simply *et tamen reddit* (e.g. Hoxley, 8b2). Sometimes, where *reddit* is used,

---

[1] But it is probable that frequently *valet* too indicates the actual amount of rent being paid.

we are not given the *valet*, and here it may be the rent was not in excess of a fair valuation. There are however two complications: first, the use in DB of *reddit* may imply that the manor was let 'at farm', but often we have no evidence that this is so; secondly, the fact that Odo was under arrest may mean that King William had let his demesne manors to those who would pay rents higher than the valuation, hoping none the less to make a profit out of the properties.

Sometimes, too, DB says nothing about a manor being rented or 'at farm', but other documents, such as the *Domesday Monachorum*, show that it was. Appledore (5a2) is in DB said to be worth £16 17s. 6d., but the *Dom. Mon.* (p. 71) shows that it is worth £12 but renders £16 17s. 6d. It is then very difficult to judge whether a DB valuation gives us all the facts, and by compression conceals the items which have gone to make up its valuation. When we find a sum additional to the valuation mentioned, the probability is that this is a premium for the lease, a *gersuma*, even though DB gives no other indication that the manor is being rented. Also, when we are told that payment is by weight of coin, or by assayed or counted coin, we may suspect that the manor is being rented.

But the information that DB gives us about values must often be deceptive. Other documents of the period show that when it says a manor was 'worth' so much, it was in fact producing a higher amount. Wingham (3b2), for example, has a value in DB and in the *Dom. Mon.* of £100, but in a schedule incorporated in the latter it is recorded that, in addition to a *firma* of £100, the manor is paying to the Archbishop of Canterbury a *gablum* of £29 10s. and also some customary dues of more than £3 (*Dom. Mon.*, pp. 83, 98).

DB does not regularly enable us to determine whether an estate was managed by a reeve or bailiff, or the nominee of its lord, or whether it was in the hands of an *entrepreneur*. Often we cannot be certain whether the sheriff, or some other royal officer, is administering royal estates by the King's order, or whether he has volunteered to farm them. We find sheriffs in charge of estates outside their own county (e.g. Harkstead, II.286b), and groups of manors with common origins administered by a steward (*dapifer* or *minister*). The Suffolk estates of

Earl Ralf passed after their confiscation to Godric the steward, and the same man administers (*servat, custodit*) a group of royal estates in Norfolk. Sometimes we find the *villani* of a manor renting it from its lord (p. 129); it is plain that the sheriff's officers (and doubtless the representatives of other men also) exacted the maximum where competition would not be acute. The *ministri* of Roger Bigot, sheriff of Suffolk, charged the free men who were in the soke of the manor of Bergholt (II.287b) with an unaccustomed rent, and his successor's *ministri* increased it. It is noticeable that a great many of the farmers of the royal estates, especially of those which have come into the King's hands through forfeitures, are men with English names, as though they are trying to hold on to former power and influence, and perhaps because their long experience of local conditions made them the most suitable of royal agents. But the obvious person to farm the royal estates was the sheriff, and it is he whom we find most often as concerned with them. Bromsgrove (172a2) had in King Edward's day rendered a farm of £18; King William's sheriff has been paying £24, 'so long as he held the woodland' – a certain source of profit. It may indeed be that almost everywhere the sheriffs were farming the counties as a whole: paying their customary commitments, general and individual, and renting the royal manors. Earl Roger is said to have 'the city of Shrewsbury and the whole county and the whole demesne which King Edward had, with twelve manors which the King had with fifty-seven berewicks belonging to them, and eleven manors also' (which he might well be farming). By way of farm these, together with the pleas of the shire and the Hundreds, are producing for the King £300, and 115s. which may be the premium for their lease the Earl is paying. The farming of the shires may be referred to in a passage which records that 'this land was thegnland but after was converted into reeveland' – land, perhaps, appropriated by the sheriff – 'and therefore the King's delegates say that this land and the rent which comes from it was illegally stolen from the King' (181a2).

Leases

Leases, for a space of from one to three lives' duration, we have already encountered (p. 139), and while DB records them infrequently, their terms are occasionally noted, especially where a newcomer had succeeded to a lease as ostensible heir of an Englishman, for the grantor was anxious to recover his property at the appropriate term. Thus it is stressed that at Wadborough (175a2) Urse, sheriff of Worcestershire, is the 'third heir', for Westminster Abbey hopes to recover the estate at his death or disgrace.[1] Of the financial side of such leases we are told little, but there was small point in granting a lease if both sides did not profit from it. A lease might be bought; it might be granted against a cash loan, or for services to be rendered; it was common to pay a premium to obtain it. The customary lease of pre-Conquest England had been one by which the landlord provided livestock and seed, but of this DB tells us nothing. Also, it conceals from us anything beyond the bare facts; that, e.g., William Hosatus was holding Charlecumbe of Bath Abbey (89b2), which a thegn had held of the Church. Documents in the Abbey cartulary show that William was paying £2 in rent, and 'was bound to go forth at the King's summons' (? to help the Abbey fulfil its quota of knight-service), to pay the King's geld, and to be 'faithful and obedient' to the Abbot. He had there at the time of lease ten oxen and sixty sheep, and 100 acres sown (or seed for that purpose). The Exeter Domesday (*186*) shows us that by 1086 the oxen had increased by two and the sheep by 140. The value had risen from a *valuit* of 50s. to £6. The Abbey was sure of its money and service, and William had obviously made a profit out of his bargain.[2] That such leases were granted in respect of demesne land is shown by the entry for Urchfont (68a2), where the reeve had leased two hides of the six hides of demesne land.[3]

---

[1] See also Selly Oak (177ai), Worthy (46b2).

[2] *Two Chartularies of the Priory of St. Peter at Bath* (ed. W. Hunt: Somerset Record Society, 1893, no. 33, pp. 37–8).

[3] On the termination of the lease, he returned all the stock to St. Mary of Winchester, who owned the manor.

Comparison of pre- and post-Conquest valuations

We must not then think that the generally higher figures of
1086 as against those of 1066 or an intermediate year indicate a
countryside become vastly more prosperous under its new
masters. Norman efficiency, or the combining of several small
estates into a single manor, may have made for an improved
economy, but the benefit was surely mostly, if not solely, the
lord's. Increased services, increased rents, would quickly
cause annual income and profit to appreciate. The information
of DB and other documents needs careful study before we can
draw conclusions. It is plain (e.g. from the Ely figures) that a
fall in manorial population did not necessarily cause a fall in
the valuation, but it must be remembered that this apparent
increase in value is often really the charging of a higher rent
from a tenant or farmer than that which had previously
obtained.

But any such increases in values had been neither continuous
nor consistent. When we are given figures for 1066 and 1086
and for some intermediate period, we can frequently see how
much the values fell in the turmoil of the Conquest and after.
They are often spectacular in the south-eastern counties, and
enabled Baring to trace what seem to be the movements of
the Conqueror's armies before and after Hastings and prior
to the surrender of London.[1] A number of estates are said to
have been 'waste' (*vasta*) 'after' (*post*) – that is, after King
Edward's death and the Conqueror's coming. Still more show
huge falls in value between 1066 and the second date concerned, with appreciation – often to a figure higher than that
of 1066 – by 1086. Mapped, they show the ravaging round
Hastings, the advance to the south bank of the Thames, the
great encircling horseshoe march into Hampshire and then
through Berkshire, Oxfordshire, Buckinghamshire, and Hertfordshire which ended at Berkhamsted. The tracks of supply
columns from Channel ports can also be seen.

Sharp declines in the Welsh marches, frequent reference to
the fact that a border estate had been waste, mark the ravages

[1] F. H. Baring: 'The Conqueror's Footprints in Domesday' (*EHR*, vol. xvii,
and *Domesday Tables*, pp. 207–16).

of Cymric tribesmen. Yorkshire, where manor after manor is waste, and without men or teams, displays the horror of the Norman punishment meted out to rebellious Northumbria; Staffordshire the passage of the army which crushed the revolt of 1069–70; Leicestershire the losses suffered in the campaign against the northern Earls in 1070–1. Even by 1086 some of the shires which had been sternly disciplined have not recovered, and mention of 'waste' is frequent. We receive occasional hints of external troubles also: nine south Devon manors were devastated by Irish pirates (*323*), and only a few have recovered former values.

We cannot, unfortunately, make any useful estimate of national prosperity or the reverse from the figures available. Comparison of entries shows that holdings with equal values do not display similar regularity as regards assessment, population, plough-teams or manorial appurtenances; the reverse is equally true. We cannot satisfactorily map the statistics, for the lack of uniformity in their presentation prevents us from knowing how to allot them. We do not, for example, know what changes in the composition of a manor may have taken place between any two of three dates implied, and often we may be given the value of a manor which since 1066 has been greatly enlarged.

Valuations of complex manors

Indeed, of the value of some holdings we know nothing. Sometimes we are given the figures for the components of a manor; sometimes it is said that the manor 'with its members' is worth so much (Bradley, 248b2). A combined value is given for Bocking with its berewick in Mersea, eighteen miles away (II.8). Holkham (II.170b) belonged to Burnham, and was valued there; that is, the value of Holkham was included in that of Burnham. We are told that the values of holdings are reckoned (*computatae*) or valued (*appretiatae*) in the parent manor (Thornage, II.192; Suffield, II.184b); that the individual values of a complex manor are 'in the price of' (*in pretio*) the *caput* of the manor (Kettleburgh, II.294).

But the individual values of components must have been known. The land of fifteen thegns had been added to the manor of Bovey Tracey (102a2, *504b*), and we are given its value – £4 2s. 6d. The value of Gappah (114bi) has apparently increased substantially; from 5s. to 30s. But fol. *502b* notes that the land of four thegns, worth 24s., has been added to the manor: the original manor has accordingly increased in value only from 5s. to 6s. Many spectacular differences in value may be because the 1066 figure is that of the manor as it was, that of 1086 as it is.

Artificial values

Some figures are plainly artificial. Many large East Yorkshire manors, each the headquarters of an extensive soke, are all said to have been worth £56 T.R.E.[1] They cannot all have been worth precisely the same sum, and the figure possibly represents a fixed rent, the tenant obtaining as profit the difference between it and his actual receipts. In 1086 they are mostly said to be worth, since the harrying of the north, only £6 or £10. In Wessex the manors on the ancient royal demesne, mostly unhidated and paying no geld, and once furnishing the whole or a proportion of a night's farm, are said to be worth or to render sums which are often very odd and never far from £100. Some of the Somerset groups of such manors pay £106 0s. 10d., others £100 10s. 9½d., one £105 17s. 4½d.; Hampshire groups in King Edward's day paid £115 5s. and by 1086 other groups £104 12s. 2d. Some payments have increased one penny less than 10,000d.[2] Of two such Wiltshire manors, one paid £100 and the other £110. The Cambridgeshire manors of King Edward pay sums varying from £10 to £25 plus the sum of £13 18s. 4d., a cash commutation for former renders in corn, honey, malt, etc., which represented three days' provisions for the royal household.

Other manors too had their renders fixed according to a now undiscoverable principle. It was Round who first noticed that the 'comital manors' of Somerset, the possession of which went with the earldom of Wessex, nearly all rendered, 'of

---

[1] £56 is half £112 – a figure which also appears – and 112 is the number of pounds in a 'hundred'weight.

[2] e.g. Barton Stacey and Broughton (38bi) seem to have paid one *feorm* of £115 5s. which rose to £156 18s. 3d.

white silver' a multiple of 23*s*. Crewkerne rendered forty of
these units, Congresbury twenty-five, Creech St. Michael
eight, Capton two.[1]

Renders in kind

A considerable number of manors, many of them royal, had
customary dues to furnish in addition to the rents and renders
valued in sums of money. Certain Gloucestershire manors
(162b2) were valued at £20 but also had to provide cows and
pigs; formerly they had had to provide honey, wheat and
barley also. These had also had to provide 3,000 loaves for
the hounds, a due commuted for a payment of 16*s*. Quenington
(167b2) had to furnish ploughshares; Kingston (179bi) had to
find a hawk; at Bach (187ai) eight Welshmen had to find a
hawk and two dogs; at Clun (258a2), two *animalia* (cows) were
required. Leominster (180ai) was worth £60, and it was said
that it would be worth £120 if it were freed from the claims
upon it – it had to maintain the nuns of a dissolved abbey.
The provision of salt, in Worcestershire and Cheshire, is a
frequent duty.

Some manors, also mostly royal, received customary payments from other manors. Axminster (100a2), for example,
had 30*d*. from Honiton and the same sum from three other
manors, but 15*d*. from Charton.

With renders in kind, especially with eels from fisheries and
mills, and with salt, we have dealt in part when considering
manorial appurtenances (pp. 183–5), and burghal dues will
be considered later (p. 271). But there are a few aspects of
these which are often more or less coupled with the stated
value of a manor; these were evidently supplementary. Honey
figures prominently in many shires: it is reckoned in terms of
the sextary or sester.[2] At *Sutreworde* (111b2) five beekeepers

---

[1] *FE*, pp. 111–2. It is probable that all are multiples of this sum, but that some
figures are defective.

[2] The extent of the sextary, used to measure both dry and liquid substances,
and which was a proper fraction of a *modius*, perhaps a peck, is not known with
certainty. There may have been six or eight sextaries to the *modius*, the equivalent
of twelve quarters. The sextary may have been the same as the horse-load known
as the seam or *summa*, the equivalent of a *mitta*, or of two *ambers*. All the quantities,
and others, appear intermittently in DB.

rendered seven sesters of honey, and the sheriff of Herefordshire received dues of honey and sheep by virtue of his office
and tenure of the manor of Linton (179bi). The largely Welsh
district of Archenfield had to produce 41 sesters of honey, and
the penalties for concealment of its existence are specified
(179a2, 181ai). Tawland and Parford (117bi, 116b2) had to
find an ox, or 30d. in lieu thereof, for the manor of South
Tawton. Ewes, or ewes each with its lamb, appear occasionally,
e.g. at North Bradon (92ai, *268b*, *269b bis*), or Bossington
(*119*, *510*), and while the value varies, here a dozen were
reckoned at 5s. Kempsford (169ai) rendered 120 weys of cheese,
presumably from ewes' milk. A render of ten sesters of wine
had been paid at Lomer (43ai,2) in King Edward's time. A
most varied collection of renders in kind from royal manors in
Bedfordshire is recorded (209a2,bi), and the accounts mention
additional payments imposed by the sheriff.

We hear too of renders of iron; each free man at Bickenhall
(92a2) and some other Somerset manors rendered a bloom of
iron, and one of the seven villeins at Alford (*277b*) eight blooms.
Pucklechurch (165a2) had to produce ninety 'masses' of iron.[1]
Ploughshares are a not uncommon contribution, e.g. from
certain Isle of Wight holdings (entries following Adgeston, 39bi,
Aviston, and Scottlesbrook, 53a2). In the Bistre entry (269a2)
we are told what King Gruffyd ap Llewelyn received when he
visited the manor – loaves, capons, vats of beer, and butter.
At High Ercall (253b2), when the lady of the manor (Earl
Edwin's wife) visited it, eighteen ounces of pence had to be
found: a similar entry (*Lene*, 179b2) adds 'that her heart might
be glad'.

Renders for parts of manors

Sometimes the payments are for use of a particular part of the
manor. The wood at Eling (38b2) rendered 280 swine and three
sesters of honey; fifty acres of pasture at Whitestaunton (265b)
four blooms of iron; the wood and pasture at Guiting (167b2)
forty hens. Charlton Horethorne (97ai) is said to have rendered
ten bacon-pigs and one hundred cheeses, and no value is

---

[1] The modern equivalent of the 'mass' and 'bloom' are not known.

recorded for the manor, but the latter was probably accidentally omitted. At King's Somborne (39bi) 17s. was received
from the pasture, and 10d. *de herbagio* – the latter may imply
grazing on meadowland. While few, if any, villages can have
been without the common pasture and wood and meadow on
which their beasts depended, here and there – perhaps more
generally than stray Domesday entries would suggest – the
lord was getting rents and dues for the villagers' privilege of
feeding their beasts on what seems to have been regarded as
his private property. It may be that often such dues were
included in the valuation given to the manor, and so we do
not hear of them. We read, for example, only thirty-seven
times of pasture in the account of all Hampshire. Every village
must have had some pasture; did the villagers pay for its use
only in these places?

Miscellaneous information

Some strange pieces of information appear in these valuations.
The reeves of Chedworth and Arlington (164ai) seem to have
'paid what they would' in 1066, but the value in 1086 was £40.
One of the Slaughter manors (162b2, 163ai) 'paid what it
would' to the sheriff in 1066, and so could not be valued. At
Droxford (41bi), 'the gain arising from the land' is mentioned;
Round thought this implied a rent. It is hard to see why
Shepshed in Leicestershire (230b2) should have had to pay £6
in rent, by the order of the Bishop of Bayeux (perhaps when
Odo was acting-regent) for the service of the Isle of Wight.[1]
Thistleton is said to be worth £3 on fol. 293bi, 50s. on fol.
358bi, where it is reckoned as part of South Witham: this
suggests independent reports from Rutland and Lincolnshire
witnesses.

Once we are given an account of the perquisites of a sheriff,
either from the estates he held in his official capacity, or by
way of profit between what he paid to the King for the privilege
of farming the shire and his actual receipts (69a2). Edward of
Salisbury obtained, among other things, 130 porkers and 32

---

[1] The island suffered much from piratical raids – including those of the House
of Godwine between 1062 and 1066 – and may have needed special revenue.

bacon-pigs, 480 hens, 1,600 eggs, 100 cheeses, 240 fleeces, and 162 acres of unreaped corn. But when the reeves could not produce all the rents due from the manors under their charge, Edward had to make up the deficiency from his own lands. It is perhaps a silent commentary upon the uncertainties of medieval rural economy.

CHAPTER XIV

The King's Geld

THE history of early taxation can never be written satisfactorily. How early 'gelds' were levied is uncertain: many must have been for some special purpose, and among these were those recurrent impositions collected to buy off Danish armies, which would in themselves be sufficient to worsen the economic position of much of English society. Only three times is the levy mentioned for the reign of the Conqueror; the *Anglo-Saxon Chronicle* notes that heavy taxes were imposed in each of its first two years, and one of 6s. upon each hide in a year it gives as 1083-4. The geld, as Professor Galbraith has suggested, was however probably 'a normal, almost annual tax', not an intermittent one.[1] Over and over again DB styles it 'the King's geld': the Inquest's investigations into liabilities, immunities, and payments were thus in the royal interest.

But DB says little of the geld except as regards this. We hear of 'the common geld which no one escapes' (30ai), and of a 'general' geld (*comuniter*), which in King Edward's day seems in Berkshire to have amounted to 7d. per hide, paid in two equal instalments before Christmas and at Pentecost (56bi). We hear too of the *herdigelt* which 'all this land renders' (28ai), which may have been the *heregeld* levied to pay the professional regular army, which in 1051 King Edward is said to have abolished.[2]

The imposition of assessments

At what date definite assessments for service and taxation were allotted to land-units is unknown. There is a very early

---

[1] This seems to receive confirmation from the entry which says that houses in Stafford gelded each year – *Rex habet de omnibus geldum per annum* (246ai).

[2] The *heregeld*, however, is sometimes equated with Danegeld: see Lennard: *Rural Eng.*, p. 167, note 1.

I.D.B.

document, known as the *Tribal Hidage*, which credits large numbers of 'hides' to the territory of peoples such as the South Saxons and the East Angles, and smaller quantities to the 'dwellers in the Peak', the 'men of Lindsey', etc. The amounts are far too large to be directly related to the figures of DB or of intervening documents, but they do suggest a mode of reckoning which endured for many centuries.

In any case, as tribal war-bands coalesced, as the kingdoms of early England were consolidated, and as the country came under the direction of a single monarch, revisions of assessments would be inevitable. Round proved beyond doubt that at some unknown period a certain round number of hides were allotted to the individual shire, and that the shire apportioned these among the districts known as Hundreds and the Hundred divided its quota among its vills.[1] There is a document, perhaps of the eleventh century (though its origins may be of earlier date), known as the *County Hidage*, which gives the hidages of thirteen shires in round numbers – 500 for Staffordshire, 1,200 for Worcestershire and Bedfordshire. It is suggestive that the number of hundred hides is often that of the Hundreds in 1086. Maitland pointed out that Northamptonshire is here said to be of 3,200 hides, and that in a geld roll for the county of 1072/8 there are twenty-two Hundreds, two double Hundreds, and four 'Hundreds-and-a-half', and $22 + 4 + 6 = 32$.[2] It is true that the figures for some shires display no sort of relationship, but we are going to see that between the date of this document and 1086 some shires altered in composition, some received reductions in their assessment, and that the composition of many Hundreds changed appreciably.

How equitable the original rating was we have no means of knowing, but by the eleventh century it had certainly become far from fair. Wiltshire had then round about 4,000 hides; Dorset, with about two-thirds of Wiltshire's acreage, some 1,700 hides less. There is no great difference in the sizes of Kent and Sussex, but Kent stands at just over 1,200 sulungs

---

[1] Round: *FE*, pp. 36–69.

[2] Maitland: *DBB*, p. 458. The 'Hundred' was never necessarily of 100 hides. In DB we find the 'Hundred and a half' of Freebridge (II.109b), the 'half-Hundred' of Earsham (II.125), the 'two Hundreds' of Ely (191bi, 192ai).

while Sussex has nearly 3,500 hides, though the sulung probably represented double or almost double the notional extent of the hide. DB shows us vills each rated at five hides with vastly differing populations and resources. Economic fluctuations must have violently disturbed any original pattern, blunting decimal and duodecimal quantities, and causing grave distress by reason of assessments no longer equitable.

Round pointed out, too, that certain principles seemed to govern the assessments of the shires. Using the Pipe Roll figures of 1130 for the number of hides and the total liability without exemptions, he found that ten counties would be due to pay at the rate of about $£\frac{1}{7}$ per square mile, and a block of adjacent shires – Bucks., Oxon., Berks., and Wilts. – at $£\frac{2}{7}$ and that Middlesex showed an almost comparable figure. But the remainder do not fit into the pattern: Nottinghamshire and Derbyshire's rate was only $£\frac{1}{17}$, Staffordshire's $£\frac{1}{27}$. Round decided that uniformity coincided with the sphere of West Saxon influence.[1]

Round's establishment of the method employed in distributing quotas of 'hides', and of the decimal and duodecimal principles involved, was a major discovery. Previously it had been argued that the hide roughly represented an area of 120 acres, and much labour had been spent on trying to reconcile the acreages of parishes as they were in the nineteenth century with the given number of hides at 120 acres for each, making some allowance for the waste – upland, moor, marsh, and unpenetrated woodland – and the unproductive portion of the village territory.

Decimal assessments and reductions

Round discovered that over much of England the total assessment of a village was five hides or a multiple thereof, and that villages with non-decimal quantities could often be combined to give a decimal figure. The Cambridgeshire Hundred of Staine, for example, consisted of five villages each rated at ten hides; elsewhere Whittlesford and Sawston, the one of twelve, the other of eight hides, formed a 20-hide unit. Codicote

[1] Round: *FE*, pp. 93–7.

and Long Stow together counted for five hides, in the proportion 1¾ : 3¼; 25 hides had been divided equally between
Eversden, Kingston, and Toft-with-Hardwick. Each individual
holding in a village had its own assessment; the vill of Hasling-
field is said to consist of twenty hides, and therein were eight
holdings, rated thus:

	Hides	Vir.	Ac.
DB fol. 189b2	7	1	0
197a2	5	0	0
200bi	3	0	0
200bi	1	3	0
194bi	1	0	15
194bi	0	2	0
194bi	0	0	12
ICC fol. 106b2[1]	1	1	3

It looks as if the Wiltshire villages of Teffont and Swallowcliff
together formed a 15-hide block; Teffont (70a2) was an un-
divided vill and was rated at 6½ hides, and at Swallowcliff the
nunnery of Wilton had 4¼ hides and two King's thegns 2⅞ and
1⅜ hides respectively (67b2, 73bi).

Round further pointed out that where the ICC indicated a
reduction of assessment, this, with very few exceptions, was at
a uniform rate. In Armingford Hundred, for example, its
total of just one hundred hides had been reduced by 20%, and
all its villages had been re-assessed in the same proportion – the
ten-hide vills becoming of eight hides, the five-hide vills of four.[2]
Since the number of ploughlands and the values of villages in
1086 vary so appreciably, and bear no relationship to the
number of hides, it follows that assessment was not dependent
upon area or value, but had been arbitrarily imposed by the
authorities. But no doubt, at the time of initial assessment, this
was not determined without reference to the equipment and
prosperity of each village.

Round and others found evidence of the five-hide unit over

---

[1] The final holding was omitted from D.B

[2] DB, as Galbraith points out (*MoDB*, pp. 127–8, 132–3) does not indicate
these reductions. Apparently irreconcilable figures elsewhere may also be
attributable to DB's silence.

a great part of England. Of the system of reductions of assessment disclosed by Cambridgeshire being applied elsewhere there is proof to be found in the Northamptonshire record. The shire, the *Anglo-Saxon Chronicle* tells us, had been cruelly ravaged during the descent upon it in 1065 of the Northumbrians in protest against Earl Tostig's misgovernment. We have said above that it appears to have been assessed originally at 3,200 hides, and the geld account of 1072/8 gives it $2,663\frac{1}{2}$. In DB it has only about 1,356. But Round, and Baring also, demonstrated that 'the ploughlands of the Northamptonshire Domesday are not ploughlands at all, but represent the old assessment before this great reduction'. They had noticed that in one part of the county the hides were 40% of whatever the number of ploughlands was, in another 50%; in a third the percentages are irregular, but most figures display reductions. It must be that the Hundreds had been empowered to relieve ravaged villages of burdens become insupportable, in proportion to their distress. We find different ratios, and sometimes no evidence of reduction, because the disaster would not have affected the whole shire equally.

The administrative and fiscal units of the Danelaw

But not all England had been what DB sometimes describes as 'divided into' or 'numbered by' hides. In the shires in which Danish influence had been paramount – those of York, Lincoln, Nottingham, Derby, and Leicester – and occasionally in other shires, which suggests that the composition of these may have altered by 1086, the unit was the carucate. This was also arithmetically of 120 acres, and was divided into eight bovates or oxgangs. The administrative unit is here the wapentake, not the Hundred. The component fractions of the townships, dispersed over DB, total three or six or nine or twelve carucates – a duodecimal instead of the decimal five-hide system.

As with the five-hide system, we find assessments, but here a multiple of six carucates, allotted to a group of villages; e.g. twelve had been shared (338ai) by Gedney (8) and Lutton (4). We find, too, that the various holdings in a village, dispersed over the folios of DB, make a duodecimal total; e.g. at Ludford we have

fol.	carucates	bovates
351ai	—	5
354a2	1	6
354a2	3	—
354a2	—	2
356b2	—	2
364a2	—	1
	6	0

This principle too was one of Round's discoveries, and he noticed also, from collation of DB with early twelfth-century Surveys, that in the Danish districts twelve carucates or a multiple thereof made a 'hundred' and that each wapentake contained a varying number of 'hundreds' – in Lincolnshire we have Yarborough with 14, Horncastle with $6\frac{1}{2}$, Ludborough with 3. The equation is even given in DB:

> In Alstoe Wapentake are two hundreds; in each there are twelve carucates for geld (293bi).

In Leicestershire we have 'hundreds' of, e.g., 36, 42, and 48 carucates, and also a 'hide' of 18 carucates, while in the district between Ribble and Mersey we are told that 'in each hide are six carucates of land' (269bi).

The arithmetical relationship seems to vary with the county, but there can be no doubt that we have here an artificial system of assessments and administrative groupings, possibly reflecting a transformation of an Old English organisation by Hundreds and hides into that of the Danelaw, with its wapentakes and carucates. It looks too as if the ploughlands of DB may reflect some lost artificiality, for each of the 'hundreds' of Alstoe has 42 of these, though DB says 'in each there can be 24 ploughs' (see p. 107). There must have been some basis governing the relationship between the carucates for geld and the ploughlands; it was Taylor's contention that it was dependent not on the whole amount ploughed in any year, but the quantity ploughed in the individual open field.[1]

Yet another indication of artificialities is the recurrent

---

[1] Isaac Taylor: 'The Ploughland and the Plough', in *Domesday Studies*, vol. I, pp. 143–86. For Round's theories, see *FE*, pp. 69–90, 196–214: see also the *VCH* for the relevant shires.

appearance in the north of units of twelve carucates in groups of seven.[1]

We do not know whether an older system of hides and Hundreds, Mercian or Northumbrian, was on the settlement of the Danelaw reconstituted by Scandinavian settlers in terms of carucates and wapentakes. We may think so, since in DB we find occasional hides in the carucated areas, and in Cheshire, an hidated but strongly Danish district, the occasional bovate.

East Anglian assessments

In East Anglia yet another artificial system had determined the liability of the individual holding. DB never tells us the number of hides at which a Norfolk or Suffolk village or holding is rated, and here the carucates recorded seem to represent the ploughlands. The villages had in each Hundred been grouped together in 'leets', and where a village was responsible for the geld of an area which must often have gone far beyond the bounds of the place named, we are simply told that when the Hundred has to pay twenty shillings of geld, the village named contributes so many pence to the required sum. Presumably it was the collecting centre for the area. Again, the amount stated bears no proportional relationship to the carucates, to the values, or to the dimensions which we are given for certain vills. As elsewhere, villages were grouped to discharge their responsibilities; there were twelve groups in Thingoe Hundred, of from one to three villages, and each group contributes twenty pence, or very near it.[2] The individual holdings are reckoned in terms of carucates and acres, and as the dimensions of some manors are given, it seems possible that these figures for the holdings indicate individual liability for geld, though owing to the impossibility of allotting their constituents to the manors or knowing when the lesser is already included in the greater, we can make no estimate of total assessment.[3]

[1] See *VCH: Lancs.*, vol. I, p. 272, and Round: *FE*, pp. 78–80.

[2] Tables showing the composition of leets and Hundreds and their liabilities are given in *VCH: Suffolk* and *VCH: Norfolk*; the arrangements for one Hundred are demonstrated in Round: *FE*, p. 100.

[3] For East Anglian assessments, see D. C. Douglas: *The Social Structure of Medieval East Anglia*, pp. 55–6.

Changes in the original assessments

It is probable that when the initial allotment of hides was made every Hundred, or group of Hundreds, received a decimal quota. But, if so, there is scant sign of this by the time of the Inquest. For each of the five south-western counties we possess copies of abstracts of financial accounts for a year which is either that of the Inquest or very near it. The number of Hundreds with a round number of hides in this is comparatively small; for example, in Wiltshire Frustfield has $11\frac{1}{8}$ hides, Swanborough $183\frac{2}{3}$, Branch $108\frac{1}{2}$, Dunlow 28, and the number of Hundreds with a decimal quantity is only eight, and never do we find 25 or 50 or 100 hides. But that Downton had once been of one hundred hides is clear.[1]

For the changes in the composition of Hundreds there would be many reasons. Each new settlement, if it received an allotment of hides, each deserted village, would disturb the pattern. It might suit many a lord to transfer stray villages he owned to a Hundred in which his influence was paramount. The process was unceasing, and DB frequently shows it to us at work. Evesham Abbey had 65 hides in the Hundred of Fishborough, and this had to be made up into a true 'Hundred' by including 20 hides from the distant Hundred of Dodingtree and the 15 hides at which the city of Worcester was rated (175bi). One hide of the Wiltshire village of Idmiston (66b2) lay in Hampshire; Waleran the Huntsman took $1\frac{1}{2}$ virgates belonging to the Hampshire village of Wellow and 'put them in Wiltshire' (50ai). Henry de Ferrers joined two Oxfordshire hides with his Gloucestershire lands (157b2). Not a few villages lay in one shire, but were taxed in a neighbouring one.[2]

---

[1] Fol. 65bi. The borough of Huntingdon at one time gelded for 50 hides as being one-quarter of the double Hundred of Hurstingstone (203ai). Even the rapes of Sussex can be grouped in blocks of eighty hides (*VCH: Sussex*, vol. I, p. 360.

[2] Land at Kimbolton in Huntingdonshire, to which county it belonged, 'always paid its tax' in Bedfordshire (211a2); at Broadholm the land lay in Newark in Nottinghamshire, but 'the service of the villeins' belonged to Saxby in Lincolnshire (291bi).

The geld accounts of the south-western shires

There survive in the LE summarised accounts of the payment of geld at the rate of 6*s*. for each hide at two 'fixed terms', one of which seems to have been Lady Day or Easter.[1] Despite the *Anglo-Saxon Chronicle*'s mention of a geld levied at this rate in 1083–4, Professor Galbraith thinks that it belonged to 1085–6, and was connected with the Domesday Inquest.[2] Collation of DB with these geld accounts often seems to argue against this hypothesis, and it may be that the inquisitors, who throughout DB display their desire that no land should escape its liabilities, investigated the results of a 'mickle geld' of two years earlier. But the probability is that gelds were imposed both in 1083–4 and 1085–6. Certainly there is a similarity in the approach, and language, of DB to that of the geld accounts. In both we read of land which had 'concealed' its liability or been 'found' – discovered to be illegally absent from authority's list of geldable property – which suggests an enquiry into liability and payments. When in the geld accounts we read of evidence given about immunity just as we read in DB of evidence given before the Commissioners – 'the thegns say it belongs to Bempstone Hundred' (*77b*); the 'English' or the 'Hundredmen' testify that certain Cornish lands were exempt (*72–3*) – that these phrases are the result of an enquiry seems plain. Also, the collectors (who are sometimes noted as not having handed over all they should) have 'given surety', 'amended their fault' to *barones*, *legati regis*: this is the very language of DB.

These geld accounts, drawn up Hundred by Hundred (though in Somerset the manor occasionally appears as the unit and once the fief is the basis), tell us the number of hides in a Hundred, how many (and these are itemised according to holder) are exempt, how many have paid, and for how much, and (again itemised) who has failed to geld, and for how much. They are not altogether consistent in content and form; their arithmetic is frequently faulty, and it is often impossible to

---

[1] LE fols. *18b, 19, 19b, 20b*.

[2] V. H. Galbraith: 'The Date of the Geld Rolls in Exon Domesday' (*EHR*, vol. lxv,) reprinted with corrections in *MoDB*: see also Chapter VII of that work. Eyton and Round both took the date to be 1083–4.

harmonise them with DB. But they have proved to be of immense service in identifying Domesday place-names, and in reconstructing the composition of the Hundreds. The only existing parallel to them is a less detailed abstract of a Northamptonshire geld of 1072/8.[1]

'Inquest' and *'Geld-account'* Hundreds

Commentators have been puzzled because occasionally Hundreds are mentioned in DB which do not seem to be among those which were Inquest units and are not found as rubricated headings, and moreover are often not to be found in post-Domesday records. In Huntingdonshire we read of Hundreds of Cresswell (207a2) and of Kimbolton (206ai,b2) in addition to the four Hundreds which were clearly the inquisitors' units. A Bedfordshire Hundred of *Odecroft* is incidentally mentioned (209bi); in Derbyshire two wapentakes are noted 'for the existence of which we have no other authority'.[2] *Thunreslau* appears twice in the Essex folios (II.77, 79), and is not heard of again.

It seems probable that some shires at least were divided into more than one category of Hundred, one of which formed units for geld-collection, and one those of the Domesday Inquest: thus each may have possessed distinct functions concealed from us. We find in the LE two lists of Hundreds for each of three south-western shires (fols. *63–4b*). Their names are not always those of the geld-account Hundreds, and it looks as if certain geld-account Hundreds were composed of a number of Inquest Hundreds.[3] A Hundred of Purbeck is incidentally mentioned in DB (82a2), but it is not one of the Hundreds of the Dorset geld accounts. In Somerset, much of the eastern part of the shire is, so far as the geld accounts are concerned, in the Hundreds of Frome and Bruton. But these

---

[1] The best texts are those given in A. J. Robertson: *Anglo-Saxon Charters* (C.U.P., 1939), or *Eng. Hist. Docts.*, II, p. 483.

[2] *VCH: Derbyshire*, vol. I, p. 294.

[3] The Devon geld-account Hundred of Ermington is *Alleriga* in the second list. There seems to have been a Hundred of Walkhampton (first list) which was part of the geld-account Hundred of Roborough. One Devon list mentions Hundreds of *Hertesberie* and of Molland recorded nowhere else.

lists of Hundreds record Wellow and Kilmersdon as well as Frome, Wincanton and Blackthorn as well as Bruton. One large geld-account Hundred is that of Yeovil, but in the account of this is mention of the fact that a holding in it pays geld *in hundreto Liet* (*79*). *Liet* (Coker) is not a geld-account Hundred, but (also as *Lieget*) is in the Somerset lists of Hundreds, as are Tintinhull, Stone, and Houndsbarrow (Houndstone) – all post-Domesday Hundreds in the Yeovil neighbourhood. It is quite clear that for Inquest purposes these four, not Yeovil, were the units; the lands within each come in different and inconsecutive parts of each relevant fief.

Further evidence is furnished by the fact that some (but not all) of the Somerset lands of Bishop Giso of Wells, though scattered about the shire, are a unit for geld accounting: they are not styled a Hundred, but 'part of the land which belongs to the honour of his bishopric' (*78b*). But in the list of Hundreds are a number of places owned by the bishopric, e.g. Wellington, Wiveliscombe, and Wells itself, which we should expect to give their names to Hundreds, and the structure in DB of the Bishop's fief does not suggest that this artificial agglomeration of properties was an Inquest unit, but merely one for payment of geld. Moreover, in DB all the holdings in a Hundred in the individual fief do not always come together; e.g. in Surrey. This could be either because the entire account of a Hundred was not always available to the compilers of the initial draft of Domesday, or because what goes by the name of a single Hundred in DB was sometimes two or more administrative or fiscal units. Occasionally, in the geld accounts, we find two Hundreds treated as one; e.g. those of Cutcombe with Minehead, or Braunton with Shirwell.

Geld-liability in Domesday Book

The IE'S list of questions includes 'how many hides are there?' Obviously it was considered to be essential to record the total liability for geld of each holding. The answer forms the opening statement of most Domesday entries. In some shires it is particularly clearly expressed: 'In Y Z had (*or* W has) *n* carucates (assessed) to the geld', or 'in the time of King Edward Y gelded (*or*, defended itself) for *n* hides'. In some, though geld is not mentioned, the implication is similar: 'Z holds Y for *n* hides', or 'there are *n* hides'.[1]

But a great many entries do more than give us the total assessment of a manor. These tell us at how many hides or carucates or sulungs some, if not all, of the components of a complex manor were rated, or indicate the assessments of pre-Conquest manors which by 1086 had been absorbed into or amalgamated with a different manor. Sometimes we can determine these by comparing an Exeter Domesday entry with the corresponding passage in *Terrae Occupatae*. But DB is often deceptive about geld-liability. Not infrequently the liability of a holding is given without any indication that this is already reckoned elsewhere in that of a manor of which it is a component. Trow Farm (73a2) is said to be rated at $7\frac{1}{2}$ hides. But this is Richard Poingiant's holding, illegally acquired, in the manor of Chalke (68ai), whose 77 hides include these $7\frac{1}{2}$, and in the account of which it is mentioned. Another instance is the Bishop of Coutances's holding at *Millescota* (*147b*), duplicated in the account of the Glastonbury manor of Mells (*168*) out of which it had been taken.

The relevant authorities naturally knew the individual liability of the possessor of every constituent of a manor, and of the *villani*, who did not normally possess holdings other than their share in the common fields.[2] Indeed, in some shires, while individual holdings are rarely recorded, we are told that so many villeins – and, on occasion, bordars also – have so many hides or virgates, and we may think the quantities represented their geld-liability. That the total of the figures for the holdings often does not coincide with the hidage of the manor suggests that the amount of cultivated land has increased since the time of the original or of the latest assessment. If there had been no exemptions from the geld (an aspect we shall be discussing almost immediately), the geld of a manor would be made up thus: the demesne, which was usually a substantial portion cultivated for the lord and in which the peasantry

---

[1] These formulae recur in, e.g., (a) Derbyshire, Lincolnshire, (b) the south, (c) Middlesex, Bucks., (d) Warwickshire, Staffs.

[2] See D. C. Douglas: *Feudal Documents from the Abbey of Bury St. Edmunds* (London, 1931).

had no share except that of labour upon it, would pay its quota; any sub-tenancies would pay their quotas; and the remainder would be discharged in accordance with each man's share of what is called the *terra villanorum*, for there was no equality of holding, no parity of numbers of strips in the common fields. Also, the higher a peasant stood in the social and economic scale, the larger his holding was likely to become.

Had the original arrangements persisted, Anglo-Saxon England would have been gelding for something like 70,000 hides. But they had not. Some manors had never paid; e.g. the twelve hides of Glastonbury (90ai), the chief holy place of Wessex. Of many royal manors, especially in Wessex, we are told that they 'never gelded'. Now 'never' may mean 'not within the memory of man', but it is probable that these, which for the most part are said to have paid the *feorm* of one night or a contribution thereto, had been exempted because they had this burden and perhaps other liabilities. The formula varies: 'it never gelded, therefore it is not known how many hides there might be'; 'it never gelded nor was divided into (or numbered by) hides'; 'they have not said how many hides there might be'; 'they did not give an account of the hides'; 'they cannot tell us the number of hides'.[1]

Other manors enjoyed what we style 'beneficial hidation', the grant of immunity from a proportion of their assessments, often because they were the Church's property. The classic example is Chilcombe (41ai), where an estate of one hundred hides was permitted to defend itself for a single hide.[2] As a rule we are not told when these privileges were first bestowed, but it is clear that many date from long before the Confessor's reign. Four of the twenty hides at Wenlock (252bi) had been 'quit of geld' since Cnut's time.

But not all these benefits had been bestowed because the land belonged to Holy Church. Fareham (40bi) was a manor of the Bishop of Winchester, but its assessment had been reduced from 30 to 20 hides because of piratical raids – 'by reason of

---

[1] The formulae are mostly found in Wessex; see especially fols. 38ai–b2.

[2] See Maitland: *DBB*, pp. 449, 496. The manor included land in a dozen villages.

the Vikings, for it is by the sea'.[1] The rating of Chippenham in Cambridgeshire (197a2) was halved because its contribution to the *feorm* was too great for it to bear. We see, too, King William lowering liability (Cowerne, 186a2), and confirming reductions made by King Edward (Alverstone, 165a2). Here and there the Church seems to have been granted the privilege of receiving what DB normally calls 'the King's geld'. The Cornish lands of St. Petrock 'never paid geld except to the Saint' (205); St. Michael had the geld of *Treuthel* (258b); and the Bishop of Worcester that from Hampton (174ai). The newly-founded Abbey of the Battle seems to have collected geld from its lands, but not paid it over to the King.[2] When £1 was levied on the Hundred for geld 'there went from the town' (of Bury St. Edmunds), 'sixty pence towards the provision of the monks': they were getting one-quarter of the geld (II.372).

Demesne land

Moreover, demesne land seems to have been exempt, at least upon occasion, from payment. How often, or how regularly, this was so, we do not know. But in those geld accounts mentioned above, and in the Northamptonshire earlier account, land *in dominio* was certainly treated as exempt, and in the south-western shires represented at least one-third of the total assessment.[3] The privilege of not paying for land which was in demesne may initially have had to be offered by a monarch in return for the support of his magnates which otherwise would not have been forthcoming. It is suggestive that it had apparently become traditional and that the Conqueror did not see fit to revoke the privilege.

Intermittently in DB, but regularly in the Exeter Domesday, we are given the hidage of land *in dominio*. But this is not always the same quantity as that indicated by the geld accounts. Upon occasion it is; e.g. the Bishop of Salisbury owned the entire Hundred of Ramsbury, which was assessed at 90 hides,

---

[1] Pirford (32a2) had its assessment reduced from 27 to 16 hides 'because Harold so pleased', but the Hundredmen had never seen or heard the King's writ sanctioning this.

[2] *VCH: Sussex*, vol. I, p. 375.

[3] In Northamptonshire it is the 'inland' (see p. 258) which is exempt.

of which 30 did not pay geld because they were in demesne. In DB the manor of Ramsbury, which occupies the whole Hundred, also has 30 hides in demesne.[1] But often, when we can with certainty identify the manors to which the geld accounts refer (these very rarely give the names of manors), the demesne of DB and the demesne of the geld accounts is not coincident, though frequently very nearly so. Sometimes, however, this is not the case. William of Mohun is in the Dorset accounts said to have in all 9 hides less 8 acres of geld-free demesne, but in DB he has 36¾ hides 28 acres *in dominio* in his various manors. The explanation is probably this: the geld accounts give us what we might call fiscal demesne, DB manorial demesne. No doubt both were originally the same in quantity, and the amount exempt was regarded as traditionally fixed, irrespective of fluctuations in the quantity of demesne.[2] For many demesnes would alter in extent; here a portion of the *terra villanorum* would for lack of ability to maintain its status be taken into demesne; there portions of the demesne would be leased to tenants; some might go out of cultivation for lack of men to work it.

DB demonstrates to us this difference of quantity between fiscal and manorial demesne: in *Lega* (*363*), the Exeter Domesday tells us, is one hide of land, and it rendered geld for half a hide, and of this hide the owner has three virgates and one ferting in demesne. Here, we may think, manorial demesne has substantially increased from what it was when exemption was first granted. In Cornwall we are almost always given two figures for the hidage of a manor; it is recorded that there are so many hides there, but that it gelded for a smaller quantity: the difference is the amount of land in fiscal demesne, and when, as we usually are, we are given the quantity of (manorial) demesne, this is usually a different amount. At Pendrim (120a2) there is a hide, but it gelded for half a hide: there is, however, not half a hide in manorial demesne, but one virgate only; for Connerton (120a2) the figures are seven hides of

---

[1] Fols. *1, 7b, 13;* 66ai.

[2] The details of DB, IE and LE must make us think that, though DB gives information only spasmodically, the hidage of every individual holding was known. Surely the manorial authorities would need to know this.

assessment, of which three geld, and one is in manorial demesne. Exemption of fiscal demesne is at least as old as the Confessor's reign: of the 6½ hides at Helston (120ai) only two rendered geld in the time of King Edward.[1]

DB indeed often tells us of what can only be fiscal demesne. 'There are five hides (liable) for geld', it says of Monkland (*Leine*, 183a2); 'one of these did not geld because it was in demesne'. Again, at Street (184bi): 'there is one hide, half of which was in the King's demesne and does not geld; the other half gelds'. Of Calcutt (73bi) it is written: 'There are five hides. T.R.E. it gelded for half a hide. Of it (the manor) four and a half hides are in demesne'; moreover its owner has 4½ hides in (fiscal) demesne in the geld account for Staple Hundred (*1, 7, 13b*). Linkenholt (43a2) 'defended itself' *tunc* (i.e. T.R.E.) for five hides and now (*modo*) for one hide; the others, says DB, are in demesne. At Tawton (*118*, 101b2) there were twelve hides of which nine rendered geld T.R.E.; the other three the Bishop had in demesne, and they never gelded.

The shire jury seems to have given evidence at the Inquest about immunity, as we find it doing in the geld accounts. Three of the seven hides of Elmbridge (176b2) are 'quit of geld, as the shire testifies'. *Quieta* is frequently used in DB to indicate exemption of part of a holding from geld-liability (e.g. on fol. 163bi). Another phrase implying this immunity is 'free as belonging to the court' – exempt as being demesne (*libera ad curiam pertinens*: Sherborne, 175bi). At Nantwich (265bi) a house was quit because of its duty of furnishing salt: the Cheshire salt-wiches, indeed, were not assessed in hides, and were, as manufacturing units with other burdens, free of geld-liability. We hear even of so small a holding as four acres of meadow being exempt from geld (Offington, 346a2).

Occasionally we seem to be reminded that the exemption of demesne is to be regarded as a privilege, not as a right. Miswell (138ai) defended itself T.R.E. for 14 hides, and now does so for 3½: 'however, there are always 14 hides' – that is, 14 hides liable for geld if the full tale is exacted.

---

[1] Trewella in Feock (120bi) gelded for 2 hides, but 'there are 12 hides' there. Maitland (*DBB*, p. 410) for some unstated reason thought that the two figures indicated a general increase of Cornish assessments imposed by the Conqueror.

DB, too, may in the south-eastern counties tell us of demesne and its exemption where the formula does not at first sight suggest it. For the majority of holdings it tells us that they gelded for so many hides *tunc*, but geld now (*modo*) for what is usually, but not invariably, a smaller quantity. This was once taken to indicate that liability had been lessened on those manors which had suffered in the campaign and march encircling London which had ended with the Conqueror's acceptance as king. But, as Baring pointed out, there would be no need for the reduction of assessment to have persisted over twenty years, for the villages would recover from the passing of an army reasonably quickly, as is perhaps shown by their recovery of or improvement upon their pre-Conquest valuations.[1] It is significant that the manors for which two contrasting figures are given are usually demesne manors; that is, those without sub-tenants, kept by the lord in his own hands. A manor may, of course, have no land at all in demesne, and in such cases we should expect no reduction. But these instances of apparent reduction may really indicate that a manor gelded for so many hides before demesnes were ever exempted, but now, when they are, for a smaller quantity, so that the difference between the two figures is the amount of fiscal demesne (which is not necessarily the amount of manorial demesne of which we are sometimes also told). Sometimes the text – as in the instance of Linkenholt mentioned above – seems to make this clear. So, perhaps, does this: 'then there were ten hides, and the villeins who dwelt there gelded for five hides. Now the abbot has five hides in demesne, but (*sed* often seems to have the effect of no more than *et* = and) they have not gelded' (Alton, 43ai).

But the exemption of demesne land did not endure: this we may gather from collating the figures of DB with those of the Pipe Roll of 1130. Surrey had in all about 1,830 hides recorded in DB, and over 1,100 there seem to be exempt, but in 1130 it paid for 1,750½, and in 1150 for 1,798. Other shires show similar figures. Some exemptions may have persisted; Cornwall was paying on less than 100 hides at the time of the

[1] F. H. Baring: 'The Conqueror's Footprints in Domesday', in *Domesday Tables*, pp. 207–16.

18   I.D.B.

geld accounts, but of a little over 400 hides, only 227½ paid in 1150.

Even if assessments were not reduced after 1066 in the south-eastern counties, they seem to have been lowered elsewhere. In Cambridgeshire there is a crescent of Hundreds in which the assessment of every vill had by 1086 been reduced by 20%, a 10-hide vill becoming one of 8, a 5-hide vill of 4. No reason is given; the formula simply says that a vill defended itself formerly for y hides, now for z, and $z = 4y/5$. It might be because of damage sustained during the local revolts of 1070 and 1075, or on account of good service rendered at those times. The reduction indicated by the Northamptonshire ploughlands has already been mentioned (p. 106). The shire had been cruelly ravaged during the Northumbrian revolt of 1065, but this might have been the reason for an initial reduction from 3,200 hides to about 2,664, while the second one may have been granted in consequence of losses suffered during the turmoil of the Conquest.[1] If we can trust the figures of the County Hidage (p. 242), other shires also had been granted substantial reductions of assessment between the time of its origin and 1086. Shropshire, for example, has lost almost half its 2,400 hides.[2] But Staffordshire, which was in a deplorable state as a result of Norman ravagings following rebellion, has lost none.

Inland

DB tells us of other immunities from the geld. Here and there it refers to what it calls 'inland'; in the Northamptonshire geld account we are told how many hides are reckoned as inland in each Hundred, and it is made clear that this inland had not paid geld. Inland, then, is virtually the equivalent of fiscal demesne. It seems indeed to be the ancient demesne of a manor, the equivalent of our 'fiscal demesne', and the difference between this and 'manorial demesne' might be land annexed by the lord, perhaps from villeins' land, or by clearing the

---

[1] The revolt of Earls Edwin and Morcar in 1071 might have been the occasion.

[2] The evidence of charters suggests reduction: in 901 Easthope had three and Patton five hides: in DB they have two and one respectively (*VCH: Salop*, vol. I, p. 282, n. 15).

waste land, and added to the total demesne. A few passages confirm this: at Watereaton (158a2), besides the five hides at which the manor was assessed, the owner had 3½ hides of inland 'which never gelded'. At Berrington (254bi) two hides 'defended the land which was inland from the geld'. But occasionally we find both demesne and inland in a manor: at Deddington (155bi) there were 11½ hides in demesne 'besides inland'. Such a phrase confirms the supposition that the inland is the original demesne, quit of geld; the 11½ hides must be land which, once tenants' or villeins' land or unsettled and uncultivated, has been made episcopal and manorial demesne. DB quite often tells us that land which is properly *terra villanorum* has become demesne land or a sub-tenancy in the manor. Once, too, we are told (Cowley, 160b2), that there is one hide of *warland* in demesne, and 'warland' is the land which should be paying its *wara*, its 'defence' – 'defending itself' by paying geld; i.e. land *not* in demesne. *Wara* or *warnode* are terms not uncommonly found in DB; we hear of land *in warnode Drogonis*, land for whose geld Drogo was liable (Thistleton, 366a2), the *warnode* of ten acres of meadow (Pickworth, 377bi). The *wara* of the Hertfordshire manor of Weston lay in the Bedfordshire Hundred of Manshead (132bi): this and similar passages show us that a holding could be physically in one shire or Hundred but liable for geld in a different one, probably because manorial structure was constantly changing. Warland is the opposite of inland: when we are told that of the four hides at Offord (204b2) one is inland, we know that the other three must 'defend themselves', pay their *wara*. The inland of Newton, a berewick of the manor of Threckingham, is said to be 'in Threckingham'; (341bi); this must mean that there was no fiscal demesne land at Threckingham, but that the lord's demesne was at an outlier of the manor.[1] Expressions of this order are not uncommon in the eastern counties; in Stonham (II.350b), for example, were 50 acres of the demesne land of the 'hall' or manor of Creeting.

---

[1] The demesne of the royal manor of Braunton seems to have been at Totleigh Barton some miles away.

Carucatae non geldantes

It seems as if the Commissioners discovered, or had reported to them, land which had never been hidated, but which was not of the order of those unassessed royal manors which had been responsible for providing the *feorm* of one night. In DB and elsewhere there are noted, with varying phraseology, *carucatae terrae* 'which were not divided by hides and which never gelded'. The principal instances are in Wessex, and some are to be found in both DB and the geld accounts.[1] Those in Wiltshire are all in royal manors; in Dorset they are the Bishop of Salisbury's or Glastonbury Abbey's; in Somerset are represented land of the King, of the Bishop of Winchester, and of Glastonbury Abbey, the three islands in the marshes belonging to Muchelney Abbey, and the estate of St. John's Church at Frome.

These can hardly be ploughlands in the normal sense of the word, and indeed the ploughlands of the manor are separately recorded for each of the relevant entries. They represent, perhaps, grants of land or reclamations from the waste made after the original 'division into hides', and never assessed. They had not been paying geld, and presumably they appear in DB and geld accounts (and once in a Summary) because unless possession of them was notified at the Inquest there was a risk that continued possession of them would not be permitted or confirmed.

It looks as if land of this character had not infrequently to be reported, and it is possible that DB omits many other instances. 'Carucates of land', as distinct from hides, appear elsewhere in the south-western folios.[2] The Huntingdonshire estates of the Abbey of Ely (204ai) are said to have 'land in demesne for *n* ploughs besides the aforesaid hides'; in each case the quantity of manorial ploughlands is also given, and this demesne land seems to parallel the 'carucates which never gelded' of Wessex. We are told here, too, that 'in Hursting-

---

[1] Round discussed these in *Domesday Studies*, vol. I. Those in Wiltshire appear only in the geld accounts, and are ignored by DB. The phrase appears also in the Dorset Glastonbury Summary (*527b*).

[2] See, e.g., fols. *83b, 150b, 191, 191b, 435b, 437, 484*, and 65bi.

stone Hundred demesne ploughlands are quit of the King's geld' (203a2), and here and there that 'apart from' the hides recorded 'there is land for *n* teams in demesne' (e.g. Stukeley, 204a2). *Carucatae terrae* appear in the hidated county of Stafford (they are, incidentally, subdivided into virgates, not bovates), and appear intermittently elsewhere. At Clapham (212ai) there are 30 ploughlands, and also 'ten carucates of land in the demesne'; there is 'land for two teams' in addition to (*super*) 34 hides at Bramley (31a2). In Buckinghamshire there are four entries which record carucates of land in demesne additional to the hides mentioned.[1] Certain other phrases in DB must imply the same thing. Fawsley (219bi) is said to have 'inland for four teams' – the land had never been 'divided into hides'. But when we are told that at Eynsham (155ai) 'there is in demesne land for two teams of inland', we seem to have an unnecessary duplication.

Since it seems as if the hidages of the individual components or divisions of a manor were normally available, it appears that these holdings, expressed in terms of the carucate, were estimated in this way because they represented land occupied after the original assessment, or at times perhaps land which had formerly gone temporarily out of occupation and whose hidage had been forgotten.

Carucated land

In one part of the country, the Welsh borderland, the territory appropriated by Norman lords since the Conquest is inevitably expressed in terms of the carucate – 'the carucate as it is reckoned in Normandy' (162a2) – for, as it had not been Mercian land, it had never been hidated. But not all which is now in Wales is carucated, for some of this had long been English; places now in Radnorshire, e.g. Pilleth and Discoed (183b2, 186b2), the country around Montgomery (e.g. Leighton and Church Stoke, 255b2, 259bi), and that part of the Hundred of Atiscros which is on the Cheshire side of Wat's Dyke (268b2). But Rhuddlan (269a2), though it had never gelded nor been hidated, had been a manor of Earl Edwin of

---

[1] Turweston, Hanslope, Newport Pagnell, Tickford (fols. 151a2, 152a2, 148b2, 149ai).

Mercia, and resembles rather the royal manors of the south; its berewicks are reckoned in terms of land for so many teams. Where land was unsuitable for settlement, no reason for assessment existed; hence we read that most of Rhos and Rhufoniog in Arvester Hundred (269b2) was woodland and moorland, and could not be ploughed. The Welsh districts of Ewias and Archenfield did not geld, for they were not yet properly included in the shire system, though reckoned as part of Herefordshire, and were described in terms of the carucate, or of land for so many teams, and were under Welsh law and observing Welsh customs.[1] Beyond the Wye, west of Gloucestershire, penetration was so recent that we do not even find expression in terms of the carucate, but groupings of thirteen or fourteen vills under a reeve, furnishing food rents (162ai). Around the castles built in newly won territory to contain the Welsh, however, the extent of the lands forming the castleries are reckoned in terms of the carucate; e.g. for those of Caerleon (185bi), Clifford (183a2), and Ewyas (184ai).

Forest land

Land which was placed 'in the Forest' paid no geld. For the Forest is something outside (*foras*) the normal administrative framework, and an area in which the beasts of the chase are the first consideration implies an absence of cultivation, and often of inhabitants in a position to earn sufficient to be taxable. King Edward had given an estate at Dean (167bi) 'quit of geld, for the purpose of looking after the Forest'. Earl William fitzOsbern put two foresters 'outside his manor' (this probably implies acquittance of geld-liability, since the manor was the gelding unit) 'for the keeping of the woods' (Hanley Castle, 180b2). But it is naturally in the account of the New Forest that we are given the clearest picture. Fawley (41b2) had defended itself for two hides; now it does so for one virgate only, 'because the other seven are in the Forest'. Over and over again we are told land has been freed of geld-liability 'because it is now in the Forest'.

---

[1] See, e.g., How Caple (181b2), Westwood (181ai).

Ownership and liability for geld

DB occasionally seems to suggest that if a man could prove he had paid the geld of a holding unclaimed by anyone else, he was entitled to the land. The statements are indeed somewhat negative: Humphrey paid the geld of a virgate at Throcking (133bi), and yet did not have the land; Anschitil held an estate at Watton (136b2) under the Archbishop of Canterbury, but Earl Alan paid its geld, (it is listed under his fief, and it had been illegally taken out of the manor); Ralph Taillebois paid the *gafol* in a case where the occupier refused payment, and so became possessed of the land (Sharnbrook, 216bi). Peter de Valognes, sheriff of Hertfordshire, took an estate at Libury (*Stuterehele*, 141ai) as a forfeiture because its sokeman-holder did not pay the King's geld, so the 'men' (the Hundred-jury?) said. But the shire-jury said that it had always been quit of geld, which explains the failure to pay.[1]

The boroughs and the geld

Earlier Robert d'Oyly's holding 42 houses in Oxford 'as one manor' was mentioned (p. 50). This practice is intelligible enough when we remember that many of the boroughs were liable, though in varying degree, for the payment of geld. Those which were or had been manors of the ancient royal demesne often indeed were not; these are among those manors which never gelded or were divided into hides. It is never said that boroughs such as Wilton or Cricklade were liable for geld, but, though the geld accounts do not indicate geld liability on their part, this silence is evidently of no value, for they were extra-hundredal. Yet Shaftesbury gelded, for twenty hides, and as a borough Shaftesbury seems to be very much on a par with Wilton. Bath both gelded, 'for twenty hides when the shire gelded', and was intra-hundredal.[2] So was, or had been,

[1] But a passage in Heming's Cartulary states that four days' grace only was allowed for the payment of geld, and that after that period had elapsed anyone who discharged the liability could take the land for himself.

[2] It appears in the geld account for Bath Hundred. The phrase that a borough gelded 'when the shire gelded' is of common occurrence; e.g. at Worcester (172ai). It probably implies that boroughs had no immunity from geld but also no special liability for geld beyond that which the shire through its vills and manors had.

Northampton, for the twenty-five hides of *byrigland* in the Hundred of Spelho in its surviving geld account are those of the borough. Cambridge gelded 'for one hundred', and whether this implies one hundred hides or as many hides as the local Hundreds contained, we do not know; Bedford for half a hundred. Huntingdon had gelded for fifty hides, as being one-quarter of the double Hundred of Hurstingstone, but 'afterwards the King set a geld of money on the borough'.[1] The burgesses 'geld and render custom', and the 100 bordars here have to help them find the geld. Exeter's geld was a mere half-mark of silver, paid only when London, Winchester, and York gelded, and paid 'for the use of the troops'; similarly the Dorset boroughs' payments were 'for the use of the housecarles': there is perhaps an echo here of the *heregeld* (p. 241). Size and prosperity seem to have had little correspondence with assessment (Buckingham gelded for a solitary hide), but the low-rated towns may have had additional charges laid upon them of which we do not happen to be told. Stamford had had to geld 'for 12½ hundreds' – these are probably the 'hundreds', each of twelve carucates, we sometimes find among carucated, not hidated, shires – 'for the army and the navy and danegeld'. It is sometimes made plain that, unless special exemption had been granted, burghal property was liable for geld. St. Benedict of Ramsey had all the customary dues from his score of burgesses at Huntingdon, but care was taken to add 'except the King's geld', and to note from which Leicester houses the King was entitled to geld; this is true of a number of other boroughs also. Again, at Lincoln the Bishop has sake and soke and toll and theam over his *mansiones* and churches, but he does not get the geld, which these 'give with the burgesses', though one *mansio* is said to be 'quit of all things' while the other two 'geld with the burgesses'. In the account of York we hear much of the arrangements for geld. There are 84 carucates of land 'in the geld of the city', each one of which gelds 'as much as one house of the city', but we are not told for how much each house gelds.

The geld had no doubt been partitioned individually

---

[1] Does this mean that it was taken out of the Hundred and made responsible for a fixed sum of money?

between the property owners and the burgesses. Some land –
perhaps 'outside the borough' – was exempt from geld, as at
Torksey and Grantham. Torksey (337ai) was responsible for
one-fifth of the city of Lincoln's geld, and one-third of Torksey's
responsibility was allotted to the neighbouring manor of
Hardwick. We are sometimes told that 'of all these houses the
King has his geld', as at Leicester and Warwick (were some
others exempt?); the Bishop of Lincoln had two houses in his
see-town which were 'in the geld with the burgesses'. The
assessment of a borough seems to have been an inelastic
quantity: the English-born burgesses of Shrewsbury complain
that it is very hard on them that they have to pay geld just as
they did in King Edward's day, though 144 burgages have
been destroyed in the construction of the castle, are waste, or
have been occupied by French burgesses, and 39, which do
not geld, have been given to the newly-founded Abbey. Six
houses are waste in the tenth ward at Cambridge, but none the
less, they 'defend themselves'; their owners have to pay the
geld. But the owners of twenty houses at Bridport are so
destitute that they cannot pay the geld. At Lincoln, we are
given a long list of persons who 'have not given the geld as they
should have done'.[1] This too may in some instances be because
their houses had been destroyed, for the next paragraph says
that 'of the aforesaid wasted *mansiones* 166 were destroyed by
reason of the castle', but the number is far greater than that
of those who have not gelded.

---

[1] This suggests that the Inquest officials had been enquiring into payments of
geld.

CHAPTER XV

Other Sources of Revenue

THE obligations of the people of England, small and great, did not cease with the aspects of manorial duties or burghal obligations already outlined. In addition to their immediate duties to the lord of the manor on which they lived, to the rents and services they owed for the occupation of borough property, they had more general obligations to the ruler of England or to those notables to whom the King might grant privileges which in the first instance had been his alone. Of these one, as has earlier been indicated (p. 141), was the right to receive the fines exacted for breaches of the law. Of this, as of the corporate obligations of the shire or borough, DB tells us something, but, as with the accounts of the boroughs themselves, the information is sporadic and by no means complete.

The customary obligations of the shires

For some counties a few notes were included with a view to recording what rights and profits the King, and to a lesser degree the local earl and sheriff, were entitled to receive. Their inclusion, and the character of the information recorded, seems to depend very much upon the 'circuit'; in the east and the south-west nothing is said about these sources of revenue or local responsibilities. For the most part they appear at or towards the close of the entry for the principal borough in the county: this too rather suggests that the 'county' borough was the last unit to be considered by the inquisitors, and that they did so at a shire-moot held therein. The information they give, too, is similar to that for the boroughs themselves.

In Berkshire (56bi) one soldier (*miles*) had to be provided from each five hides if the King sent an army anywhere, and every hide had to give, not to the King, but to the soldier

himself, 4*s*. for his food and upkeep for two months.[1] If anyone
was summoned to the host and did not go, his whole land was
forfeit to the King: this was the penalty in Worcestershire
(172ai) also if he was 'so free a man that he had his sake and
soke'. However, if anyone found a substitute, and the substitute
failed to go, his lord was quit of blame on paying a fine of 50*s*.[2]
But if a Worcestershire man had a lord, and the lord had to
find a substitute, the lord was none the less liable to a 40*s*. fine,
and had to pay it over to the King. No doubt he recompensed
himself where he could.

A Berkshire man who slew anyone who was 'within the
King's peace' forfeited his body and all his goods to the King.
The same law was current in Oxfordshire, but here it is added
that if the offender could not be arrested he should be deemed
to be an outlaw, and anyone killing him obtained his goods.
Here, too, if a man killed another within his house or his
'court' (*curia*), the murderer's body, and all his goods, save his
wife's dowry, if he was married, were at the King's disposal. In
Worcestershire a man who wittingly broke the King's peace
was automatically adjudged outlaw, but if the peace had been
given by the sheriff, he paid a fine of 100*s*. In Nottinghamshire
and Derbyshire (280bi) a breach of the King's peace 'given
under his hand or seal' had to be compensated by a fine of £8
from each of eighteen 'hundreds', of which the King received
two-thirds and the earl one-third.[3]

If, in Berkshire, anyone 'broke the city' by night, the King
and not the sheriff had the consequent fine of 100*s*. In Oxfordshire, if anyone violently broke into the house or 'court' of
another and slew or wounded or attacked a man, a similar fine
was payable to the King. Housebreaking or assault on the
highway in Worcestershire involved the same sum; rape,
however, could not be atoned for by payment of a fine, but
only by surrendering the offender's body to justice. King
Edward had given the profits of fines to St. Peter of Westminster

[1] This saved the royal officials the trouble of collecting it, and making good
deficiencies.

[2] Failure to go with the host when warned cost an Oxfordshire or Warwickshire
absentee 50/–, payable to the King (154b2, 238ai).

[3] This was exacted in Yorkshire and Lincolnshire also. The 'hundred' is that
of twelve carucates.

where this church owned Worcestershire manors. But in the Hundred of Derby 'between Ribble and Mersey' (269b2) all three crimes, or an infringement of the King's peace, could be purged by a payment of 40s. Here, too, if blood was shed or a woman raped, or a man without reasonable excuse failed to attend the shire-moot, a fine of 10s. was exacted; only half that sum was payable for staying away from the Hundred-moot or for non-attendance at 'pleas' if the reeve so ordered. But it is noted that the owners of certain manors in this and other Hundreds were quit of all customary dues except six – the fines for breach of the peace, assault on the highway, house-breaking, theft, failure to attend at the deer-hays, and fighting after oath-taking, which cost 40s. They had also to pay the King's geld.[1] In Derbyshire and Nottinghamshire, if a thegn who possessed sake and soke forfeited his land, the King and the Earl between them had half his land and goods or stock (*pecunia*), and his lawful wife and legitimate heirs the remaining half.[2]

In Berkshire, when a thegn or a 'King's soldier' was dying, he sent his heir to hand over to the King, by way of heriot or relief, all his weapons, together with one horse with its saddle and another without. If the King would accept them, his hounds and his hawk, if he had them, also had to be handed over. In Derby Hundred the heir had to pay 40s. if he wished to succeed to his father's land; if he did not, the King got all the father's land and goods. In the northern shires, a thegn with more than six manors had only to pay the King £8 by way of heriot. But if he had six or less, he paid the sheriff three silver marks, whether he lived in the borough or not.[3] If a stranger lived in Oxford, and possessed a house, but died leaving no relatives, the King had all he owned.

A few times we are told of payments which elsewhere we find attached to a royal manor.[4] Worcestershire, through its

---

[1] Others were quit of geld and the forfeitures for bloodshed and rape, or of pannage-dues. Failure to pay a debt when the reeve so decreed is also mentioned.

[2] This suggests that concubinage and bastardy were common. The *VCH* translates *pecunia* as 'money'.

[3] This passage occurs for all the shires composing the northern 'circuit'.

[4] For example, the 'third penny' – one-third of the profits of justice – throughout Dorset was attached to the royal manor of Puddletown (75ai); the royal manor of Cleeve (86b2) had the third penny of the 'burh-right' of four Somerset Hundreds.

sheriff, rendered £17 by weight and (? or) £16 in counted coin, which were from the pleas of the shire- and Hundred-courts, and if it was not paid to him, he had to find it out of his own money. He was no doubt farming the borough and the royal demesne manors, from which he had to find £23 5s. from the former and £123 4s. from the latter.[1] The county of Oxford had to find a three nights' farm, reckoned at £150, and other payments, including £23 'for the hounds' and six sextaries of honey. Northamptonshire (219ai) also had to find a three nights' farm, but of £30 only by weight, and £42 'of blanched money at 20d. to the ounce for the hounds'.[2]

On fol. 1ai, after the account of Dover, we are told something of the customs which obtained in four of the Kentish lathes. The King received a 100s. fine if anyone narrowed the public way – the King's highway – by making a fence or a ditch, or let fall a tree standing outside the road and took branch or twig therefrom. If the offender went home and was not arrested, nor found a surety, it was the King's bailiff's duty to pursue him. We are told of 'forfeitures' which the King enjoyed over all the allodial tenants and their men, but he did not have the heriot of these in the lands of the Holy Trinity (Canterbury) and of SS. Augustine and Martin, or in those of certain named Saxons. The King, except in the above Church lands, had the man's fine in cases of adultery; the Archbishop had the woman's. The former had half of the goods of a man condemned to death for theft; from what has been said earlier, his heirs may have had the remainder. The men of certain lands in Wye had to guard the King for three days if he visited Canterbury or Sandwich; other dues are also mentioned. From certain other lands six days' service was required, but if the guard did not receive food and drink from the King as was laid down, it could go away without incurring any penalty.

One set of customs is especially full; those of the formerly Welsh district of Archenfield (179a2, 181ai), which was as yet

---

[1] He also had to find £16 – £5 of this for the Queen – but he could substitute a Norway hawk for £10 of it.

[2] The purpose of the dues, if not the amounts, are common to several counties, £10 for a hawk being frequently mentioned. Usually the shires of a particular 'circuit' record similar responsibilities.

not completely incorporated into Herefordshire. The priests of the King's three churches had to bear his messages to Wales and sing two masses for his soul each week. When one died, the King had 20s. from his estate. When a free man died, the King had his horse and his weapons, and an ox when a villein died. If a Welshman was convicted of stealing a horse or an ox or a cow, he had to return it upon conviction and then pay a 20s. fine; so did a woman. The theft of sheep or of a bundle of sheaves involved a 2s. fine. If a man of the King was slain, the guilty party paid the King 20s. as bloodwite or compensation for the loss of his services, and a further fine of 100s. for the commission of the crime was exacted. If it was 'another man's' thegn who was killed, his lord got only 10s. But if a Welshman killed a fellow-Welshman, the relatives of the deceased were to gather and despoil the slayer and his neighbours, and were permitted to burn their houses until noon of the burial-day. The King got one-third of the proceeds of the confiscation, and the aggrieved the rest, apparently tax-free (*quietum*). Anyone accused of burning a house had to bring forty men to his defence.[1] If he could not do so, he paid a fine of 20s. to the King. If anyone 'concealed' (i.e. failed to render) the customary due of honey, and his offence was proved, he had to render the quantity fivefold; apparently the ninety-six men above peasant status had to produce 41 sextaries. When the sheriff sent out a summons to the shire-moot, six or seven of the best men of the district were to go with him. Anyone who failed to do so forfeited 2s. or an ox to the King, and the same fine was exacted for failure to attend the Hundred-moot, and for failure to respond to the sheriff's summons to accompany him into Wales.[2] When the army went forth to war, the men of Archenfield formed the advance guard, and in retreat the rearguard. This was according to custom; and it is further stated that these were the customs and customary dues of the inhabitants of Archenfield in King Edward's day. They did not pay geld, or any render other than those mentioned above, except that they

---

[1] That is, he had to produce forty men to protest his innocence, or perhaps guarantee his fine would be paid. A survival of Celtic tribal law is suggested.

[2] Presumably this implies military service. If the sheriff did not go, none was bound to go.

had to pay 20s. 'for sheep' (for pasturage?) and 10s. for carrying loads, and to fight among the King's troops.

The reason for the inclusion of such information is that it was on the proceeds of such customary dues that the King largely supported himself, far more so than by whatever taxation was intermittently imposed. In some instances the sums or goods might be received by the royal reeves, but primarily it was the King's sheriffs' duty to see that he received all that was due to him, and to render account of collection and payment. But just as royal (and other) manors were farmed, so the principle of farming the shire or the borough had been established. The King knew that he would receive a fixed sum at a stated time, and the sheriff (or, where relevant, the earl of the county) would do his utmost to ensure that he would acquire more than the amount for which he was liable. We have seen that if he failed to furnish the King's dues in full, he was personally responsible for finding the balance.

The customary obligations of the boroughs

If we hear very little of the inhabitants of the boroughs, we learn a good deal of their varied obligations. Of those in some towns we indeed hear nothing, for the accounts are too meagre, or the existence of the borough too incidental, for them to be recorded. The entries, too, sometimes include what are customary dues not from the burghal inhabitants, but those which involve the whole shire, and these have already been considered.

'Of anything that could be called the constitution of the boroughs', wrote Maitland, 'next to nothing can we learn'.[1] We have learnt little more since his day, for the passages in DB which hint at burghal organisation and government are few and disjointed. It looks as if each major borough had its own court of law, but we cannot be sure that all the inhabitants were bound to attend this and no other court. When we read of the King and his magnates having sake and soke over burgesses, or over the 'houses' which imply burgesses, they may, if they possessed sufficient of these, have organised an internal court in which to do justice upon them, or the barons may have

[1] *DBB*, p. 209.

been empowered to judge them in the court of a manor to which burgesses were attached. Maitland saw in the tenth-century regulation which ordained that in every borough there should be a panel of witnesses, who could testify to the legality of sales and contracts, the origins of the 'lawmen' (*lagemanni*) and judges (*judices*) or 'doomsmen' mentioned in DB. Lincoln and Stamford had twelve of the former, and there were thegns who were lawmen at Cambridge; there were four 'judges' at York and twelve at Chester, and these last included men of the King, of the palatine Earl, and of the Bishop.[1]

Something of the laws and customs obtaining in the Chester of 1086 and earlier is revealed to us. The list of legal offences is the most comprehensive DB furnishes, and the reason for its inclusion comes at the very end; the King received two-thirds, and the Earl of the palatine county one-third, of the majority of the fines levied. They begin with breaches of the King's peace 'whether given by his hand or his writ or his legate', and cost the offender a hundred shillings. The King got the whole of this, but if it was the Earl who 'ordered this peace', he had a right to one-third of the fine. But if it was given by the King's reeve or the Earl's official, the fine was only 40s., and the Earl had one-third of it.

If one of the King's freemen broke into another man's house and killed him, his land and the whole of his goods were forfeit to the King, and he was outlawed. Only the King could receive an outlaw into the protection of his peace again; this was beyond the Earl's or sheriff's powers. There follow the fines for slaughter or bloodshed, and these offences cost more if committed between noon on Saturday and Monday morning or on the Twelve Days of Christmas, the Feasts of the Purification, Easter, Pentecost, the Ascension, and the Assumption and Nativity of the Virgin Mary or All Saints' Day. It cost £4 to kill a man then, 40s. on other days; mere bloodshed was half the price.

The fines for minor offences are recorded. Assault on the highway (*forestel*) or housebreaking (*heinfare*) involved a fine of

---

[1] The dozen at Stamford had been reduced to nine by the time of DB: perhaps the effects of the Conquest had been to decrease the number of those potentially eligible for the position.

20*s*., but this was doubled if the crime took place on the above days. The offences include robbery, rape, and fornication – the fine for the last of these was twice as high if a widow was involved as it was in the case of a maiden. The crime of *hang-wite* – allowing a thief to escape, or failing to raise the alarm in case of theft – involved a double fine if the guilty party was a King's or the Earl's reeve.

Anyone who forcibly possessed himself of another's property in land and who was unable to prove his right to it was fined 40*s*., but if the objector could not prove *his* right, he too was fined 40*s*. Anyone failing to pay his rent (*gablum*) by the appointed day was liable to a fine of ten shillings, and if he could not or would not pay it, the King's reeve was to take his land.[1] If a house caught fire and so damaged others, the owner had to pay 'three ounces of pence', and 2*s*. to his nearest neighbour. Ships coming to or leaving the port without the King's leave were liable to a forty-shilling fine for each man involved; if they came lawfully they might sell the goods they carried peacefully, but fourpence was paid for each 'last' on departure. But if they brought marten-skins they might not sell them until the King's reeve had had his pick, if he so desired, and non-observance of this custom cost 40*s*. Persons of either sex who gave false measure were fined 4*s*., and the penalty for brewing bad ale was 4*s*. or being ducked by means of the ducking-stool. All such fines and tolls seem to have been collected by the King's or the Bishop's or the Earl's officials according to the territory in which the crime was committed, and if they were not paid within three nights, a forty-shilling penalty resulted.

For the Bishop too had his peculiar territorial rights within what would later have been known as his 'liberty'. If a freeman worked on a feast day, the Bishop had 8*s*. from him; if a male or female slave did so, 4*s*. He had a 4*s*. fine from a merchant breaking open bales of goods for sale at prohibited times without leave; and if one of his men found anyone leading carted goods within the boundary of his portion of the city, the Bishop had 4*s*., or two oxen by way of forfeiture for prohibited ploughing.

[1] There must always remain a suspicion that *gablum* could be geld as well as a property-rent.

A number of these penalties are recorded in the accounts of other cities also, and it is certain that similar ones were exacted elsewhere even though we hear nothing of them. The accounts of some cities, e.g. Hereford and Shrewsbury, have much to say about the fines for breaches of the law and urban customs; in others, e.g. those in the south-west, we hear nothing. Also, there is variation in their application. The Shrewsbury entry says that King Edward had had 'the three forfeitures' – for breach of his peace, assault on the highway, and housebreaking – throughout England 'outside places at farm', that for Hereford that he had them 'within his demesne'.[1] At Romney (4bi), the Archbishop of Canterbury had the fines resulting from robbery, a breach of the peace, or assault delivered on the King's highway, but sake and soke over the burgesses was the King's, and the King had the unspecified services they were due to render. But the burgesses themselves received the customary dues and the other forfeitures for breaches of the law in consideration of the services connected with the sea that they rendered. The fines payable for the commission of certain crimes at Lewes (26ai) are specified; 7s. 4d. for murder, 8s. 4d. for rape, adultery, or as penalty from a captive fugitive: the King had two-thirds of the proceeds, the Earl one-third, but the King had the man's fine in cases of adultery, and the Archbishop the woman's.[2] At Southwark (32a2) the King had the fine from a man accused of a trespass; but if the man escaped to within the jurisdiction of the lord who had sake and soke over him, the lord obtained it. This is more or less paralleled by the statement that if anyone shed blood at Wallingford and escaped into the houses of certain men who received the *gablum* for these, the owner of the house received the fine exacted, the 'bloodwite'. But this system did not obtain on a Saturday, when the King got such a fine, 'because of the market'. It looks as if one of the conditions for establishing trading privileges, for intensifying 'the King's peace' to ensure that commerce may be conducted without fear of violence or robbery or fraud, has been that the grantor of the franchise

---

[1] But this, we have seen (p. 228), might mean very much the same thing.

[2] 7s. 4d. may be a scribal error for 8s. 4d.: adultery would hardly cost *more* than murder did.

shall receive the profits for a breach of it. These men also had the fines for robbery and adultery. At Dover the King's peace existed from the Feast of St. Michael to that of St. Andrew; that is, during the herring season.

One duty frequently mentioned, which is recorded in connection with Malmesbury, is that of contributing to the royal host by land and sea. When the King 'went with his army by land', Leicester sent twelve burgesses to accompany him; if he went by sea, it sent four horses to London to carry weapons 'or other things of which there might be need'. Maldon (II.48) had to find a horse for the army, and provide a ship. Twenty Oxford burgesses 'went with the King for all the rest', or £20 was paid for non-fulfilment of this duty, when they were quit of it. When the King wished to send forth a land-army or fleet, the inhabitants of Exeter had to 'serve for the quantity of five hides', which seems a light duty. Warwick sent ten burgesses 'by land', and provided four boatswains (*butsueins*) or £4 for their support. Dover furnished the King with twenty ships, each containing twenty-one men, for fifteen days in the year, and for this service they had been freed from the King's jurisdiction. For their services, too, the Dover men were free of toll throughout England. If the King wished merely to guard the coasts, without carrying out a campaign, Lewes provided 20*s*. a man for the fleet's armament and guards. If the sheriff of Herefordshire went into Wales with an army, the burgesses of the city had to go with him, and were fined 40*s*. apiece if they failed to go after receiving his summons. The borough of Bedford had to send, for either a land or a sea expedition, the quota for the half-Hundred at which it was assessed.[1]

A bodyguard of twelve burgesses had to be found for the King when he visted Shrewsbury, and those who did not possess 'whole masures' at Hereford had to find a guard for the King's hall when he was in the city. The men of Torksey, when the King's messengers came thither, had to conduct them to York with their ships and means of navigation, and the Lincoln-shire sheriff had to find food for the messengers and the sailors.

---

[1] The quota was presumably ten men – one for each five hides. The sokeland of the manor of Keisby (368ai) – not a borough – rendered nothing but helped in the King's land and sea forces.

When the King's messengers came to Dover, the burgesses paid threepence in summer and twopence in winter for horse-transport; they also had to find a pilot and his assistant. Another duty at Shrewsbury was that when the King left the city the sheriff sent twenty-four horsemen with him as far as Leintwardine, or as far as the first (presumably royal) manor in Staffordshire.

The relief or heriot payable by the heir as a form of death-duty is often mentioned. A Shrewsbury burgess on the King's demesne paid 10s. by way of relief. The King had the horse and arms of a Hereford burgess, but if he had no horse, then he had 10s. or his land with his house. The lawmen of Cambridge gave the sheriff £8, a palfrey, and a soldier's weapons. But the burgesses of York did not pay a relief. If a citizen of Hereford wished to leave the town, he could grant or sell his house to another man willing to perform the service due from it, and the reeve got a third of the price. If he was too poor to perform the services ordained, he could hand over his house to the reeve without cost to himself, and it was the reeve's business to see it did not stand empty. A Torksey man could depart or sell his house without notifying the reeve or obtaining his permission. If a Lewes house was sold, buyer and seller each paid the reeve a penny.

The most miscellaneous obligations are recorded. The holder of an entire Hereford masure within the wall had to pay 7½d., and 4d. for hiring horses, do three days' reaping at the royal manor of Maurdine and one day's haymaking where the sheriff wished; those living without gave only 3½d. A man owning a horse had to go three times a year with the sheriff to the hearing of pleas and to the Wormley Hundred-moot. Every man whose wife brewed ale within or without the city had to pay tenpence: the six smiths each had to make 120 horseshoes from the King's iron; they paid one penny each from the proceeds of their forges and threepence by way of customary dues, and for all this they were quit of all other service. At Shrewsbury, a maiden paid 10s. on her marriage, but a widow twice that sum. Other customs recorded for these two cities were no doubt in force elsewhere also. From every Hereford house 'one man went to his station in the wood' to drive the deer when the King hunted, and at Shrewsbury the burgesses who possessed horses guarded him, while thirty-six others went on foot to give their services towards ensuring the success of the drive. The Wallingford burgesses 'did the King's service' – his errands – 'with horses or by water as far as Blewbury, Reading, Sutton, and Bensington'. No one might reduce the breadth of the King's highway at Canterbury by erecting a fence or digging a ditch, or cut down a tree or remove wood in its neighbourhood, under pain of a fine of one hundred shillings. Violence committed on the highways passing through the city, or for the space of one league, three perches, and three feet beyond it, resulted in a fine which went to the King, but outside the city to the Archbishop where the roads ran through his own lands. The Canterbury and Kentish details include a list of those who receive the profits of justice where their tenants offend against the law, and the relief from the heir on succession, but it is made plain that the King gets the fines for certain reserved offences. The Nottingham burgesses had to guard or look after the waterway by Trent, the ditch, and the road to York; if anyone impeded the progress of ships, or made a ditch within two perches of the King's highway, he was fined £8. At York the King had three 'ways' by land and one by water, and the King and the Earl had all fines for offences connected with them, whether they ran through the King's or the Archbishop's or the Earl's land.

At Southwark, King Edward had had two-thirds of the dues of the port – the wharf-dues, probably – and Earl Godwine one-third (32ai). The inhabitants testified that T.R.E. the King alone received the tolls levied along the Thames strand and near the river. Such tolls and port dues were worth, at Pevensey (20ai), 45s.

Of renders in kind we hear a good deal. Warwick produced 36 sesters of honey for the King, Norwich a palfrey for the Queen, Leicester £10 in lieu of a hawk and 20s. for a sumpter-horse. Warwick furnished the same as Leicester, and also £23 as commutation for an earlier due of providing for the King's hounds, and 100s. for a *gersuma* for the Queen – a premium for the use of her property. Norwich provided a bear and six dogs for baiting it, Thetford honey and goat-skins and ox-hides,

Beccles 60,000 herrings – a due doubled from what it had been in 1066. Renders at Lewes included 38,000 herrings and 500 porpoises, and the Canterbury monks received 40,000 herrings from Sandwich (3ai). Gloucester, rendering in 1066 £36 by tale together with honey and iron and rods of iron from which nails for the King's ships were made, had by 1086 had its dues commuted into a single render of £60 at 20*d*. to the ounce.

At Rhuddlan (269a2), where there were both a new castle and a new borough, the burgesses lived under the same laws and customs as those applicable to Hereford and to the Norman town of Breteuil, and except in cases of manslaughter, theft, and premeditated housebreaking, they paid fines of twelve pence only.[1]

The renders of the boroughs had often been increased since the Conquest. The Wallingford of 1066 was valued at £30; this had increased first to £40 and later to £60, but it was in fact producing £80. That of Norwich had gone up from £30 to £90; of Oxford from £30 to £60. Here, perhaps, may be seen the mark of the royal sheriffs at work.

Such, then, is Domesday Book, a vast collection of information which gives us so much and yet so little, which is full of detail and yet hardly ever states general principles. Its use for interpretation of conditions both long before and long after its compilation is almost incalculable, and at the same time it has to be used with continual caution, for it is self-contradictory, imperfect in execution, and painfully easy to misinterpret. But in appreciating its limitations, we have this to remember also: that not only is it a unique record, but a powerful tribute to the men who, in face of poor communications and pressure and patent opposition, accomplished their task far better than anyone had any reason to expect. An England which could achieve a production of this magnitude and comprehensiveness is something to revere.

[1] Whence did the burgesses in a 'new borough' come? Was a surplus element or those with inadequate opportunity in a neighbouring city, invited to settle there? Or did local merchants congregate by reason of the security offered? An alternative suggestion is made on p. 160. The 'laws of Breteuil' governed many of the later medieval towns. They are described in *EHR*, vols. xv and xx (*see* Bibliography under Ballard, A. and Bateson, M.).

BIBLIOGRAPHY

(a) *Works of fundamental importance, or which are concerned largely with Domesday Book, in order of publication.*

WEBB, P.C. *A Short Account of Some Particulars concerning Domesday Book*, London, 1756.

KELHAM, R. *Domesday Book Illustrated*, London, 1788. Includes lists and short biographies of tenants-in-chief, grouped by counties, and explanations of 'difficult phrases', on which no reliance can be placed.

ELLIS, SIR H. *A General Introduction to Domesday Book*, London, 1816. Produced to accompany the 'Record' edition of the text and reissued in two volumes in 1833; gives statistics of population (which are not always accurate), lists of tenants-in-chief, and general information, much of which is still useful.

EYTON, R. W. *Notes on Domesday*, Bristol, 1880. Includes views on the manner in which the Inquest was held and Domesday Book made which Round was on the whole prepared to accept.

BIRCH, W. DE G. *Domesday Book*, London, 1887. A collection of disjointed chapters, the views expressed in many of which are now obsolete.

DOVE, P. E. (Ed.) *Domesday Studies* (2 vols.), London, 1888–91. Papers produced in connection with the Domesday Commemoration of 1886, and which include:

ROUND, J. H.   'Danegeld and the Finance of Domesday'
                'Notes on Domesday Measures of land'
TAYLOR, I.   'Domesday Survivals'
                'Wapentakes and Hundreds'
                'The Ploughland and the Plough'

Most of the other papers are now of small interest, and those of O. C. Pell have from the outset been stigmatised as worthless.

ROUND, J. H. *Feudal England*, London, 1895. The first chapter of this book furnished entirely new conceptions of Domesday Book and its background, and remains essential to the student. Other papers include one on the Northamptonshire Geld Roll, several on post-Domesday Surveys which can be linked with Domesday Book, and one on the introduction of Knight Service into England.

MAITLAND, F. W. *Domesday Book and Beyond*, Cambridge, 1897. Though some of the views expressed are now considered to be obsolete, this vivid and stimulating book remains as essential to the student as are Round's discoveries, and much ground is covered on which Round did no original work. It has recently been reissued in a cheap edition with a preface by E. Miller (London, 1960).

BALLARD, A. *The Domesday Boroughs*, Oxford, 1904. Not all subsequent commentators have agreed with Ballard's conclusions, and while it remains the only book concerned solely with the boroughs of Domesday Book, it is doubtful if Ballard allowed himself sufficient space to be really comprehensive.

BALLARD, A. *The Domesday Inquest*, London, 1906. A revised edition was issued in 1923, and while much it includes is at variance with modern conceptions, it is the best, though a severely compressed, 'popular' account which has appeared.

BARING, F. H. *Domesday Tables*, London, 1909. Contains tables analysing much of the material for the counties of Surrey, Berkshire, Middlesex, Hertfordshire, Buckinghamshire, and Bedfordshire, together with reprints of some of his articles, especially that on the New Forest and that in which he deduced the movements of the Conqueror's armies in 1066.

DARBY, H. C. (Ed.). *Historical Geography of England*, Cambridge, 1936. Includes a chapter on 'Domesday England' and much besides which will be of value to the student of Domesday.

STENTON, SIR F. M. *Anglo-Saxon England*, Oxford, 1942. The pages concerned with the Domesday Inquest and Domesday Book are necessarily few (Chapter XVII), but provide a useful short introduction to the subject.

GALBRAITH, V. H. *Studies in the Public Records*, Oxford, 1948. Chapter IV in part summarises an earlier *EHR* article by the author, and in part develops the conclusions there expressed. It is vital as a corrective to some of the views of Round and Maitland.

DARBY, H. C. (Ed.) *The Domesday Geography of England*, Cambridge, 1952 onwards. Five volumes – Eastern, Midland, South-Eastern, Northern, and South-Western England – are to cover the country, with a sixth volume to include the general conclusions. Each county has its own chapter, the system of sub-divisions being uniform throughout, and the text is copiously illustrated by maps. All the geographical aspects of the material are dealt with. A seventh volume will provide a Domesday Gazeteer with maps and an index to all place-names.

(Public Record Office). *Domesday Re-Bound*, London, 1954. Provides, together with much other material (e.g. on the make-up and bindings), a useful introduction to the study of Domesday Book.

LENNARD, R. *Rural England: 1086–1135*, Oxford, 1959. Deals in some detail with, e.g., manorial valuations and the farming of manors, sokeland, manorial appurtenances, and the peasantry and their holdings.

FINN, R. WELLDON *The Domesday Inquest and the Making of Domesday Book*, London, 1961. Concerned principally with the reasons for holding the Domesday Inquest, the scope and manner of its work, and the actual construction of Domesday Book in its various stages.

GALBRAITH, V. H. *The Making of Domesday Book*, Oxford, 1961. Examines afresh the procedure of the Inquest, and the manner in which its findings were recorded, stage by stage, in the various drafts and final form of Domesday Book. It corrects many of Round's unsatisfactory hypotheses.

Publication of the *Victoria County Histories* began in 1900, and for practically every county an introduction and translation of the Domesday text has been published. Most (but not all) are to be found in vol. i for the individual county.

The two volumes of the 'Exchequer' Domesday – what we usually think of as and call 'Domesday Book' – were printed and published in 1783 under the title *Domesday Book, seu Liber Censualis Willelmi Primi Regis Angliae*.[1] The Record Commissioners published Indices to these in 1811, reissued in 1816 with a 'General Introduction' by Sir Henry Ellis (*q.v.*). In 1816 they published an *Additamenta* volume, including the *Liber Exoniensis* and part of MS. A of the *Inquisitio Eliensis*. Between 1861 and 1863 a facsimile edition of the 'Exchequer' text was produced, county by county, by photozincography at the Ordnance Survey Office, Southampton; in the latter year the whole was issued in two volumes. There are numerous extended texts with translations for the various counties, but these are not always reliable.

---

[1] It must be remembered that vol. II is not an 'Exchequer' text, but the final *provincial draft*.

The following articles are concerned with the general aspects of Domesday Book:

DOUGLAS, D. C. 'The Domesday Survey', *History*, New Series, vol. xxi (1937).

GALBRAITH, V. H. 'The Making of Domesday Book', *EHR*, vol. lvii (1942).

POLLOCK, SIR F. 'A Brief Survey of Domesday', *EHR*, vol. xi (1896).

STEPHENSON, C. 'Notes on the Composition and Interpretation of Domesday Book', *Speculum*, vol. xxii (1947).

The Cambridge Medieval History (vol. v, pp. 481–520) contains a Summary of W. J. Corbett's unpublished analyses of Domesday Book.

(b) *The following are the principal texts relevant to the Domesday Inquest and its period.*

(1)

Domesday Monachorum of Christ Church, Canterbury, D. C. DOUGLAS, (Ed.) London, 1944.

Inquisitio Comitatus Cantabrigiensis . . . subjicitur Inquisitio Eliensis, N. E. S. A. HAMILTON, (Ed.) London, 1886.

St. Augustine's, Canterbury: An Eleventh Century Inquisition of, A. BALLARD, (Ed.) Oxford, 1920.

Textus Roffensis, T. HEARNE (Ed.), London, 1720 (Notes on the *Textus Roffensis* by F. Liebermann: *Archaeol. Cant.*, vol. xxiii— London, 1898.)

Evesham A, a Domesday Text, P. H. SAWYER, Worcs. Hist. Soc. Miscellany I (Worcester and London, 1960).

(2)

Anglo-Saxon Chronicle, G. GARMONSWAY (Ed.) (Texts also in *English Historical Documents, q.v.*), London, 1935.

(3)

Chronicon Monasterii de Abingdon, STEVENSON, J. (Rolls Series), London, 1858.

'Herefordshire Domesday', GALBRAITH, V. H., and TAIT, J. (*Pipe Roll Soc.*, New Series, vol. xxv), London, 1950.

St. Augustine's Canterbury: Register of, TURNER, G. T., and SALTER, H. E., London, 1915.

The following include charters and writs, etc., a number of which supplement the entries of Domesday Book:

(1)

DAVIS, H. W. C. *Regesta Regum Anglo-Normannorum: 1066–1154,* Oxford, 1913.

DOUGLAS, D. C., and GREENAWAY, G. W. *English Historical Documents,* 1042–1189, London, 1953.

ROUND, J. H. *Calendar of Documents preserved in France,* London, 1899.

(2)

BALLARD, A. *British Borough Charters, 1042–1216,* Cambridge, 1913.

BATES, E. H. (Ed.) *Cartulary of Muchelney and Athelney Abbeys,* Bath, 1899.

BIGELOW, M. M. *Placita Anglo-Normannica,* London, 1879.

BIRCH, W. DE G. *Cartularium Saxonicum,* London, 1885–93.

EARLE, J. *A Handbook to the Land Charters,* Oxford, 1888.

HARMER, F. E. *Select English Historical Documents,* Cambridge, 1914. *Anglo-Saxon Writs,* Manchester, 1952.

HART, C. *Some Early Charters of Essex,* Leicester, 1957.

FINBERG, H. P. R. *The Early Charters of the West Midlands,* Leicester, 1961.

KEMBLE, J. M. *Codex Diplomaticus Aevi Saxonici,* London, 1839–48.

NAPIER, A. S. and STEVENSON, W. H. *The Crawford Collection of Early Charters and Documents,* Oxford, 1895.

ROBERTSON, A. J. *Anglo-Saxon Charters,* Cambridge, 1939.

STENTON, SIR F. M. *Documents illustrative of the Social and Economic History of the Danelaw,* Oxford, 1920. *The Latin Charters of the Anglo-Saxon Period,* Oxford, 1955.

THORPE, B. *Diplomatarium Anglicum,* London, 1865.

WHITELOCK, D. *Anglo-Saxon Wills,* Cambridge, 1930.

(c) *The publications in the first group which follows contain much material relevant to the study of Domesday Book; those in the second group all contain matter which is concerned with its contents or interpretation.*

(1)

DOUGLAS, D. C. *Feudal Documents from the Abbey of Bury St. Edmunds,* London, 1932. *The Social Structure of Medieval East Anglia,* Oxford, 1927.

HOYT, R. S. *The Royal Demesne in English Constitutional History*, Ithaca, N.Y., 1950.

MORRIS, W. A. *The Medieval English Sheriff to 1300*, Manchester, 1927.

STENTON, SIR F. M. *The First Century of English Feudalism*, Oxford, 1931.
Types of Manorial Structure in the Northern Danelaw, Oxford, 1910.
William the Conqueror, London, 1908.

TAIT, J. *The Medieval English Borough*, Manchester, 1936.

VINOGRADOFF, SIR P. *English Society in the Eleventh Century*, Oxford, 1908.
The Growth of the Manor, Oxford, 1905.
Villainage in England, Oxford, 1892.

(2)

ANDERSON (later ARNGART), O.S. *The English Hundred Names*, Lund, 1934–9.

ASHDOWN, M. *English and Norse Documents*, Cambridge, 1922.

ATTENBOROUGH, F. L. *The Laws of the Earliest English Kings*, Cambridge, 1922.

BARLOW, F. *The Feudal Kingdom of England 1042–1216*, London, 1955.

CAM, H. M. *The Hundred and the Hundred Rolls*, London, 1930.

CHADWICK, H. M. *Studies on Anglo-Saxon Institutions*, Cambridge, 1905.

CHEW, H. M. *English Ecclesiastical Tenants-in-Chief and Knight Service*, Oxford, 1932.

CHRIMES, S. B. *An Introduction to the Administrative History of Medieval England*, Oxford, 1952.

COX, J. C. *The Royal Forests of England*, London, 1905.

EKWALL, E. *Oxford Dictionary of English Place-Names*, Oxford, fourth edn., 1960.

FARRER, W. *Book of Fees*, London, 1920–31.

FEILITZEN, O. VON *The Pre-Conquest Personal Names of Domesday*, Uppsala, 1937.

FREEMAN, E. A. *History of the Norman Conquest* (vol. v), Oxford, 1876.

GRAY, H. L. *English Field Systems*, Cambridge, Mass., 1915.

HASKINS, C. H. *Norman Institutions*, Harvard, 1918.

JOLLIFFE, J. E. A. *Constitutional History of Medieval England*, London, 1937.
Pre-Feudal England: The Jutes, Oxford, 1933.

KNOWLES, D. *The Monastic Orders in England*, Cambridge, 1940.

LARSON, L. M. *The King's Household in England before the Norman Conquest*, Madison, Wis., 1904.

MAITLAND, F. W. *Township and Borough*, Cambridge, 1898.

ORWIN, C. S. and C. S. *The Open Fields*, Oxford, 1938.

ROBERTSON, A. J. *The Laws of the Kings of England from Edmund to Henry I*, Cambridge, 1925.

SEEBOHM, F. *The English Village Community*, Cambridge, 1833.

STENTON, LADY D. M. *English Society in the Early Middle Ages*, London, 1951.

STEPHENSON, C. *Borough and Town: A study of urban origins in England*, Cambridge, Mass., 1933.

WEBB, P. C. *A Short Account of Danegeld*, London, 1756.

WHITELOCK, D. *The Beginnings of English Society*, London, 1952.

SAYLES, G. O. *The Medieval Foundations of England*, London, 1948.

(d) *The following articles deal for the most part with Domesday material and problems* (*EHR* = 'English Historical Review'; *BJRL* = 'Bulletin of the John Rylands Library').

BALLARD, A. 'The Laws of Breteuil', *EHR*, vol. xx (1905).
'The Burgesses of Domesday', *EHR*, vol. xxi (1906).

BARING, F. H. 'Domesday and some Twelfth Century Surveys', *EHR*, vol. xii (1897).
'The Hidation of some Southern Counties', *EHR*, vol. xiv (1899).
'The Exeter Domesday', *EHR*, vol. xxvii (1912).

BATESON, M. 'The Laws of Breteuil', *EHR*, vols. xv, xvi (1900–1).

CAM, H. M. *Manerium cum Hundredo*, *EHR*, vol. xlvii (1932).

DEMAREST, E. B. 'The Hundred-Pennies', *EHR*, vol. xxxiii (1918)·
'The *Firma Unius Noctis*', *EHR*, vol xxxv (1920).

DODWELL, B. 'East Anglian Commendation', *EHR*, vol. lxiii (1948).

FINN, R. WELLDON 'The Evolution of Successive Versions of Domesday Book', *EHR*, vol. lxvi (1951).
'The *Inquisitio Eliensis* Reconsidered', *EHR*, vol. lxxv (1960).
'The Immediate Sources of the Exchequer Domesday', *BJRL*, vol. xl (1957).
'The Construction of the Exeter Domesday', *BJRL*, vol. xlii (1959)·

GALBRAITH, V. H. 'The Date of the Geld Rolls in Exon Domesday', *EHR*, vol. lxv (1950).

HODGEN, M. T. 'Domesday Water Mills', *Antiquity*, vol xiii (1939).

LENNARD, R. 'A Neglected Domesday Satellite', *EHR*, vol. lviii (1943).
'The Hidation of "Demesne" in some Domesday Entries', *Econ. Hist. Rev.*, vol. vii (second series) (1954).
'The Economic Position of the Bordars and Cottars of Domesday Book', *Econ. Journ.* vol. lxi (1951).
'The Economic Position of the Domesday Villani', *Econ. Journ.*, vol. lvi (1946).
'The Economic Position of the Domesday Sokeman', *Econ. Journ.*, vol. lvii (1947).

LEVISON, W. 'A Report on the Pinnenden Trial', *EHR*, vol. xxviii (1913).

MAITLAND, F. W. 'The Origin of the Borough', *EHR*, vol. xi (1896).

MILLER, E. 'The Ely Land Pleas in the Reign of William I', *EHR*, vol. xliii (1947).

MORRIS, W. A. 'The Office of Sheriff in the Anglo-Saxon Period', *EHR*, vol. xxxi (1916).
'The Office of Sheriff in the Early Norman Period', *EHR*, vol. xxxiii (1918).

PAGE, W. 'Some Remarks on the Churches of the Domesday Survey', *Archaeologia*, vol. lxvi (1915).

ROUND, J. H. 'The Introduction of Knight Service into England', *EHR*, vol. vi (1891).
Carucata Terra, *EHR*, vol. vii (1892).
'The Hundred and the Geld', *EHR*, vol. x (1895).
'The Domesday Manor', *EHR*, vol. xv (1900).
'The Castles of the Conquest', *Archaeologia*, vol. lviii (1902).
'The Officers of Edward the Confessor', *EHR*, vol. xix (1904).
'The Domesday *Ora*', *EHR*, vol. xxiii (1908).
'The "Tertius Denarius" of a Borough', *EHR*, vol. xxiv (1919).
' "Domesday" or "Doomesday" ', *EHR*, vol. xxxviii (1923).

SAWYER, P. H. 'The "Original Returns" and "Domesday Book"', *EHR*, vol. lxx (1955).
'The Place-Names of Domesday Book', *BJRL*, vol. xxxviii (1955).

STENTON, SIR F. M. 'Sokemen and the Village Waste', *EHR*, vol. xxxiii (1918).

STEPHENSON, C. 'The *Firma Unius Noctis* and the Custom of the Hundred', *EHR*, vol. xxxix (1924).
'Commendation and Related Problems in Domesday', *EHR*, vol. lix (1944).
'English Families and the Norman Conquest', *Trans. Roy. Hist. Soc.*, vol. xxvi (1944).

STEVENSON, W. H. 'A Contemporary Description of the Domesday Survey', *EHR*, vol. xxii (1907).

TURNER, G. J. 'William the Conqueror's March to London in 1066', *EHR*, vol. xxvii (1912).

VINOGRADOFF, SIR P. 'Sulung and Hide', *EHR*, vol. xix (1904).

The material following is concerned with the individual county or group of counties, arranged alphabetically by counties. Those items marked * are concerned with more than one county. A short bibliography for each county (concerned largely with aspects of Domesday geography) will be found in the volumes of the 'Domesday Geography of England'.

Bedfordshire (see also under BARING, F. H.)

AIRY, W. *A Digest of the Domesday of Bedfordshire*, Bedford (1881).

FOWLER, G. H. 'Bedfordshire in 1066: An analysis and synthesis of Domesday Book', *Beds. Hist. Rec. Soc.*, Aspley Guise (1922).
'The Devastation of Bedfordshire and the neighbouring counties in 1065 and 1066'*, *Archaeologia*, vol. lxxii (1922).

Buckinghamshire (see also under BARING, F. H.)

BARING, F. H. 'Note on the Hidation of Buckinghamshire', *EHR*, vol. xv (1900).

DAVIES, A. M. 'The Hundreds of Buckinghamshire and Oxfordshire'*, *Records of Bucks.*, vol. xv (1950).

Cambridgeshire

CAM, H. M. 'On the Origins of the Borough of Cambridge', *Proc. Cambs. Ant. Soc.*, vol. xxxv (1935).

MILLER, E. *The Abbey and Bishopric of Ely**, Cambridge (1953).

FINN, R. WELLDON 'Some Reflections on the Cambridgeshire Domesday', *Proc. Cambs. Ant. Soc.* (1960).

Cheshire

BROWNBILL, J. 'Cheshire in Domesday Book', *Trans. Hist. Soc. Lancs. and Chesh.*, vol. li (1899).

TAIT, J. 'The Domesday Survey of Cheshire', *Chetham Soc.* (1916).

Cornwall (see also under DEVONSHIRE)

MICHEL WHITLEY, H. 'The Cornwall Domesday and the Geld Inquest', *Journ. Roy. Corn. Inst.* (1865).

ALEXANDER, J. J. 'The Hundreds of Cornwall', *Dev. and Corn. Notes and Queries* (1934).

HENDERSON, C. *Essays in Cornish History*, Oxford (1935).

HOYT, R. S. 'The *Terrae Occupatae* of Cornwall and the Exon Domesday', *Traditio*, vol. ix (1953).

Devonshire

REICHEL, O. J. 'The Devonshire Domesday and the Geld Roll' *Trans. Dev. Assn.*, vol. xxvii (1895).
'The Hundreds of Devon', *TDA*, vols. xxvi–xlvii (1894–1915).

WHALE, T. W. 'Analysis of the Devonshire Domesday', *TDA*, vol. xxviii (1896).
'Principles of Domesday'*, *TDA*, vol. xxxii (1902).
'History of the Exon Domesday'*, *TDA*, vol. xxxvii (1905).

HOSKINS, W. G. and FINBERG, H. P. R. *Devonshire Studies*, London (1952).

FINBERG, H. P. R. *Tavistock Abbey**, Cambridge (1953).

FINN, R. WELLDON 'The Making of the Devonshire Domesdays', *Trans. Dev. Assn.* vol. lxxxix (1957).

Dorset

EYTON, R. W. *A Key to Domesday*, London and Dorchester (1878).

FINN, R. WELLDON 'The Making of the Dorset Domesdays', *Proc. Dors. Nat. Hist. and Arch. Soc.*, vol. lxxxi (1960).

Essex

ROUND, J. H. 'The Domesday Hidation of Essex', *EHR*, vol. xxix (1914).

DEMAREST, E. B. '*Consuetudo Regis* in Essex, Norfolk and Suffolk'*, *EHR*, vol. xlii (1927).

Flintshire

TAIT, J. 'Flintshire in Domesday Book', *Flints. Hist. Soc. Pubns.*, vol. xi (1925).

Gloucestershire

TAYLOR, C. S. *An Analysis of the Domesday Survey of Gloucestershire*, Bristol (1889).

'The Pre-Domesday Hide of Gloucestershire', *Trans. Brist. and Gloucs. Arch. Soc.*, vol. xviii (1894).
'The Norman Settlement of Gloucestershire', *Trans. Brist. and Gloucs. Arch. Soc.*, vol. xl (1917).

Hampshire

BARING, F. H. 'The Making of the New Forest', *Papers and Proc. Hants. Field Club*, vol. vi (1910).
'William the Conqueror's march through Hampshire in 1066', *Papers and Proc. Hants. Field Club*, vol. vii (1915).
KARSLAKE, J. B. 'The Watermills of Hampshire', *Papers and Proc. Hants. Field Club*, vol. xiv (1938).

Herefordshire

BANISTER, A. T. 'The Herefordshire Domesday', *Trans. Woolhope Field Nat. Club* (1904).

Hertfordshire (see also under BARING, F. H.)

JOHNSON, W. B. 'Hertfordshire 900 years ago', *Herts. Countryside*, vol. viii (1953).

Huntingdonshire

LADDS, S. INSKIP 'The Borough of Huntingdon and Domesday Book', *Trans. Cambs. and Hunts. Arch. Soc.* (1937).

Kent

JOLLIFFE, J. E. A. 'The origin of the hundred in Kent', in *Hist. Essays in honour of James Tait* (1933).
JOLLIFFE, J. E. A. 'The hidation of Kent', *EHR*, vol. xliv (1929).
DOUGLAS, D. C. 'Odo, Lanfranc, and the Domesday Survey', in *Hist. Essays in honour of James Tait* (1933).

Lancashire

DEMAREST, E. B. *Inter Ripam et Mersam, EHR*, vol. xxxviii (1923).

Leicestershire

HOSKINS, W. G. 'The Anglian and Scandinavian Settlement of Leicestershire', *Trans. Leics. Arch. Soc.* (1935).
Essays in Leicestershire History, Liverpool (1950).

Lincolnshire

MASSINGBERD, W. 'The Lincolnshire Sokemen', *EHR*, vol. xx (1905).

I.D B.

FARRER, W. 'The Sheriffs of Lincolnshire and Yorkshire, 1066–1130'*, *EHR*, vol. xxx (1915).

FOSTER, C. W. and LONGLEY, T. *The Lincolnshire Domesday*, Horncastle (1924).

Middlesex (see also under BARING, F. H.)

DAVIES, A. M. 'The Domesday Hidation of Middlesex', *Home Counties Mag.*, vol. iii (1901).

SHARPE, SIR M. 'Middlesex in Domesday Book' *Trans. Lond. and Msx. Arch. Soc.*, *N.S.*, vol. vii (1937).
Middlesex in the Eleventh Century, Brentford (1941).

Norfolk (see also under CAMBS., DOUGLAS, D. C., DODWELL, B.)

ROUND, J. H. 'The Early Sheriffs of Norfolk', *EHR*, vol. xxxv (1920).

TINGEY, J. C. 'Some Notes on the Domesday Assessment of Norfolk', *Norf. Arch.*, vol. xxi (1923).

DODWELL, B. 'The Free Peasantry of East Anglia in Domesday', *Trans. Norf. & Norwich Arch. Soc.*, vol. xxvii (1939).

DAVIS, R. H. C. 'East Anglia and the Danelaw' *Trans. Roy. Hist. Soc.*, fifth ser., vol. v (1955).

Northamptonshire

ROUND, J. H. 'The Hidation of Northants', *EHR*, vol. xv (1900).

BARING, F. H. 'The Pre-Domesday Hidation of Northants', *EHR*, vol. xvii (1902).

Oxfordshire (See also under DAVIES, A. M.)

MOWAT, J. L. G. *Notes on the Oxfordshire Domesday*, Oxford (1892).

Shropshire

SYLVESTER, D. 'Rural Settlement in Domesday Shropshire', *Sociological Review*, vol. xxv (1933).

SLACK, W. J. 'The Shropshire Ploughmen of Domesday Book', *Trans. Shrop. Arch. and Nat. Hist. Soc.* (1939).

Somerset (see also under DEVONSHIRE)

EYTON, R. W. *Domesday Studies: An Analysis and Digest of the Somerset Survey*, Bristol (1880).

WHALE, T. W. 'Principles of the Somerset Domesday', *Bath Nat. Hist. and Inst. Field Club*, vol. x (1902).

FINN, R. WELLDON 'The Making of the Somerset Domesdays', *Proc. Som. Arch. and Nat. Hist. Soc.*, vols. xcix–c (1954–5).

MORLAND, S. C. 'Some Domesday Manors', *Proc. Som. Arch. and Nat. Hist. Soc.*, vols. xcix–c (1954–5).

Staffordshire

EYTON, R. W. *Domesday Studies: An Analysis and Digest of the Staffordshire Survey*, London (1881).

WEDGWOOD, J. C. 'Early Staffordshire History', *Staffs. Rec. Soc.* (1916).

BRIDGMAN, C. G. O. and MANDER, G. P. 'The Staffordshire Hidation', *Collections for a History of Staffordshire* (1919).

BRIDGMAN, C. G. O. 'The Five-Hide Unit in Staffordshire' (1919).

Suffolk (see Norfolk)

Surrey (see also under BARING, F. H.)

MALDEN, H. E. 'The Domesday Survey of Surrey', in *Domesday Studies*, vol. ii (1891).

Sussex

ROUND, J. H. and HOWARTH, H. H. 'The Sussex Rapes', *Archaeol. Rev.*, vol. i (1888).

SAWYER, F. E. 'The Rapes and their origins', *Archaeol. Rev.*, vol. i (1888).

JOLLIFFE, J. E. A. 'The Domesday Hidation of Sussex and the rapes', *EHR*, vol. clxxvii (1930).

SALZMANN, L. F. 'The rapes of Sussex', *Sussex Arch. Collns.*, vol. lxxii (1931).

CLARKE, D. K. 'The Saxon hundreds of Sussex', *Sussex Arch. Collns.*, vol. lxxiv (1933).

POOLE, H. 'The Domesday Book Churches of Sussex', *Sussex Arch. Collns.*, vol. lxxxvii (1948).

Warwickshire

WALKER, B. 'Some notes on Domesday Book for Warwickshire', *Trans. Birm. Arch. Soc.*, vol. xxvi (1900).
'The Hundreds of Warwickshire', *Trans. Birm. Arch. Soc.*, vol. xxvi (1900).
'The Hundreds of Warwickshire at the time of the Domesday Survey', *Antiquary*, vol. xxxix (1903).

Kinvig, R. H. 'The Birmingham District in Domesday Times'*, *Brit. Assn.* (1950).

Wiltshire

Jones, W. H. *Domesday for Wiltshire*, London and Bath (1865).

Ballard, A. 'The Walls of Malmesbury', *EHR*, vol. xxi (1906).

Bateson, M. 'The Burgesses of Domesday and the Malmesbury Walls', *EHR*, vol. xxi (1906).

Finn, R. Welldon 'The Assessment of Wiltshire in 1083 and 1086', *Wilts. Arch. and Nat. Hist. Mag.*, vol. l (1946).
'The Making of the Wiltshire Domesday', *Wilts. Arch. and Nat. Hist. Mag.*, vol. lii (1948).

Yorkshire (see also under Lincs. and Taylor, I.)

Bishop, T. A. M. 'The Norman Settlement of Yorkshire', in *Studies in Med. Hist.* presented to F. M. Powicke (1948).

Maxwell, I. S. 'The Geographical Identification of Domesday Vills', *Trans. Inst. Brit. Geog.*, vol. xvi (1950).

INDEX

Names of towns and villages which make only incidental appearance in the text have not been included. Names of laymen (those incidentally mentioned have not been included) are to be found under the places from which their owners derived their style; e.g. Roger de Beaumont is indexed under 'Beaumont'; of ecclesiastics, under Christian names; e.g. Osbern, Bishop of Exeter, is under 'Osbern'. But where reference is to an office, not the individual, see under, e.g. Exeter, Bishopric of. Domesday Book is abbreviated as DB.